D1572243

SEEKING HOPE:

Stories of the Suicide Bereaved

Edited by
Michelle Linn-Gust, Ph.D.
&
Julie Cerel, Ph.D.

ꕥ

Seeking Hope: Stories of the Suicide Bereaved

ISBN: 978-09723318-4-5
Library of Congress Control Number: 2011900258

Chellehead Works books are available at special discounts when purchased in bulk for premiums and sales promotions as well as fundraising and educational use.

For details, contact the Special Sales Director at:
info@chelleheadworks.com
505-266-3134 (voice)
Albuquerque, New Mexico

Printed in the United States of America
First printing March 2011

Designed by Megan Herndon

American Association of Suicidology

AAS is a membership organization for all those involved in suicide prevention and intervention, or touched by suicide. AAS leads the advancement of scientific and programmatic efforts in suicide prevention through research, education and training, the development of standards and resources, and survivor support services.

The proceeds from this book, *Seeking Hope: Stories of the Suicide Bereaved*, will be donated to a fund at AAS called the "Seeking Hope Suicide Bereavement Research Fund" to support research with the goal of easing the grief journey for the many people left behind after the suicide of a loved one. Donations also are appreciated to this fund. See www.suicidology.org and click on "Donate Now" to find out more.

"This compilation of the grief journeys of individuals whose loved one died by suicide conveys accounts of what these bereaved by suicide experienced after the death and how they survived the loss. Each person's actions involved responding to the death in a manner that assisted their own grief, but that of others with similar loss as well. These individual accounts in the aftermath of suicide give us the detailed experiences, feelings, and events that occurred in a way that group-based research findings and characterizations cannot fully capture. Each survivor tells a personal, honest, and powerful story of loss, but more importantly, one of hope, surviving, and healing. Both survivors of suicide and those who want to help survivors with their loss will benefit tremendously from the insights and accounts presented here."

~ John L. McIntosh, Ph.D.
Associate Vice Chancellor for Academic Affairs and Professor of Psychology, Indiana University South Bend, past president of the American Association of Suicidology, and co-editor of Grief After Suicide *(2011, Routledge) and* Suicide and Its Aftermath *(1987, Norton).*

ACKNOWLEDGEMENTS

The editors would like to thank everyone involved in making *Seeking Hope* a reality. To tell one's story of survival after the suicide loss of a loved one can be a daunting task but these fourteen authors did it, even when they didn't think it was possible. We wish to thank our families for their support. Also, a big thanks to designer extraordinaire Megan Herndon and web guru Tim Mickey. Finally, thanks to David "Idea Guy" Davis who initially conceived this idea and threw it by Michelle one day letting her make it happen several years later.

TABLE OF CONTENTS

FOREWORD

"These days are the winter of the soul...
But spring comes
And brings new life and beauty...
Because of the growth of the roots in the dark."
~ Sarah Graves Reeves

Everyone has a personal life story. The gift of sharing that story...and the gift of receiving it...are two of life's blessings.

The following pages are proof of this. Fourteen courageous people and two editors wrote their incredible stories to be published in this book, *Seeking Hope: Stories of the Suicide Bereaved.*

You are holding a treasure in your hands. Hold it with tender respect as you read. Hold yourself with gentleness. The stories will touch your heart. You will be awestruck and inspired by the resilience of humanity.

The authors contributed writings after each experienced the life-shattering death of a loved one by suicide. Life changed forever. This devastating event left them bereft and traumatized. Each person shares with you the powerful phases of handling the crisis, dealing with the aftermath, and finding meaning and purpose in their life. These are stories of healing and hope.

If you, too, have been bereaved by suicide, the sharing will be especially meaningful and comforting. It may enhance your own healing. If you have not experienced this event in your life, we are all grateful. Learning about suicide and the impact of this kind of loss may bring unexpected sensitivity and compassion to your soul.

Sharing stories takes many forms. One-on-one is the most intimate perhaps. It honors another person through daring to speak of deep personal pain. To trust the confidentiality of another takes courage. Telling the story repeatedly brings one face to face with the fact of suicide in one's life, yet this cathartic relief often brings comfort.

To listen without judgment or a need to give council may evoke empathy and gratitude. When someone reveals their deepest pain, it brings to the fore the privilege and preciousness of holding in one's hands...a broken heart. To validate that pain is a gift. A treasure beyond rubies and diamonds, this suspended moment in time builds a sacred trust for a lifetime.

Sharing in a self-help group, or a support group may take even more courage, or more longing to be with other bereaved suicide survivors. Most emotionally connected people need to share their stories. They need to learn from one another what helps and what does not. They need to be re-assured that it is possible to go on living without their loved one after being slammed with suicide.

LaRita Archibald says in her chapter, people are "thirsty to be in the presence of others who understand the anguish of losing a loved one to suicide."

Writing or speaking about one's story to the public requires bravery and enormous trust. It requires a desire to help others in spite of vulnerability. Each bereaved survivor knows the pitfalls of the voyage ahead. They are privileged to be a guide through unfamiliar waters for the newly bereaved.

In a culture only recently addressing this mysterious malady, there is often shame and fear of being judged. The ignorance of the general population can be overcome by risk-taking and bold determination to speak out. Stigma must be eliminated. Education and advocacy are imperative. As the stigma of cancer has disappeared over time, the same must evolve for suicide.

The authors in this collection of stories are contributing to this effort. I applaud them and admire the honest eloquence of their words. There are themes and threads in the writings that weave people together in universal consciousness. Of course, there are differences; but the similarities join their wounds in compassion. There comes a knowing beyond understanding... beyond words... a gift to us all.

My story is their story...

On February 19, 1977, my twenty-year-old son, Curtis Mitchell Bolton, took his life by gunshot. This inexplicable act shattered our family like a bomb destroying its target. My husband, our three other sons, and I, became the horrific center of wildfire gossip and speculation ... and, at the same time, of love and compassion. In those days suicide was a forbidden word. Stigma demanded that families hide their pain and perhaps the truth about the death. No one stood before us to guide us.

At that time I was the Director of The Link Counseling Center in Atlanta, Georgia, a non-profit counseling center for individuals, families, and groups. Our work at The Link was well known for professionalism. It was one of the first agencies in the country to provide family therapy.

The nightmarish impact of our son's death was felt in our community, mainly because we told the truth about what happened. We spoke openly about Mitch's hidden struggle with depression. He kept his secret from everyone, including us. He was a superb actor; but he may have felt like an imposter, always pretending to be happy-go-lucky. He may have had clinical depression, which we did not recognize.

We thought his sadness was due to the break-up with his girlfriend. That sadness may have masked a deeper depression. We will never know. After years of searching for answers, we have learned to live with unanswered questions. We live with hunches and guesses, with partial answers; enough to put to rest the tortuous question, "Why?"

We were to learn, after the fact, that Mitch had four girlfriends. The only one known to us broke up with him three weeks prior to his death. He had apparently promised marriage to two of the young women. This was only one of several losses and pressures which may have contributed to his depression. He struggled with academics in high school, then college, in spite of his genius level IQ. He was later diagnosed with a learning disability, for which he received professional help.

He was a talented musician, frustrated by his impatience to be a success. He obviously had trouble with relationships. Yet, Mitch was charming, funny, and beloved by his peers–described as "the life of the party." His low self-esteem and his perfectionism, his sense of being a failure and a burden, as well as the catastrophic pain he hid, combined to create a conflicted and hopeless young man.

Mitch shot himself in his bedroom of our home...determined, I believe, to end unbearable pain, caused by a combination of sources. From what I've learned since then, most people don't really want to die. There is ambiguity. They believe they cannot go on living with the pain, but they don't want to die. Finally, in their mind, when the pain becomes too much to bear, the choice to end it, sadly, becomes the only option they see.

My journey of healing involved years of grief work. The decision to go on living, the resolution to let the process unfold, and the powerful encouragement of family, friends and peers, sustained me. I searched my Soul in therapy with a wise, sensitive psychiatrist. I earned a master's degree in Suicidology from Emory University. I found my life's direction.

In 1977 there were no known support groups, locally or nationally, for loss or grief. An Atlanta minister asked me to help him start one. I put him off for three months.

Finally, in August of 1977, six months after Mitch's death, I agreed to help. The next year, 1988, we formed one of the first support groups in the country specifically for people bereaved by suicide. We called it SOS, Survivors of Suicide. I believe that the collective unconscious was at work. The response manifested ... was growing all over this country. Groups were formed by bereaved laypeople, giving comfort and solace to hundreds of newly bereaved survivors of suicide.

A movement in this country, sparked by those bereaved by suicide, began pushing against the "vow of silence" and against the stigma. Today, local and national government supports some funding for research and projects on suicide prevention and intervention. Clinicians and researchers touched by experience, and determined bereaved suicide survivors, now encourage attention to bereavement after suicide.

Currently, I speak about suicide prevention and aftercare in this country and abroad. Suicide education and bereaved survivor healing continues to be my life's work. My story, in the book, *My Son...My Son...A Guide to Healing After Death, Loss or Suicide*, offers to others one family's path to healing.

Kudos to editors Michelle Linn-Gust and Julie Cerel, for the loving energy it took to produce this book. Proceeds will fund survivor research through The

American Association of Suicidology. This collection of poignant stories will make a profound difference in the lives of the newly bereaved.

Psychiatrist Drew Slaby, from New York City, once said, "When there is one death by suicide, we are all diminished." I believe when one life is saved we are all touched by grace.

To be transformed by the experience of a suicide event in one's life is possible, not inevitable. It is a choice, an initiation which will test an individual's body, mind and spirit. This monumental trauma presents an invitation to die to one's old patterns and to replenish life with meaning and purpose. It is about resilience. It has a unique timetable. It reevaluates priorities. It calls one to value the preciousness of life.

On a visit to Australia, I learned from the Aboriginals a formula for living: "Live in service. Live without judgment; and live in forgiveness."

Our authors bravely exemplify these words. They have received the restorative healing properties of speaking their truth, of resurrecting their lives and sharing their wisdom with others. They now live in service by helping others. They released their loved one and themselves from judgment. They are witness to forgiveness.

They earn your listening heart.

Iris Bolton
Atlanta, Georgia

What We Know and Need to Know About Suicide Bereavement: Why This Book

By Julie Cerel, Ph.D.
Kentucky, USA

Approximately 33,000 people in the United States die by suicide each year. If you're reading this book, it is likely you knew someone who died by suicide or are trying to help someone who cared about someone who died by suicide.

I am a researcher. I'm trained as a clinical psychologist and work as a faculty member in the College of Social Work at the University of Kentucky. I've been doing research on suicide bereavement since 1996. I did not know this would be my life's work when I started.

I was working on a study of children who had experienced all types of parental death and realized that so little was known about the experience of children who lose a parent to suicide. When I tell people my work focuses on suicide survivors, people bereaved by the suicide death of someone close to them, I get one of two reactions. One reaction is of shock and sometimes disgust, often followed by a "That's so sad. How can you do that kind of work?" Sometimes this is even a conversation stopper. The second, and much more common, reaction is exemplified by the disclosure from my childhood friend's father when I told him what I do. He told me about his father who died by suicide when my friend and I were in elementary school and said something like, "I guess we never told any of you kids how he died." Both of these reactions are why I do the work I do. I respond to the first kind of people with what they probably think is way too much information about suicide and the consequences for people left behind. For the second type of person, I tell them that they are not alone and their stories fuel my work. Since I started doing research on suicide survivors, I have learned that many of my friends have lost loved ones to suicide and even that there were suicides in my family I did not know about.

How common is the experience of losing someone to suicide

You've likely read somewhere that for everyone that dies by suicide, there are six people left behind. These people are often referred to as "survivors" or people bereaved by the suicide. The term survivor comes from the language of obituaries– "he was survived by his wife and..." If we count only six survivors for every suicide, it would make one in every 64 Americans (1.5%) a survivor of suicide (see http://mypage.iusb.edu/~jmcintos/2007datapgsv2b.pdf). In reality, when a suicide occurs, it's not just those intimate family members who are affected. Each death by suicide has the potential to have a profound impact on parents, siblings, grandparents, spouses or partners, aunts and uncles, cousins, neighbors, friends, classmates, co-workers, therapists, and countless other people who might never be included in the six. We really don't know how many survivors exist. Research to determine that is one of the reasons for this book.

In the last few years, my research group has conducted yearly phone studies of residents of my state. In these studies, numbers were randomly dialed in order to get the widest representation of residents across our state. We asked, "Do you know anyone who has attempted or died by suicide?" to which 64% of the people agreed they had. We then asked them, "Did they die by suicide?" Forty percent of people stated they knew at least one person who had died by suicide. Individuals also were asked, "Do you consider yourself a survivor of suicide, that is, someone whose life has been personally affected by a suicide?" Over a third of people (34%) agreed with this label. We also did a similar study online with college students and the findings were almost the same. What this tells me is that most people have experience with someone they know attempting or dying by suicide, almost half of people know someone who has died, and up to a third of people feel like a suicide has had an impact on their lives. The people who reported that they were survivors were the most likely to report they were very close with the person who died but the actual relationship type did not seem to matter (for example, child, friend, cousin). Research like this can help people feel less alone knowing that, even though each suicide is different, you are not the only person who has experienced the suicide of someone you care about.

Another thing we do not know is what kind of help people need following the suicide of a loved one. Many people search out the Internet or books like this to read about other peoples' experiences. Some research has been done on who receives treatment after a suicide. From 1999-2005, 257 suicides occurred in East Baton Rouge Parish (Louisiana), an average of thirty-seven per year. In the same time period, 374 adults were seen for treatment following a suicide. Based on this, for every suicide in the Parish, 1.45 adults sought treatment. The survivors seeking treatment fell into forty-five unique categories based on their relationship to the deceased. The top ten relationships accounted for 79.3% of all relationships. These top ten relationships comprise ones not typically covered in the six closest kinship relationship categories and included mother of the deceased, sister of the deceased, wife of the deceased, daughter of the deceased, son of the deceased (tied for fifth), friend of the deceased (tied for fifth), father of the deceased, brother of the deceased, girlfriend of the deceased (tied for ninth) and husband of the deceased (tied for ninth). So we know that a wide variety of people feel they need help after someone close to them dies by suicide. However, people seeking treatment do not represent everyone who is profoundly affected by suicide.

What do we know about survivors?

The grief process for suicide survivors has been described as more difficult and as drastically different than for those mourning a loved one through other causes of death. However, there has been little research to examine the longitudinal course of bereavement, what grief is like over time, for survivors. Survivors of suicide have many similar difficulties to individuals bereaved from other types of traumatic, sudden death such as car accidents or homicide. However, they also must deal with problems which are unique to suicide bereavement. These often include a search for the reason for the suicide (the whys), a misplaced sense of responsibility for the death and feelings about not having been able to prevent it, and intense feelings of blame for the suicide or the problems that led to it. Family members also often feel blamed by others for not having done enough to help the person before he or she made the decision to end his or her own life.

Some research shows us that a person is more likely to die by suicide or attempt suicide if a family member has died by suicide or has a history of psychiatric illness. This seems to be a result of both genetics and imitation.

While some people who experience the suicide of someone close to them experience depression, there is no research which shows us that depression is more common in suicide survivors compared to other bereaved people. Suicide survivors are at higher risk for post-traumatic stress disorder (PTSD) than people who experience other types of deaths. What is also probably more common for suicide survivors is complicated grief.

Complicated grief has been coined by Holly Prigerson, Ph.D. of the Dana-Farber Cancer Institute Harvard University. It shares features of PTSD and depression and also involves intrusive yearning, longing for, or searching for the deceased. Symptoms that may be present include avoidance of reminders of the person who died, a feeling of purposelessness or futility, difficulty imagining life without the deceased, numbness, detachment, feelings of being stunned, dazed or shocked, feeling like life is empty or meaningless, feeling like part of oneself has died, disbelief, excessive death-related bitterness or anger, and identification with symptoms or harmful behaviors resembling those the person who died experienced before his or her death. Complicated grief has been shown to occur following the suicide of a family member. It also has been shown to increase the risk of suicidal ideation for those bereaved by a suicide as well as appears to be related to the onset of depression, the prolonged course of depression, and PTSD. More research is needed on the course of bereavement following suicide to fully understand who has what types of problems following the suicide of someone they care about.

Interventions for Survivors

The literature on interventions for survivors of suicide is sparse. Most survivors do not seek out mental health treatment, formal or informal interventions. At this point, there is no one treatment which has been recommended for survivors. Psychotherapy or counseling, both in individual or family format, is preferred by some survivors and may be helpful. Support groups, often called SOS (Survivor of Suicide) groups are the most common form of intervention received by survivors. Many view participation in support groups as an essential part of "working through" bereavement following suicide. Support groups can be located through the website of the American Association of Suicidology (www.suicidology.org) and the American Foundation for Suicide Prevention (www.afsp.org). There are over 400 support groups for survivors in America with at least one group in each state and several online support groups available for people who prefer the anonymity and convenience of online support. Support groups may be helpful because they allow members to feel a sense of identification with other group members who may have experienced similar situations. People in support groups can feel like they are benefitting both themselves and others from sharing their own experiences and listening and providing advice to people newer to the process. Over time, people who have been in the group and who have been survivors for a longer period of time can help newer members as they describe ways they made it through especially difficult times or handled sensitive topics. This becomes a form of social support which often extends to friendships outside the group itself. This social support may be helpful for survivors coping with depression, loneliness, or life stress.

Advocacy has been a source of support for some survivors either on its own or in combination with individual or group therapy. By using their grief to advocate for local, regional, or national change, survivors have been at the forefront of the suicide prevention movement. These efforts have led to a variety of legislative successes including the introduction of Congressional resolutions recognizing suicide as a serious problem in the 1990s and the passage of the Garrett Lee Smith Memorial Act in 2004. The Garrett Lee Smith Memorial Act, named after the son of the United States Senator from Oregon who died by suicide, was the first ever national authorization and appropriation for youth suicide prevention. The Garrett Lee Smith Act authorized $82 million over three years for youth suicide prevention programs including grants to states, American Indian Tribes, and colleges to support suicide prevention efforts. Services for survivors are part of these funds. Some survivors have reported that the act of creating political will and seeing changes becomes a part of their healing experience. Other survivors use their grief to work in suicide prevention with the hope that other families do not have to experience the pain of losing a family member to suicide. There has been no research to date about the effect of survivors engaging in advocacy or prevention work.

Some survivors may experience what has been termed Posttraumatic Growth. Posttraumatic Growth is a concept that has been described as psychological change for the better that occurs as the result of a person's struggle with a stressful and traumatic event. This is an area which needs further research to determine which survivors or what situations might be most associated with growth following the suicide. As awful as the experience is of losing someone we care about to suicide, there are people who come out of the experience changed for the better for it.

Why Research?

We really don't have a great deal of information about how suicide impacts people. We don't know how many survivors exist in the United States or worldwide. We don't know who is really affected by a suicide of someone they care about or who needs help following a suicide. We don't know what types of help works best overall or for some people in particular.

As I see it, there are several reasons research has not yet been conducted to answer these questions. First, people see survivors as vulnerable individuals who might be injured by being asked to participate in research. This has not been my experience. Many survivors are very willing to participate in anything that better helps them understand and share their experience. And, participation in research is always voluntary. Second, research takes a long time. Most research is funded by grants which can take years to obtain. Then, the study needs to be approved by what is called an Institutional Review Board (IRB) that makes sure that participants in research are being treated ethically. IRB reviews slow down the process which can be frustrating for people who are hurting now and who want answers before anyone else dies by suicide. But they are necessary to make sure the research does not cause harm. Once a study is conducted, it can take years for the results to get published in scientific journals due to a process called "peer review" in which the articles are read by other scientists to make sure the study was done in a way that the results make sense. And these scientific publications often don't end up readily available to non-scientists so they can learn the results of studies. Finally, research takes money. Suicide bereavement research has not been funded at high levels because no one has done research to show that people bereaved by suicide are at special risk. It's a kind of catch-22.

Why this book?

We decided to write this book for three main reasons. The first is to instill hope in people bereaved by suicide or those people who care about them. All of the chapters in this book are about people who have survived one of the worst losses imaginable, the suicide of someone in their family or someone very close to them. Each contributor did more than just survive. The people who contributed to this book have all taken the suicide of their loved one and turned it into something that has changed their lives and, in many cases, inspired them to help change the lives of others.

The most unique reason for this book is to provide funding for research which will help us better understand the experience of suicide bereavement and to determine what kinds of treatment, support, and resources work best for which survivors. The majority of proceeds from this book will go into a special fund housed at the American Association of Suicidology which only will fund research on suicide survivors. People also can contribute directly to this fund by going to www.suicidology.org and clicking on "donate now." It is called the "Seeking Hope Suicide Bereavement Research Fund."

This book would not have been possible without the stories from each contributor. I know each author traveled a journey to get their story from memory onto paper. Thanks to them for sharing the stories of their losses and the journeys they have traveled to find hope following suicide.

Thank you for reading and I wish this book leaves you with a little more hope than you experienced prior to picking it up.

Traveling Through Suicide Grief

By Michelle Linn-Gust, Ph.D.
New Mexico, USA

Before my sister died in 1993, the closest deaths to me had been both my grandfathers. My paternal grandfather died in 1985 and my maternal grandfather in 1989. Both died in their sleep, but the effect on me was limited. I didn't know them well; they weren't part of my everyday life. Mostly, their deaths felt awkward.

However, when Denise ended her life in 1993, just two weeks before her eighteenth birthday when I was twenty-one, her death turned my world upside down. She was the girl I shared a room with for ten years, we wrote letters while I was at college (as these were the days before email), and she knew more about me than anyone else. I didn't understand what grief was and couldn't comprehend the emotions that the journey forced me to travel through.

I had no idea that grief was a process, one that would take time to go through, that wouldn't just last a year, as I'd heard in "a year of mourning." I didn't realize it was normal to feel sad and that the peaks and valleys of grief were normal. I didn't understand that my yearning to reconnect with my sister was typical in grief when someone we care about has died. And I didn't understand that the bond between my sister and me wasn't broken, instead it had changed. My only regret for my grief road is that I didn't understand it at all, but my hope now is that by educating other people, perhaps I can offer a road map that wasn't available for me.

Although each of us experiences grief uniquely because of who we are (our personal histories), our relationship to the person who died, our views of suicide and death, and what is going on in our lives at the time when the person died (good and bad), there are parts to the journey that all of us might experience, or will see our loved ones travel through. Having some idea of what the grief journey entails, particularly after suicide, helps the road feel less confusing and overwhelming. It also helps us to feel "normal," that we aren't verging on some sort of a mental breakdown because our emotions feel out of control.

To lose someone to suicide is complex and confusing. It's unique from other ways people die because someone ended his or her own life. They made a choice and that leaves those of us left behind wondering if there is something we could have done to change that choice. Often, there were mental health issues involved that also could have included substance abuse. There is not only one factor that goes into a suicide death. Each of the stories that follow this chapter describes the unique aspects of the losses although there also are parallels that run through all of them.

Our reactions to suicide loss begin with our view and attitude of suicide. If we were raised to believe it is a sin (culturally and/or through religion) or a crime, we often still feel that stigma. And we feel fear that we don't know where our loved one went after he or she died or what will become of us because we fear telling anyone what happened. Or if our loved one coped with a mental illness, we might believe the suicide was inevitable. Many of the emotions we feel can be traced back to our past experiences of death and suicide (Do we have any? What have they been like?). Even death is a taboo in many families and to top it with suicide makes people more uncomfortable.

Who we are and what's going on in our lives when the person dies also affects how we grieve. We could be going through some difficult circumstances in our lives, but we also might be experiencing happy events (like a new marriage, new job, or the birth of a child) and the loss tempers them. What was our relationship with the person who died? Were we close to them? Had we shared a history with them? There are many factors to sort through during the processing of a loss and what it means in our lives.

The emotions of suicide grief are endless. By trying to include them all, we inevitably would forget some of them. Instead, here are some of the major ones that people often experience:

Guilt

It's very common for survivors to feel guilty after a suicide death, where people wonder what else they could have done, or what could have made the outcome different. The reality is that, although we believe we might think would have been different if we had done things another way, there's no way of knowing that. Guilt is an emotion that sometimes overwhelms people, but it's one that needs processing to let go and realize we did all we could to help them.

Why Question

One significant place on the suicide journey is the asking of the Why? question. This can go on for some time as we try to place all the puzzle pieces together after a loved one has died. The reality is that the person who died often took some (or most) of the pieces with them, and we never will truly know why they ended their lives. But it's important that we ask ourselves this question as it is part of traveling on the road of suicide grief.

Relief

While not usually discussed, sometimes there is relief when a loved one has ended his or her life. If the person was severely mentally ill or struggled with everyday life, some families feel relieved that they don't have to worry about a loved one anymore. But with the relief comes guilt for feeling relieved that they have ended their life. Know that relief is common and it doesn't make you miss your loved one any less if you feel that way.

Blame/Anger

What is there not to be angry about? A loved one has left us. We feel hurt and that manifests itself into anger. As human beings, we have a tendency to look for someone and/or something to blame. We usually do this in our anger because we're trying to make sense of what has happened. We are trying to understand why our loved one has left us. Often, though, our anger and blame are misdirected and hurt the people we care about the most. It's okay to feel angry about the choice your loved one made to end his or her life.

Sadness

Sadness is a fundamental part of grief. We feel sad that our loved one has chosen to end his or her life and is no longer with us. Sadness is a very common emotion of any grief journey because we must acknowledge what we don't have our loved one with us anymore.

Abandonment

In suicide grief, abandonment also can be a very common emotion. We feel like our loved one left us and didn't consult us. We might feel that to be left in this world without them (because they were so important to us) is painful and difficult.

Loneliness

Suicide grief is lonely. We all have to travel our own roads, even when we are part of a family or have many connections in our lives. We also feel lonely because someone significant to us is gone. And we feel lonely because often we don't have anyone to share the road with us. Our family members might not be in the same emotional place we are, our friends might not understand, and/or we just aren't sure how we can connect with others who have been through something like we have.

The Holistic Self

As human beings, we have a tendency to see ourselves in pieces. We forget that our body, mind, and all the other aspects of us work together. When we grieve the loss of a loved one, particularly after a suicide, we feel it emotionally. We can't stop crying. We don't understand. We feel confused. But we also feel tired and exhausted.

Grief is hard work and we must process it in the many pieces that make us holistic beings. Often we talk about how we emotionally cope with grief, but it's much more than that. We also must be aware of ourselves physically to keep from getting sick as we travel our grief journey. It's important to eat balanced meals and try to get sufficient sleep and exercise. It can feel overwhelming to think about these things when we feel like our world is crashing down, but it also can give us a much-needed focus.

And we should nurture our spiritual selves. Again, this can be like a burdensome task especially because we might be angry with God or our Higher Power. We might doubt that anyone exists beyond the here and now where we live. But asking these questions is part of the grief journey, especially after suicide when a loved one has ended his or her life. The questions feel larger, more difficult to answer. By reaching out spiritually we are allowing ourselves to find help and hope in ways we might not have thought of before.

Routine

We often discount the importance of routine in our lives. When we have a suicide loss, it throws life as we know it out the window. We don't realize how much we miss our routine until it has been stripped away. We are creatures of habit and often we complain about our routines, about the seemingly flatness of daily life, because we are looking forward to the "big" parts of life– the holidays, the vacations. We forget that life is really about savoring the simple aspects and when our loved one dies, we often feel like we missed out on something.

Hope

In this confusing and often lonely journey we call suicide grief, there is one aspect that sustains us and guides us although much of the time it feels hidden from us. Hope. It is hope that keeps us forging forward. Hope helps us to know deep down somewhere inside of us we will one day feel good again. What we each define as hope will vary among us, but the most important part is that we all know it is there. Hope is what life ultimately is about.

For some of us, there is hope that we will see our loved one again in another life, for others it's feeling the presence of our loved one in some way in our life. And yet for others it's the sense that we will find purpose in our lives again.

To have hope in our lives, we also have smaller symbols of hope that sustain us in times of sadness and difficulty. This symbol can be as basic as the sun rising in the morning. There is hope in seeing the sun come up, in seeing a new day with a clean slate. While some people might find dread in a new day, the ultimate comfort is knowing that we have a chance to have another opportunity at a new day. Other symbols of hope in our lives can be children, pets, material objects– whatever is important to us in our lives that we grasp when we are in pain and need something to give us relief. For some people, reaching out to others through suicide prevention advocacy, helping people grieve a suicide loss, or in another helpful manner is a way to find hope again.

The grief journey we must travel after suicide often is treacherous because we aren't sure what to expect. Life never prepares us for the kind of grief (and the reactions that tumble after it) that suicide loss brings. We also don't realize that we don't have to travel it alone. There are many other people out there who are going through a similar journey (or are much further along on the road) and would welcome some company or a chance to help us. Ultimately, we must find our own way and our own hope and peace, but it's there waiting for us to discover it.

It would be impossible to include everything there is about the grief journey because the journeys are unique to each of us. However, the chapters that follow take us along the grief journeys of fourteen people and their families. You will see similarities and differences in their stories but most of all, there will be hope.

A Man of Few Words

By Diana Sands, Ph.D.
Australia

On a small island with the rhythmic sound of waves washing against the rocks, and a gentle breeze rustling the grasses, we gathered to remember our loved ones lost to suicide. The gathering was part of International Survivor Day, and together we survivors planted a sturdy Sydney Red Gum seedling as a symbol of growth. I wrote my grandfather's name in gold on a small pebble and carefully placed it at the base of the tree, pushing it firmly into the gritty, Australian soil. Finally, my grandfather has a place among our family. He would approve of this small, rocky island surrounded by water, reminiscent of the Hebridean Island from which our family originated.

I have always known that my grandfather took his own life. I can't recall who told me or how I knew because it was not something talked about in our family. It has been said that telling is a process, not an event, and as a child growing up with the absence of family conversations about my grandfather, it is a complex and lengthy process making meaning of his death. Earlier this year I travelled from Australia to visit family in Scotland, and gathering my courage breached no-man's land, to ask where my grandfather was buried. In response, my elderly aunt looked at me, paused, and said, "My daddy killed himself," and for that moment I could see in her eyes the confused young girl she was when this happened. If there had once been a grave, the location of it had been lost in the heavy blanket of silence surrounding my grandfather.

My aunt's fragility reminded me of my mother's admission in a rare moment in which she spoke of her father, telling me, "I think about him every day." When I asked what she was thinking, she told me in a small voice, "I think about how could he do that to me." Seventy years of silent rumination on her daddy's death. I, too, ponder how he could have done that to those he loved, how he could have left his wife and his three children in the way he did. From my perspective, his death and the consequences of that event within our family have significantly influenced choices I have made in my long professional career as a clinician, researcher, and educator specializing in suicide bereavement. My grandfather's powerful presence in my life is puzzling, separated by two generations. He died before I was born. We never met, but the manner of his leaving formed a constant and painful base theme that is part of the fabric of our family life. And in the way that children know, I knew about this pain because I grew up among it and I saw and felt the experience of those I loved. The space he left in the family was not an empty vacuum, but one filled with a heavy sense of poignant tragedy and loss. Most significantly, I think the manner of his dying spread a shadow of uncertainty about the value of living that still weaves through the texture of our family. I believe our family would have been strengthened had he stayed and stood behind the generation before me, contributing his resilience and continuity to anchor the value of life.

At different times in my life I have found myself "trying on my grandfather's shoes" as I reflected and engaged with questions about the intentional nature of his death that linger like dangerous holes within our family (Sands, Jordan, & Neimeyer, 2010, p. 265). I have been told, "He was always a sad man." He was a man who had experienced "a very hard life," and the evidence for the accumulated burden of a lifetime of hardship begins with his early years. My grandfather Matthew was born in Scotland into a family of six children, a shale miner's son with hunger and poverty always close. He started work in the mines at the age of twelve. Shortly afterward, he lost his father and older brother in a tragic accident. The early loss of his father and the consequent weight of responsibility as sole breadwinner for the family was an overwhelming and frightening burden for a young boy and became an integral part of the man he grew to be. His youngest sister died during this period due to lack of medical treatment and I have been told her death weighed heavily on his heart. The hardships he endured in his life also take account of his years as a soldier serving in WWI, years of economic depression before and between the two wars, the constant threat of unemployment that tenaciously followed him throughout his life and the death in infancy of his son.

Significantly, despite these hardships, I have found through my reflections, evidence for a remarkable resourcefulness and resilience in the way my grandfather battled the odds life dealt him. The slaughter of millions of soldiers which took place in WWI resulted in estimated deaths for all those countries involved, of between 9 million to 16.5 million, with 21 million wounded. My grandfather, however, having served in the Army from September 1914, until demobilization in March 1920, returned to marry his sweetheart. As further evidence of his resourcefulness, although unemployment fears were a constant companion, he worked two jobs during the day and night after he immigrated to New York City throughout the awful years of the Great Depression. So I ask myself why, at this particular point in his life, at the age of forty-nine years, having negotiated all these hardships, did he give up on himself?

In my efforts to answer this question and integrate the knowledge of his death, I have, like many of those bereaved by suicide, found myself doing an inter-generational version of "walking in his shoes" (Sands, Jordan, & Neimeyer, 2010, p. 266) trying to understand his life, the world he lived in and the pain and hurt he carried within himself. What kind of man was my grandfather? Would I have liked him?

Would we have had anything in common? What was his mindset at the time of his death and what events in his life caused him to find himself in that place? I have been told he was a shy, reserved man– a thinker given to quiet reflection. He was a self-taught man of few words. And he was a man born into a time in history of great economic, social, and political upheaval and change. It is hard for me to imagine his world from this side of two world wars. With so much change in the intervening years, much of his world has vanished with little trace. Miraculously, however, his Army Service Records, although damaged in the bombing of London in 1940, are among the less than 40 percent of records salvaged. On the first page is his home address, the same as his mother's address, listed as next of kin. But I am too late when I visit– the rows of cottages rented to the shale miners were bulldozed many years ago. The Royal Commission into Housing in Industrial Areas of Scotland Report (1918) does, however, provide insight into the cramped, unsanitary living conditions in these cottages. Despite the hardships and meager wages, people flocked from the highlands of Scotland and Ireland to work in Scottish mines during the 1870s.

By 1910, my grandfather was made a foreman in the mines and a few years later he met my grandmother, a woman considerably younger than himself. Apparently my pretty grandmother was quite a flirt, and she and her sisters would get dressed in their best outfits and walk around the golf course. I've been told my grandfather was a handsome man who looked like the actor Randolph Scott. An introduction was made and they commenced to "walk out," a term for courting, but I think that most of the courting involved walks as there was little else to do. My grandmother was a petite, dynamic woman with beautiful blue eyes and a stunning head of chestnut hair. Her family owned a dairy farm outside the village. Born into a large family of eight children, she was blessed with an optimistic, outgoing personality and possessed a firm, practical footing in the world.

Apart from a few photos, I have only two linking objects to help me connect with my grandfather and these are very important to me. I have a lovely Victorian gold locket holding both their photos, a gift from him to my grandmother, and a beautiful ivory white silk scarf that she made and gave to him. The locket and scarf were clearly gifts they exchanged when he was leaving for the war. These tangible, tactile objects have a presence far greater than the objects themselves. They speak to me of the richness of lived experience and the language of the heart, and hold for me many nuances and meanings about my grandparents' love for each other. I wonder how many times over the long years of his absence during the war my grandmother touched the locket, opening it to look at their two young faces, my grandfather in his uniform ready to embark. I think about him among rough Army conditions, far from home, slipping his hand into his kit pack and running his hand over the silk scarf and thinking of my grandmother's beautiful hair. I imagine my grandmother with a needle selecting each thread and working it out to make the beautiful fringe to the scarf and her careful stitching hemming the material. My grandmother had worked as a maid in a large house from the age of twelve so I also think of the sacrifice of her scant shillings spent on the silk to make the scarf. I imagine him shy and diffident, presenting her with the locket– or perhaps on their day off they went on the train for a special outing to Edinburgh and chose it together. I like to linger on this image of them both so in love, young, and full of hope despite their world on the verge of plunging into a war that would kill and maim so many of their generation.

My grandfather enlisted in the 25th Middlesex Regiment Pioneer battalion under the command of Trade Unionist, John Ward. Later, while serving in Siberia, this battalion became known as the "Diehards" (Ward, 1920). The "Diehards" were sent to Siberia, paradoxically, to support the White forces of Admiral Koltchak during the Russian Civil War and were the first allied support troops to arrive in Vladivostok. When they arrived in August 1919, they marched through the streets with crowds cheering and music playing to be housed in the old Siberian barracks. I like to linger on this moment in my grandfather's life, such a long way from the shale mine in Scotland, marching up the street in Vladivostok with the crowds cheering. It was at this time that my grandfather received a Meritorious Service Medal (London Gazette, 1920). I remember being told that the medal was awarded for his outstanding skills in managing the Army horses during a violent storm at sea. John Ward's (1920) account of the Ping Suie being battered by strong typhoon winds and heavy sea conditions en route to Vladivostok offers support for this family lore. I wonder at this "horse whispering" aspect of his personality. It seems to be an important key to who he was, a good man to rely on to keep his head in a difficult situation. A man who perhaps had few words for people, but could understand and soothe animals.

The first thing my grandfather did on his return from the war, even before he was officially demobilized in March 1920, was to marry my grandmother on the 12th of December 1919. I have a studio photo taken at the time of their marriage in which they both look surprisingly animated despite the stiff, distant quality of studio photos of that period. I wonder if they had already talked about leaving to build a new life in America because it looks as though they have their eyes set on the future. Although unemployment was soaring in Scotland, my grandfather resumed his old position as foreman at the mines. It was during this time that their firstborn child, a daughter, was born. I reflect on the kind of optimism required to bring a baby into the world in the face of the catastrophic numbers of deaths during WWI. How did my grandfather reconcile the birth of his baby with his experiences in Siberia? I like to think of my grandfather still getting used to civilian life, holding their newborn baby daughter with love, wonder, and perhaps some awkwardness, vowing to himself that he would always protect her from harm.

Sadly, it was not long after this that they suffered the tragic death of their second child, a son who died from meningitis. Perhaps it was the death of their son, or maybe they were discouraged by the harsh economic conditions, but it seems they were restless and hoped for more opportunity in America. By 1922, with their little girl and a new baby daughter, my mother, they joined the courageous ranks of their countrymen reaching back to the forced emigration of families during the Clearances, a relentless tide of people leaving Scotland in search of a better life. They left Britain immersed in mourning for the unprecedented number of deaths in the war, symbolized by bringing "The Unknown Warrior" home to be buried in Westminster Abbey in 1920.

They settled in New York City and my grandfather found work with the New York City Railways and later extra shift work as a security patrol guard. Throughout these years, true to his beliefs, he fulfilled the position of Trade Union Secretary. Special outings were a visit to Central Park, Coney Island, or a trip along the Hudson River to Hook Mountain, or Bear Mountain for picnics. I have a photo of my grandfather at the beach wearing a hat, with his shirt sleeves rolled up, watching his children playing in their swimsuits enjoying a childhood a far cry from his own. I think he must have felt pleasure that he was able to give his children quite simply a childhood he never had. These were good years for my grandparents with their young family. The American economy was producing more than a third of the world's goods and talking movies were a source of wonder and entertainment. The optimism of the period is captured in the construction of the Empire State Building, at that time the tallest skyscraper in the world.

Yet these were also turbulent times, and New York City was a violent place to live. During the years of Prohibition, the Italian-American Mafia was growing stronger in New York's Lower East Side and the streets where the family lived were the scene of gunfights, with the citizens of New York running for cover. By 1928, as Eddie Cantor beat out the tune for "Makin' Whoopee," there were the first worrying cracks in the government's laissez-faire approach to the economy that was showing a marked decrease in consumer spending. The Great Depression was heralded by the day the Wall Street Markets crashed, Black Thursday, October 27, 1929. The lines from a popular song of that period captured the sense of despair "No more money in the Bank/what's to do about it/let's put out the light and go to sleep." Suicide deaths and crime escalated as large numbers of people were forced into begging and sleeping on the streets. In the midst of this, my grandfather was trying to care for and keep safe his family. I imagine it must have been like living in a war-ravaged country and I wonder how disillusioned my grandfather was, having served in the Great War, the war that was to create a better world, a world fit for heroes.

Ostensibly the decision to relocate to Scotland was to do with my grandfather's concern about reaching retirement age and being unable to get a job. But the decision also had to do with his worries about the violence in New York, and what he perceived as, the lax moral attitudes in New York City. He was a strict father, a moral man, who at the movies when an inappropriate scene was screened, would insist that the whole family get up and leave. A further reason was that from his early years in the shale-mining village he had nurtured a dream. The warmest most congenial place in that desolate mining village had been the local pub. It had been the village pub from the century before the shale mining company moved into the area and it was the central gathering place for all the miners. When WWI broke out this is where they bought each other drinks prior to leaving for Army training, and this was where those who survived came back to raise their glasses and remember those who hadn't made it. My grandfather wanted to be the person providing that place of companionship and refuge from a harsh world. He dreamed of owning his own pub, and to that end, he had for years worked two jobs, diligently placing savings aside.

They returned to Scotland in December 1936. I have a photo of their last Christmas together and I notice that his shoulders are bent and he seems to be lingering to the back of the photo, as if absenting himself from the family. There was dissension in the family about the move to Scotland. The children were angry with their father and not talking to him because they had not wanted to leave their schools and friends, and my grandmother was worried about how she would adjust to the staid atmosphere of regional Scotland. There also were worries about moving to Britain because of indicators that Germany was again gearing up for war. All this was distressing, but the major blow was the discovery that their savings were not sufficient to purchase a pub. Other options would have to be explored. My grandfather was brought low by this knowledge and didn't know what to do. He had no contingency plan. For such a long time he had quietly nurtured his dream, and now what? Nevertheless, the decision was made to remain in Scotland and my grandfather returned on his own to New York to finalize things and arrange for their possessions to be sent to Scotland.

I guess, as with all suicides, we can never really know what he was thinking or whether he had been planning his death. He didn't tell anyone or give my grandmother a chance to help. After many years of listening to those bereaved by suicide, I think it is not one single event but many events, factors, and circumstances that come together in that moment to eventuate in the final tragic act of despair. My grandfather had reached his limit of endurance and could go no further. I believe nobody can know or make judgment about what the limit of endurance is for another human being because each person and the life he or she lives is unique. I believe he was worried about finances and his employment prospects and confused about which way to turn. Moreover, in this weakened state, perhaps the pain of early trauma weighed heavily upon him. On a chilly winter day, he lost heart and went alone to the basement of the building where they had lived in New York and, with his bible opened at Matthew 6:10-14, The Lord's Prayer, he hung himself. The Lord's Prayer is one of the best-known and most beautifully worded Christian prayers. Eloquent in its simplicity, the words that stand out for me are those that speak of forgiveness. I like to think that my grandfather, a man of few words, chose to use the words of this beautiful prayer to ask forgiveness of his family for leaving them in this way.

However, as I know from my clinical experience, forgiveness is generally a complicated and lengthy process. My grandfather's suicide left a raw wound filled with broken trust and unanswered questions, a wound corroded by social stigma that has left my grandfather shrouded in silence for all these years, marked tragically only by the way he died. Not knowing how to talk about his death, the family stopped talking of him, and by the time I was a child, he was simply a vague, shadowy figure. All the hard-won achievements of his life, wrested with great difficulty like the back-breaking work of hacking and hauling shale from tortuous seams, slipped away and were lost to the family. In my group work and counseling with those bereaved by suicide, I have found narrative therapy to be extremely helpful (Neimeyer & Sands, in press). I also have come to understand the importance of constructing a "healing container" to foster narrative efforts, a space that has enough safety, support, and trust to nurture positive meaning-making possibilities as the bereaved initially "try on the shoes" and then "walk in the shoes" (Sands, 2009, pp. 13-14). In this process, there comes a time to "take off the shoes" (Sands, 2009, p. 14) and, like forgiveness, "taking off the shoes" is a process as people move backwards and forward integrating new meanings into their narrative. Sometimes in searching for meaning among the broken pieces, the complex layers of metaphoric stories can capture essential themes and subtle truths that offer guidance.

In terms of my own quest, a story that speaks to me is the Brothers Grimm tale "The Six Swans." In this story, six brothers are turned into swans by an evil stepmother. To return her brothers to their human form, their sister must spin a prickly plant into threads that can be woven to make six garments, one for each brother. The sister must complete this task in silence and without help. Over time, the fear is that her brothers will gradually lose their ability to assume human awareness and decline into the primitive mind of the swan. The plant is full of prickles, and as the sister pursues her task her hands become covered in sores due to tiny, fine thorns embedded in her hands. Many difficulties impede the completion of her task and to overcome these she must draw on her strength, courage, determination, compassion, and love before the task is finally achieved and she is free at last to speak and tell her tale. The vow of silence and the manner in which she continues with her task, alone, never knowing if the goal is achievable, resonates for me.

Also inherent in metaphoric stories is the concept that every story is intended to bear many meanings. For the swan girl's story intersects with the individual stories of each of the six brothers. There are many different meanings for each character in a story and also for those who listen to it. I have endeavored not to be presumptuous in writing this story and have tried to proceed with respect, compassion, and a well-intentioned curiosity, recognizing that others would place emphasis on different pieces and perhaps tell a different story. It has been a difficult and lonely journey for me to find a way to meet with my grandfather, a serious and quiet man of few words, across the gulf of time. However, I feel I have reached a place of understanding and the valuable resource that is his story has now become a part not only of my story but of our family story. My grandfather has been brought home to take his place within our family, a place denied to him in his death.

Having valued his achievements and honored and laid to rest the pain he carried in his life, I find myself in a tranquil space of positive valuing in which broken trust can be soothed and healed and the family tapestry repaired. Out of the confusion, sadness, and missing pieces, my quest has brought a knowing about my grandfather far deeper and more profound than words can describe. Another blessing to come out of this tragedy is the experience and learning I take into my work as a clinician, educator, and researcher. I am privileged to have been able to work with those bereaved by suicide for so many years and to be significant in the establishment of an association in Australia for those bereaved by suicide– The Wings of Hope. Particularly, I hope that my book and DVD, *Red Chocolate Elephants: For Children Bereaved by Suicide* (Sands, 2010), a combination of text, illustrations, children's wisdom, and practical activities comforts and supports children dealing with this kind of grief. I wish a resource like this had been available for my mother and her siblings when their daddy died. In the spirit of this transformative space, I have taken myself on several pilgrimages and lit candles in sacred places around the world, from Australia to Scotland to America, and prayed for my grandfather and our family. I have reached across the generations to my grandfather's time and gathered the essence of his life, his love, hope, idealism, courage, and perseverance; the innocent and shining moments that are the best of him, and woven these into something good and strong. In this gesture of love and redemption, we have come to know each other. There is so much worthiness in this quiet man, so much to be valued by current and future generations. I offer this story in the hope of promoting conversations that will build connection and strength within our family and perhaps also for others.

References

Grimm, J., & Grimm, W. (2003). *The complete fairy tales of the brothers Grimm.* (Transl. J. Zipes). New York: Bantam Books.

London Gazette (22:1:1920). *Supplement to the London Gazette* (p. 946). London: His Majesty's Stationery Office.

Neimeyer, R. A., & Sands, D. C. (in press). Meaning reconstruction in bereavement: From principles to practice. In D. Harris, R. A. Neimeyer, & H. Winokuer (Eds.), *Grief and bereavement in contemporary society: Bridging research and practice.* Routledge.

Sands, D. (2009). A tripartite model of suicide grief: Meaning-making and the relationship with the deceased. *Grief Matters: The Australian Journal of Grief and Bereavement,* 12, 10-17.

Sands, D. (2010). *Red chocolate elephants: For children bereaved by suicide.* Sydney: Karridale.

Sands, D. C., Jordan, J. R., & Neimeyer, R. A. (2010). The meanings of suicide: A narrative approach to healing. In J. R. Jordan & J. L. McIntosh (Eds.), *Grief after suicide: Understanding the consequences and caring for the survivors* (pp. 249-282). New York: Routledge.

Ward. J. (1920). *With the "Die-Hards" in Siberia.* Dodo Press, UK.

When Love Was Not Enough

By Mark A. Wilson
Louisiana, USA

This is the story of my experience surviving my dad's death by suicide. It also is the unfinished story, as it has unfolded so far, of my relationship with my dad during his time here on earth and since he departed, March 11, 1972, at the age of forty-one. I was seventeen at the time of his death– my older sister was eighteen, younger one was sixteen, my little brother was seven, and my mother was thirty-five.

The majority of the relationship I have had with my dad has been after his death, when I have been forced to deal with and heal the relationship without his presence. As I write this, at age fifty-five, I have been without my dad's presence for some thirty-eight years, and we were only together for about seventeen, most of which were strained and painful. However, I knew that I was the "apple of my dad's eye" and we loved each other deeply, intensely, and it has continued to this day.

My purpose for sharing this story is simply this– my family and I survived the most traumatic, devastating family illness and circumstance, and have managed to find healing and functional lives, in spite of overwhelming odds against us. I would like to share this story as a message of hope for those who still suffer. And, speaking for myself, I have found peace, love, and acceptance towards my dad– his life, his death, and its impacts on me– such that we found and continue a relationship to this day. Our relationship now is characterized by love, peace, and intimacy, and I would like others who have suffered similar losses to know how this amazing transformation occurred. I'd like to think that now my dad can rest in peace and I can live in peace, free of the gut wrenching trauma and nightmarish imagery that haunted me for so many years. I hope he also found the peace he sought here on earth.

I share this story of illness and the misery that spawned out of it, with a boundless respect for my dad, his courage and judgment, and for my family that has suffered so and has struggled so for many years, to find healing and meaning in our lives. I do not judge my dad for ending his life and causing such unbearable pain to those he loved so deeply. I have come to understand, I think, in nearly forty years of contemplation, the dilemma of the suffering: chronic alcoholism; literally on fire mentally, physically, and emotionally; and unable to comprehend any relief except cessation of consciousness. I have made peace, as incomprehensible as it remains to me to this day, with his decision to take a .38 revolver, and shoot himself in the mouth, alone in a rented motel room, choosing the time of his death, in order to serve his family and end his suffering.

My dad, Harry Allan Wilson, was the seventh and last child in his family, many years later than his next sibling. He was a surprise, as they say. When my father was born, his dad was in his fifties and passed when my dad was very young. But his siblings all doted on him and spoiled him rotten– he was never without an audience or attention. Raised in the paper mill town of Bogalusa, La., in the southeastern part of the state, known far and wide for the local football team, the Lumberjacks, of which my dad was a star performer. Dashing and handsome, he worked at the YMCA as a young man, and always had a huge smile. Graduating from high school, he moved to Baton Rouge to start school at Louisiana State University where he continued a long-distance relationship with my mother, Barbara Ann Varnado, a year or two behind him. A year into college, he dropped out to join the Navy and pursue his dream of becoming a naval aviator and flying Navy jets. Reading the love letters my mother saved from this period in the early 1950s provides a glimpse into the vernacular of the time and the urgency of young love (both not yet twenty at the time) as my dad went through the training and exercises to become a pilot. They soon married, and in rapid succession three babies followed, each nine months apart. My mother remained on Navy bases in Jacksonville and then Pensacola, Fla., while my dad was on Navy cruises traveling the world. My mother, considered a beauty and a Paper Doll Queen back in Bogalusa (Bogalusa being a paper mill town, all things were paper-related, and the Paper Dolls were Bogalusa's dance and spirit team) went from her pampered lifestyle in high school to a married mother of three living on base all alone on subsistence wages. She must have felt a long way from home. In those early years, I remember us toddlers piled up in the car driving back and forth between Louisiana and Florida for visits, singing non-stop at the top of our lungs. I still to this day remember the words to all sorts of songs like "Marines' Hymn" lyrics "from the halls of Montezuma to shores of Tripoli" that we sang over and over. Happy days. There were many breakfasts on the beaches of Pensacola as a family of five playing in the sand and water.

Considered to be an ace pilot, Lt. Harry Wilson had gotten his beloved aviators wings and achieved elite status. Suddenly, he passed out in the cockpit one day and discovered he had adult onset Type II diabetes, at about age twenty-five, which would immediately and unceremoniously ground him and result in a medical discharge from the Navy. This was a blow from which Dad would never really recover. Transitioned into the business world, my dad was a gifted salesman, bright, handsome, well-liked, and immediately successful in any endeavor– that is until he lost interest. In these years his alcoholism, which had probably been there from the earlier years, began to take hold and take a toll. Once he started drinking, he would usually not stop until he passed out. Things done and said during the drinking episodes created terrible remorse and guilt that would take him days to get over. Jobs were lost, financial pressure built, homes were lost, and family was relocated over and over. The binges seemed to always come at the worst possible time, such as Christmas, or before or after a family commitment.

Through my dad's thirties, now back in Bogalusa gaining and losing one job after the other, with three teenagers at home and a brand new baby son, our family life was in terrible disarray and constant tension due to my dad's more and more frequent drinking binges and increasing depression. Wrecked cars, chronic financial stress, missed commitments, overwhelming remorse and guilt. It was very difficult for my dad to manage his diabetes with his daily insulin shots, drinking as he was. When the family moved from Bogalusa to Baton Rouge for a new position, hopes were high things would get better. Things did seem to inch better before lurching backwards. Depression, drinking all night two or three days a week, complications from diabetes, extreme financial pressure, and terrible family upheavals began to take their toll on my dad, and he started to talk in terms of suicide to my mother– driving off bridges, taking middle of the night trips to emergency rooms, etc.

For at least five years before his death, my dad knew he was not functional and was sinking deeper and deeper into the quicksand. However, even in the midst of this dysfunction and the extreme financial woes, when I, as a teenager, would go to my dad and ask him for $4 or $5 so that I could go out with my friends, he would invariably reach into his pocket and give me twice what I had asked. He always made me feel that what he had was mine, and I knew even then how little he had. His generosity towards me always, and to this day, moves me to tears, and I do my best to pay it forward. The family was in the full-blown dysfunction that all families of alcoholics eventually descend into. All family members were coping in various dysfunctional ways– little brother, for example, had extreme stomach pains in his early years, brought about by the stress. Many nights during these years, my mother and I would drive from bar to bar looking for my dad to try to get him home before he wrecked the car or something terrible happened. We never did find him during those searches, but to look for him was a nightmare, wondering what was going to happen if we should find him. The few times I saw my dad drunk were horrifying to me.

The fighting between my mother and dad had gotten so bad that my dad had moved out of the house. The last time I saw him, I had asked him to meet me at the Yellow Stamps redemption office. I had gathered up twelve books of stamps to redeem for a .22 rifle; I needed his help as I was underage to acquire a gun. He helped me, and afterwards, on the sidewalk, tried to engage me in conversation about my football scholarship prospects and other things. At the time, I was so angry at him that I gave him the coldest shoulder I could manage, to try to express to him how angry and fearful I was at what was happening. I could not talk to him about it. I just gave him the meanest looks I could manage and then hurried off, leaving him on the sidewalk.

My sister reported a similar final encounter with him later that day as he came by the house to get his handgun, and they briefly spoke. None of us knew what was about to happen. That weekend, after writing a letter to my mother, the words of which to this day cut me like a razor, my dad shot and killed himself in the motel and was discovered Monday by a housekeeper. My dad had concluded he was more harm to our family alive than dead, that my mother could find another more suitable husband, that perhaps the Navy would see his death as service-connected and thus the family could receive benefits. He outlined the commissions he felt he was due in his work as a realtor, noted the outstanding bills, and said his "I'm sorry and good byes" before ending his life. The very idea of my dad sitting down and working out the details of his life that he wanted to be followed up indicated to me that his death was premeditated, and that he was consciously preparing for the end, for an appreciable amount of time. His was not an impulse of the moment and this somehow felt even more painful to me to consider.

Even after all these years, the thought of my dad suffering alone as he did in that motel room, simply tears my heart out of my chest. It reduces me to heaving sobs of sorrow. I cannot bear the thought of it. I know I played a part in his pain and hopelessness and if there is any one thing I could change in my life, it would be on that sidewalk at the Yellow Stamp store, where I would give him a huge hug and tell him how much I loved him. Even if the outcome would all be the same, I would want to be able to let him know I loved and respected him and thanked him for all he had done for me. The truth is I have come to a place of accepting what happened, and I accept that for him it was what he chose needed to happen, outside of my control. After so many years of trying in vain and frustration to try to work out historical events in my mind where I could make them come out differently, this was torture. I don't even go there anymore. However, unable to change all that happened, I was destined to privately grieve and remain tormented for every waking and sleeping minute for many more years to come. The thought that love was not enough to save a person or a family, tormented and frustrated me, and I replayed events over and over and over in my mind, trying for a different outcome.

I was sitting in class at Robert E. Lee High School that Monday morning in March when I was summoned along with the rest of the family and told I needed to get home. There was a tangible feeling of dread and despair over the news that I feared. Hysteria and shock erupted in my home over the news of what had happened. I remember a feeling of free falling into a bottomless pit of fear, sorrow, anguish and torment as images of the scene, of my dad's face, of his suffering, would involuntarily appear. My dad's still bloody revolver was carelessly placed in his briefcase for us to find as we went through his things that were retrieved from the motel. (Many years later, that handgun had remained for some reason in his things, and I had it melted down by a metal smith and made into a wind chime).

Nothing had prepared our family for this outcome – it seemed we had traded one nightmare for an even worse one. We got through the funeral in Bogalusa, and started trying to sort through the financial ruins of our family. I have no idea where my mother got the strength to get through those days– in 1972 the stigma associated to suicide was in full bloom and we felt it as shocked friends and family kept their distance, as they just didn't "know what to say." At seventeen, I was the designated one to deal with social security about the benefits and to run down the commissions my dad felt were due him. I do not think any of them panned out. We made the case and, eventually, after lengthy and protracted petitions, the Navy did rule my dad's death was service-connected, due mostly, I think, to the way and means with which he was separated from the Navy after the diabetes was discovered. This period of time in the immediate aftermath of my dad's death– perhaps two to four years– as I was graduating high school and starting school at LSU, is a blur as I went from one horror to the next, without any help to process the loss or make sense of it.

Well on my way already to drinking alcoholically before he died, I began to drink and eventually use drugs with a vengeance from the time of his death on. Drinking provided the only relief I knew, for a least a brief moment in time, the gut-wrenching anguish would feel diminished until I got over the edge and it came out in drunken heaves and sobs even worse than sober. I did not draw a sober breath between seventeen and twenty-seven. Midway in this period, I discovered cocaine and using immense quantities, this drug provided the only relief from the anguish and ruminating I knew. The relief was intense for a short time, but then, as is the case with drugs, it brought on even more and bigger problems than it solved, leading me to a state of terrible depression and hopelessness. If the only relief I knew did not work, what then? Once I started drinking or drugging, I could not, would not stop, for days. I had, in my mind, given myself over to the drinking and drugging, and determined in my case it was medicinal and mandatory to just be able to sleep or breathe. To some extent, I was able to function during these years, graduating from LSU and getting and managing to keep a good job, but on the inside I was corroding and aging rapidly. By the time I was twenty-seven, I had not spoken of my dad's death but it was on my mind 24/7. I had the classic split personality– functioning out there in the world, appearing reasonably okay, but on the inside I was craving the next drink and increasingly seeking oblivion, the cessation of my own consciousness, while leaving a wide trail of destruction. I had gotten to the point where I could no longer imagine life with, or without, the drugs and alcohol.

During these years following my dad's death, my siblings, mother, and I did not speak over a twenty-year-period about Dad. It was just too painful and too raw a subject to bring up. No one wanted to upset another so we joined in the so-called conspiracy of silence, agreeing not to speak of the pink elephant in the middle of room. One of the very sad results of this is that our dad's life was sort of erased. For example, there were few if any pictures of him in any of our homes. It was not until we met privately as a group at the Baton Rouge Crisis Intervention Center, twenty-plus years after my dad's death, that we spoke to one another about our memories and feelings. We then went on to participate in a documentary that was filmed about surviving suicide, and in the filming of this documentary, we continued the process of sharing with each other feelings and facts, that, it turned out, much of which was unknown to the others. The feeling of intimacy in the sharing of these feelings was immense and it brought all of us, but particularly our mother, in the year before her death, enormous satisfaction that, finally, it appeared our wounds were healing.

By the time I stopped drinking and drugging on November 2, 1981, (as I write this, I am now approaching twenty-nine years of continuous sobriety) at twenty-seven, I was feeling very old, very tired, very much ready for the end. I fantasized about overdosing and on one hand, ached for the end of the suffering, and on the other, recoiled from the idea of this, aware of the unbearable suffering my death would cause my mother and loved ones. I generally felt that the option of ending my life had been taken from me, and that I had been "sentenced to live." All I wanted to do was to drink myself into unconsciousness. But by a strange turn of events, I got "invited" by people who were concerned about me, to consider my drug using and drinking, and spend some time in a Chemical Dependency Unit, which I agreed to do. Initially in complete denial about the nature of my drinking and drugging, it took me all of an hour to "see" what had been going on for a very long time in my life. I initially stopped drinking on November 2, 1981, and stayed sober, have been continuously involved in AA, therapy, sponsors, healthy living, and got married and had two children. I started and ran a business, and went along like this for another ten years, still unable to speak of my dad. I could not look at a picture of him and had only a private internal relationship with him characterized by anguish and torment. I wondered if his fate would be my own? Could I survive failure and disappointment? Over every relationship I formed hovered the cloud, "When and how was the subject of fathers going to come up; how was I going to tell them about my dad when they asked:" "How did he die so young?" They all seemed to want to know.

Twenty years after my dad's death, when I was ten years sober, in the quiet aftermath after a business I owned failed and I was watching myself to see if I could survive it, I read a story about the Suicide Survivors Support Group at the Baton Rouge Crisis Intervention Center. Survivors like me told their stories of the sorrow and anguish and the relief they got speaking with others who understood, as only others who have been there, could understand. Making the appointment to go to the Center and speak with the Director, Dr. Frank Campbell, and talk about perhaps joining the group, was maybe the most frightening act of my entire life, before or since. It was like taking myself back to the scene and reliving it in Technicolor that which had only swirled around silently inside of me for twenty years. No one before Frank had ever asked me what happened, in detail, and had stepped me through the facts and feelings. It was like being hit in the face by a bazooka for me. Not one fragment had been forgotten or healed. All the bloody trauma and wreckage was still smoking and smoldering. I joined the group and felt the immense relief and kinship as we survivors all feel when listening to others speak about what we have shared.

My turn came and amidst much sweat, tears, and snot, I told the story between heaving sobs. I began to tell what had happened, what it all had felt like, all the secret misery and torment and anguish. I told it over and over in all the ways I needed to, but now I was on the path towards healing. Words that I could not say, like "daddy," or "suicide," or many others gradually were desensitized and I began to thaw out and feel lighter and more free. But for six months at least, a veritable river of tears flowed out of me nearly all day and night, as years and years of sorrows and frustration expressed themselves. I did not know if I was losing my mind, or finding it. I just knew I could not go on one more minute like I had been. I had a sense, the same sort of sense I had when I first appeared in Alcoholics Anonymous and knew that I was found, that the Survivors Group was for me a defining moment of grace and that I could trust the people and the process with my life, which is what I did. I do not know if I have ever been more vulnerable, as when I voluntarily, at thirty-seven, took myself back to seventeen, to re-experience and fully feel all the blindingly painful events and feelings in the company of people in the group. It was, for me, the ultimate leap of faith.

For several years, I attended and shared in the group, found more peace than I had ever dreamed possible, and began to act as a peer facilitator and share more deeply with others. I began to see how my experience could help others. I sought out those with whom I could share. From the perspective of alcoholism, my dad's as well as my own, as well being a teenager and surviving my dad's suicide, I had lived a story that many others had lived or could relate to. Being able to share my story of recovery and survival and healing accelerated my healing and brought me a sense of meaning and purpose and joy beyond my wildest dreams. As the LOSS Team (Local Outreach to Survivors of Suicide) was formed at the Baton Rouge Crisis Intervention Center, I got involved as a team member and visited over a period of years with hundreds of families more or less immediately after the discovery or notification of a death by suicide. Dr. Campbell's premise in creating the LOSS group, that "postvention is prevention," that by helping families immediately after they are impacted by suicide (postvention), you would actually be helping prevent the next generation of suicides (prevention). By having survivors visit immediately with the impacted families, this was shortening the time for them to seek and receive help, from years to weeks. I knew from my case that this was certainly true and would save lives. And, I had suffered in silence for twenty long, excruciating years before getting help, and at any point in those twenty years I could have easily ended my life.

In my own experience with my dad's life and then death, there were many gaps in my mental map, in the pictures I could draw of what happened. For example, I did not see the scene where my dad died. Not that I wanted to, but my mind for many years struggled with what the scene looked like. As a member of the LOSS team over the years, we were on rotating call, available to go out to a scene whenever a call came in. The calls that I responded to during my years on the team seemed miraculously sent to put me in a position to experience first hand a scene or circumstance that was essential to my healing, to help put my mind to rest. I saw the scenes resulting from gunshot wounds, I saw motel rooms, I saw many traumatized teenage sons and daughters. I visited one scene where a twenty-two-year-old young man had shot and killed himself with the same gun his dad had used some years earlier, the younger man traumatized and blinded by grief, eventually becoming hopeless and despondent– exactly as my own story could have gone except for the graces I had known. I saw everything I needed to see, to help me complete the tapestry, and finally set my mind to rest. So though I was there to help others, it was me who was the primary beneficiary. I can think of no more overwhelming scene to enter than that of visiting with a family that has just been notified of the traumatic death by suicide of a child or parent or spouse or loved one– to enter that family's home and offer love and guidance and support. It is truly a privilege to be a participant in the most intimate, most sacred exchange of human emotion imaginable. Everyone is changed and healed by it. Graces that happen in that environment are beyond words.

In these intervening years, continuing therapy has helped me sort out the myths and false beliefs I picked up as a child living in the insanity of an alcoholic home, and the sense of over-responsibility I picked up in my teenage years that continued to haunt my adult life. When asked by a therapist at one point to describe my life at age ten, I realized I had no memories, not one, that preceded about age thirteen or fourteen, about the age the anger set in. As part of the exercise to go back and explore all that, I found pictures of myself at ages such as three, five, eight, ten, and twelve, and mounted them on a board that I kept with me always, at my desk working, next to my bed sleeping. Gradually I began to thaw out and see and feel what was going on in those early years that had prompted my mind to shut down. The family stress and disarray in those early years was intense and beyond the ability of a young one to make sense of it all so I just blocked it all out. For example, my clearest memory of one phase in our early life, when I was about six or eight, was of me standing against the wall in the kitchen, of our rather ramshackle house without heat, in the days of powered milk and government cheese, with my mother frustrated and banging pots and pans, and me wishing I could just disappear, just evaporate, just cease to be. It was such a powerful urge.

I came to see that I learned, at an early age, to hold myself responsible for the things that were happening, things that I couldn't even begin to control, but somehow or another in my mind, I "should have seen it coming and should have been able to fix or prevent it." This was particularly true as we got older and I saw my sisters, mother, and little brother suffering with the family dysfunction– for some reason I felt like I should have been able to "fix it" and save them from their suffering. But since I couldn't, then I had failed them. I began at an early age to see myself as having failed my loved ones and there would be no pardon for me, ever, for these failures. The climax of this was of course my dad's death. In my mind, I felt, that at seventeen, I should have seen this coming and thus should have prevented it, and since I did not, I was the guilty party here and would be forever responsible for all the suffering. Including my dad's. My love for my dad and his for me, should have been enough to save him and all of us, was my thought. This deep-seated sense of failure and responsibility was intrinsic and unconscious to me, but I began to see myself over the years as undeserving and thus would undermine any good thing that would appear in my life. I felt I did not deserve to have love in my life or success or happiness, so unconsciously, I created relationships that were doomed from the outset and found various ways to sabotage my life professionally and otherwise. All the while this was a mystery to me as I did not understand that much of my adult behavior was governed by early childhood beliefs.

By going back to each of the earlier years and recalling the circumstances and feeling the feelings and listening to what I learned to believe about the circumstances, I could see where the false beliefs began. I could see how I started holding myself responsible for what the adults around me were doing, even at age eight, as if I had some power to control or change things. Illuminating all this twisted logic, step by step, over many months and feeling terrifying feelings of fear, loneliness, anger, and disappointment, began to free me of these destructive thinking habits. I began to understand I was not responsible for the adults and what they did, or did not do. I was a child and an innocent one at that. When I saw the beauty and the innocence of my own seventeen-year-old son, I could see myself in a new light. I could no more have saved my father and mother from their fate than my son could have me. What seems obvious now was very obscured from me for many years. I have come to see myself in a more realistic light concerning the life I was born into and how I have responded to it all. I don't feel responsible for other's decisions or sufferings, however, I do see where now as an adult, I can choose to help alleviate suffering any way or place I can, such as what I am doing here today by telling this story.

As I write this today, in August 2010, I have come to understand that our relationships with important people in our life do not end at the grave. The connections and impacts go on forever, such as the respect and admiration and love that I have for my mother, who passed seven years ago now. The respect and appreciation I have for the courage, devotion, and determination she mustered to gather, protect, and love and serve her children, when she was beyond overwhelmed, is beyond words. She was devotion personified and I still draw strength from her every day. The respect and admiration and love that I have for my two sisters and brother, for finding the courage and strength and grace to survive unbearable suffering, and raise children and contribute to life and help others, is beyond words. The thought of them inspires me.

The respect and admiration and love that I have for my dad, for the generosity and kindness and perseverance he showed during his struggles, and his willingness to give his final act of sacrifice for his family, is beyond words. I know that in his mind, his death was meant as a blessing to his loved ones that was meant to help, not hurt. I believe to some very large extent, my own sobriety, and healing and joy and happiness and very purpose in life, were bought by his sacrifice and by his suffering. I have been and remain devoted to the disciplines of discovery, feeling and healing, and attend meetings and do everything I can to preserve my mental and emotional health and to help others. I feel that we in my family are all blessed beyond words and I am grateful for this opportunity to share with you this story. I shudder to think where my family and I would be, absent the Baton Rouge Crisis Intervention Center, and all the loving people there, who, without asking for a dime, have loved us back to health. I hope this story gives you hope and helps you on your healing journey.

Finding Meaning and Purpose

By LaRita Archibald
Colorado, USA

I became a surviving mother in a time when suicide was a sordid, unspeakable act. Some of our extended family and friends were uncomfortable with our openness, but to deny the way my son died was to deny that he had lived and the uniqueness of his personhood. From early the terrible day he ended his life, I was determined to somehow channel his despair and my inconsolable loss into meaningful and productive energy that might spare another mother pain such as mine. I pray that in reading how I have worn my grief over the past thirty years you will not judge me as "blowing my own horn" but, rather, accept what I share for what it is intended, encouragement to invest your own grief energy into meaningful work. Every step is painful, but by leaning into the strength God provides, unbelievable things can be accomplished and the healing to be achieved... beyond measure.

It was my good fortune to be a stay-at-home mom while I was raising my children during the 1950s, 60s, and 70s. After school every day I heard five different voices holler, "Hi, Mom! I'm home." I had time to be a 4-H leader, the perpetual Boy Scout den mother, school room mother, and the neighborhood Kool Aid and peanut butter/jelly sandwich mom. Summers were filled with Little League, swim meets, cookouts, usually a family trip, and a kids-only stay at Grandpa and Grandma's. Our children were healthy, bright, mischievous, and deeply loved. We lived modestly, but comfortably. Life was good.

My husband, Eldon, and I had been raised with strong ethics and values and made every effort to pass them on to our children. We applauded good grades and restricted social activity when obligations were not met. We guided our four sons and our daughter to appreciate hard work done well. We knew their friends. There were rules and privileges. We participated in church activities and often had discussions with our children about their faith and holding fast to their beliefs. We talked with them about sex; about the difference between lust and love, about the responsibilities one assumes upon becoming sexually active. We talked about unwed pregnancy and emphasized the benefits of abstaining from sexual activity until they were mature enough for marriage and parenthood.

Drugs became frighteningly accessible during those years. I learned everything I could about the mind-crippling impact of various street drugs that might be offered my children, often finding they were better informed than I. We attended drug seminars together and discussed peer pressure to try drugs and the courage and strength it might take to resist.

We tried to set high but reasonable standards as a foundation for good lives...as all conscientious parents strive to do. Very likely we had discussions and disagreements about every issue that ever pertained to growing up. But we never discussed depression. We never attended a seminar about it, if there was such a thing. I never sought out or read articles about depression, if there were any. It never occurred to me there was a need to. No one within my family was depressed or had any reason to be! And suicide!! We most certainly never had conversations with our children about the senseless, deplorable act of suicide!

During those kid-busy years, I would have dispassionately defined suicide as the act of deliberately killing oneself, if I gave its meaning any thought at all. I would likely have viewed suicide as an unfortunate, infrequent occurrence among the irretrievably mentally ill, the pain-ridden terminal, or the solitary elderly. I might have described the act as a bizarre incident among the destitute and deprived, the unloved and rejected, the weak in character, the morally corrupt or the spiritually void; obscure happenings separated from me and my family by a blinding hedge of ignorance, indifference, and complacency. Far beyond my punitive attitude toward those who had thoughts and feelings of deliberate self-destruction, my judgment and condemnation of those who acted upon them and my fleeting compassion for the families that were left to grieve them, I had no knowledge or understanding of depression, of mental illness, or the pain that precedes suicide. And I had no wish or need for any, for I had believed that suicide didn't happen to "nice" people from "good" families. Not in families where there was love, laughter, and loyalty; where there was acceptance and appreciation and where there were disciplined standards and values reinforced by deep spiritual convictions. Certainly, not in families like mine.

In the wee hours of the morning of August 30, 1978, the serenity of my smug, family-focused little world was shattered by the sound of a gunshot and my husband found our bright, handsome 24-year old second-oldest son, Kent, lying on our basement family room floor, mortally wounded by a deliberately self-inflicted shotgun wound to his belly.

Gone were indifference and complacency! In that instant, my definition of suicide exploded into a hellish nightmare, horrendous beyond description; into a great morass of smothering anguish, confusing angers, and an agonizing sense of guilt and responsibility; into an alien, isolated world that reverberated with incessant echoes of WHY? Why had this happened? What had gone so terribly wrong in his life that he wanted to die? Why hadn't we known? Why hadn't he told us? Why hadn't we been able to foresee and take action to prevent his death? How could this terrible tragedy have happened in our family?

Less than a week following Kent's funeral, I was at the city library to learn why he had killed himself. There were few books on the subject of suicide and none that gave me the answers I sought. From Albert Cain's book, *Survivors of Suicide*, addressing those left behind after suicide, I learned our family had a label, an identity. I was deeply disturbed by a message in that book from suicidologist, Dr. Edwin Schniedman, indicating... family members of a suicide are at great risk of suicide themselves. Was I to lose another family member in this manner?

In the early agonizing months of my search for reasons and causes of suicide, I read there was to be a convening of the American Association of Suicidology in Denver, Colorado, in May 1979. Despite concern expressed by my husband and children, I was determined to attend. For there, among the nation's suicide experts, I would surely learn why Kent had ended his life.

What I learned in those three days was very painful. I learned that much of what I had thought I knew about suicide was false; that there nearly always were clues or signals indicating suicidal risk. This was a devastating revelation! Why had I been uninformed about such a tremendously important fact? I learned there was no simple or single cause of suicide, but that suicide is often the result of a buildup of unresolved negatives that erodes one's ability to cope, leaving them feeling helpless, defeated, and in desperate need of relief from the pain of an overwhelming sense of hopelessness.

When Kent was a shy little boy I had felt the pain of my son's search for acceptance and friendship each year as he entered a new grade. I had disagreed with a teacher who declared him "slow," and requested testing that indicated a nearly genius level I.Q. We were so proud when Kent was selected for "Sing Out America" and the beautiful music they made. Recognizing him as an underachiever, I was very angry at his high school counselor who repeatedly assured us that everything was in order scholastically, then toward the end of Kent's last high school semester advised him he did not have enough credits to graduate. I recalled the respect we felt when he opted to return the next year, after his friends and classmates were gone, to earn his diploma.

And, yes, I had saw my son's disappointment when a relapse following Victoria A flu caused him to miss classes, fall behind, then drop out of college after he had moved back home to attend. I saw his discouragement as he hunted for a job to recoup lost tuition during the recession of that time. I knew movies and eating out with his parents didn't compensate for interaction with people his age...he had to have been lonely, but his high school friends had moved on/away. In an effort to be supportive, I had asked if we needed to find someone for him to talk with. His response was, "Mom, I don't need a shrink. I need a job. I need to feel like a man. I need to be somebody." Were these words indicators of his deep despair? Why hadn't I known that even after he found a job, the pressure to make quotas caused him constant fear of losing it? Why hadn't I known that the dozens of disappointments and setbacks he had suffered throughout his life were viewed as huge failures and unworthiness through his eyes? I never asked him if he had suicidal thoughts. All I offered were empty reassurances...that he was smart, had a great personality, a lot to offer, and a family that loved him, that "things" would get better, just give "it" time.

I learned about being a survivor of suicide at this conference. For the first time since it was established in 1968, the American Association of Suicidology had expanded their mission of "suicide prevention, intervention, and postvention (survivor aftercare; preventing perpetuation of suicide among survivors)" to provide a forty-minute session for survivors of suicide. The session presenter opened with the chilling statement that she was a substitute for the scheduled presenter who had lost her daughter to suicide two years earlier and had ended her own life the week before she was to speak at the conference. The six or eight suicide bereaved in attendance were joined by a few counselors and hotline workers. Except for her initial shocking self-introduction, I have no recollection of the content of the speaker's presentation. However, I vividly recall meeting Vicki, another mother, near my age, who also had lost a son in his twenties to suicide. Finally! Someone beyond my family could validate the meaning of having a child kill himself. We spent hours in the coffee shop sharing our tragedies and tears...cathartic, freeing, healing tears.

Vicki had been divorced when her two sons were small. Her ex-husband attended their son's funeral but was not a source of comfort to her. Her surviving son had alienated himself from the family during his teens, several years before his brother's death, and his return to the family was sporadic and infrequent. Vicki was an only child. Her parents, elderly and quite dependent upon her, were sympathetic, but physically and emotionally unable to console and support her. Vicki was very alone in her grief. I, on the other hand, had a husband who shared the anguish of our son's self-inflicted death, who wept with me, and held me in the night. We had four surviving children who deeply grieved their brother's death. My parents, my brothers, my husband's widowed mother and his siblings were all there for us, assuring us that we were good parents. I realized that, in the midst of my terrible loss and grief, I was truly blessed to be surrounded by an abundance of love and support in comparison to Vicki's solitary journey. The time with Vicki comforted and strengthened me with the reassurance that what I was feeling was being felt by another mother. I had longed to talk to another parent who had a lost a child to suicide. Somehow it was a relief to learn how many common feelings we shared; to know I wasn't the only mother who thought somehow she had failed her child, that felt guilty for not having recognized the depth of pain that lay behind a mask of well-being, and who was overwhelmed with anguish from knowing her child had hurt so badly he sought relief in death...and she had been oblivious to the scope of his pain.

The bitterest but most significant truth gleaned from my first AAS conference was that lack of knowledge and awareness allowed my son to die. For, although my son's death resulted from his deliberately self-inflicted shotgun blast, he also died of ignorance...his own, for not knowing that there was help...medication, treatment, and therapy that could have eased his depression; for believing that dying was his only avenue to peace; for not being able to rationalize that bad times pass, but death is forever. And mine! My own terrible ignorance! I had been completely ignorant of signs and symptoms of suicide risk. Ignorance blinded me to his symptoms of depression and his signals of despair and hopelessness...vague and veiled though they were. I had ignored the unease I had felt at times because I didn't know how to confront him about his thoughts and feelings. I had relied upon old misconceptions and bias and they robbed me of action that might have saved his life. Ignorance and lost opportunity are indescribably painful realizations to live with.

I wanted others to know what I had not known that cost me so dearly. Through my AAS membership I received information I used to develop a presentation around the symptoms and signals of life-threatening depression. I began by asking to address the congregation of my church. Most who attended were polite, curious, uncomfortable, and nearly all conveyed that while this was very interesting, it was not an issue related to themselves or their family or even to the church. Toward the end of my half-hour presentation, a gentleman stood and proclaimed, "What we are forgetting here is...if this young man had been a Christian he would not have killed himself." I was stunned; speechless. Needless to say, before that day was over I was prepared with a response should something similar occur again. This response stated the fact that faith and devotion does not make one immune to depression, despair, or suicide. It emphatically affirmed an All-Knowing, All-Loving, All-Forgiving God that had known my son's state of mind, had offered him other choices, but forgave the choice he made.

I prayed for direction. What was I to do with what I was learning? My son was a person of great worth, his life had had limitless value and potential; there had to be a way I could use his death and my loss and pain to help others. Or was what I had in mind merely a frustrated need to compensate for the suicide in my family and my own lacks? I knew that for my increasing knowledge to make a difference in other families my efforts must be God's will...and not just my own. I gave my uncertainty to God, trusting Him to use me how and where He would.

I visited the Pikes Peak Health Association, a local organization that served as an umbrella for several health-related agencies and talked with Janet, the director. I told her of Kent's death, about the judgment I experienced speaking openly of how he died, of my wish to use our tragedy and my growing knowledge in the hope of saving another mother's child. I asked if the agency could help. She reached across her desk, laid her hand on mine and said, "Absolutely. Not many people know this, but my father ended his life when I was fifteen. It has to be any family's most horrendous calamity." This visit initiated the next thirty-plus years of my work in suicide prevention, intervention, and postvention.

During my second AAS conference (Albuquerque, 1980), I was impressed by a session addressing Suicide Prevention Education in Schools presented by Dr. Tom Barrett and Dr. Bill Porter of Denver's Cherry Creek Schools. I told them of my son's suicide, my determination to use what I was learning to inform others, and my tentativeness due to my fear that I would do harm. They agreed to come to Colorado Springs to make a presentation at a local high school, appropriately, the school where my son graduated. The auditorium was packed; the students weren't shy with their questions. They were anxious to hear the straight goods about suicide and to learn how to help a friend that might be considering killing his/herself. With their gift of a very inclusive suicide prevention/intervention manual Drs. Barrett and Porter had compiled and their strong encouragement to follow through with my resolve to inform students and their parents about the "unspeakable"...suicide, I developed a presentation that would allow interaction from the students.

With help from Janet's staff, I designed a "Suicide: Fact & Fiction" brochure to reinforce speaking presentations I hoped to make. I contacted the volunteer coordinator of the largest school district in my community, telling of what I had learned since the tragedy of my son's suicide, giving Janet as a reference, Drs. Barrett and Porter as my mentors, and made myself available to speak to parents in the district. I quickly learned that parents had little interest in what I had to say, but health class teachers were anxious for me to speak to their students. I strongly believed that I had a divine partner in this work and prayed before each presentation for guidance, that my voice be sure, my knees be stilled so I could provide the words and knowledge needed for that class. Within a few months, I was addressing classrooms of teenagers several times a week. They took what I had to tell them very seriously. Many shared their concerns for friends or family members. A few had had someone close end their lives. Occasionally, a student would approach me to speak of his or her own suicidal ideation. Nearly all the students with thoughts of suicide went willingly with me to their counselor's office.

The Health Association operated a local HELP-line. Janet suggested any calls from suicide bereaved be screened for authenticity and forwarded to me for response. The calls weren't frequent, but when they came the callers were very relieved to talk with someone who had some of the same feelings, the same despair, the same sense of futility and fear. It seemed to be important for them to know they weren't alone, crazy, or some nasty, twisted piece of humanity to have had suicide happen in their family. It was not unusual when a caller asked, nay begged, for reassurance that there would be a time when they wouldn't feel the tremendous anguish they presently experienced. Nearly all had suffered unimaginable trauma, and for some, the trauma had been magnified by hurtful words or actions from first responders at the scene.

My thoughts returned again and again to the comfort it would bring if these callers could help one another, but the Help-line agreement forbade me from sharing caller's phone numbers. And even if I could connect them, was it a safe thing to do or would it be harmful, even risky, bringing so much pain together? After all, I was not a trained counselor, I had no professional training in helping people, just the experience of losing my son to suicide and the willingness to be there for others like me. One afternoon, sitting in my office, weary from considering ways suicide bereaved could share their grief, I put my face in my hands and said, "Please, God, I need a sign to show me the way I should go." I hadn't completed that prayer when the telephone rang. It was a call forwarded from the HELP-line from a mother whose daughter had ended her life. The first thing she asked was, "Do you have meetings? I would very much like to meet others who understand what I've been through and what I feel." No one will ever convince me that God did not use AT&T to give me the encouragement I needed to start group meetings.

I named the group HEARTBEAT Survivors After Suicide because for such a long time it was almost a physical effort to make one heartbeat follow another. The name HEARTBEAT is an acronym describing a philosophy of healing after suicide. H– healthy coping techniques through, E– empathy and understanding reinforced by, A– acceptance without judgment and affirmation of self-worth, R- resolution of conflict and reinvestment in life, T– truth...responsibility for this death must be allowed to rest with the one who made the choice, B– be a "reach out" to new survivors E– effect public prevention education and A– acknowledgement of suicide as a health problem of considerable proportion within our community, T– transforming our recovery into positive action that will diminish the number of these deaths. I felt inadequate in addressing such severely traumatized people and decided to ask for help from a professional– a clergy person or a mental health professional. Calls I made asking assistance in facilitating a suicide bereavement group were met with a range of negative response. None were willing to become involved in such a controversial endeavor. Some were askance at my audacity for considering such an undertaking.

Again the Health Association came through by offering a meeting room, publicizing the formation of a peer group for survivors after suicide, providing copy access and, later, accounting assistance and a small annual stipend. I asked my husband if he would help me with a group. He said, "Yes, but I don't want you to be hurt and disappointed if no one comes."

In November 1980, at the first HEARTBEAT meeting, two persons attended in addition to my husband and me. Word spread and by the following spring there were twenty, then thirty, and more suicide bereaved attending every meeting. They came from the west across the mountains, east from the plains, from communities to the north and south, some driving well over a hundred miles to share two hours, all thirsting to be in the presence of others who understood the anguish of losing a loved one to suicide.

Within two years of the initial HEARTBEAT meeting, the Grief Education Institute of Denver asked to start a HEARTBEAT chapter to serve suicide bereaved in that metropolitan area. This first chapter was duplicated in Pueblo; Greeley; Cheyenne; Bird City, Kan.; Hastings, Neb.; and so on. Requests for guidelines to form chapters was the impetus for writing a manual that helped start HEARTBEAT chapters and peer support groups by a variety of names across the country. Some of the initial HEARTBEAT chapters still offer comfort and encouragement to survivors after suicide. A few chapters in small communities fulfilled their purpose and discontinued meeting due to the fortunate lack of new survivors. New chapters continue to form across the nation and two in foreign countries, keeping the total organization consistently at about forty-five chapters. My husband seems to enjoy telling of the doubts he had that anyone would attend and of the pride he feels from being a part of turning our terrible tragedy and loss into something positive and beneficial.

Serving on the Colorado Governor's Commission for Children & Their Families presented frequent opportunity to discuss with Drs. Barrett and Porter our mutual concern for the lack of any organized effort to combat the very high rate of suicide in Colorado. We took these discussions back to our local administrators, mental health professionals, and survivors. In 1983, these discussions resulted in the founding of SPARE (Suicide Prevention Allied Regional Effort), uniting concerned Coloradoans to fight a common enemy: suicide. SPARE dissolved after seven years due to a disappointing lack of funding support, but the work accomplished and awareness created was not in vain for it caused Colorado citizenry to acknowledge suicide as a preventable health problem and laid a foundation for efforts that followed, including the current Colorado Office of Suicide Prevention and Colorado Coalition for Suicide Prevention.

Membership in the American Association of Suicidology provided me the opportunity to be among pioneering suicide survivors who established the AAS National Survivor Committee in 1984. Iris Bolton, an Atlanta survivor-clinician-author and the first suicide survivor elected to the AAS Board of Directors, shared the frustration of survivor members who felt they had much to offer, but no voice in the organization. Iris worked to give survivors equity in AAS and to generate sensitivity to survivor issues among the professional membership. "A Healing After Suicide Day" was allocated during annual conferences with plans for the next year's Healing Day usually outlined over farewell drinks with Stephanie Weber, Marilyn

Koenig, Karen Dunne-Maxim, Mary Douglas Kraut, and Iris Bolton. During his AAS presidency, Dr. John McIntosh appointed Stephanie and me as Survivor Committee co-chairs. We served two years encouraging other survivors to become active in suicide prevention through AAS committee involvement, conference presentations, support groups formation, and education advocacy. The original Survivor Committee has matured from that small group of wounded people needing their losses and hard-earned knowledge validated into a well-organized component of the first and leading suicide prevention organization in the nation.

The local chapter of the National Mental Health Association operated under the umbrella of the Health Association. I was introduced to the chapter president, Susan Golden, a mental health counselor with Peterson Air Force Base Family Support Service, and very knowledgeable about suicide prevention and intervention. Susan and I joined forces to create awareness in our community of suicide as a considerable health problem and to provide suicide risk recognition and intervention training. Despite our unshakeable belief that a suicide-informed public would save lives and our numerous opportunities to make educational presentations, the area suicide rate continued to rise, causing us to ask ourselves if we were making a difference or just stirring dust. A void in our community was an agency specifically for the purpose of providing suicide prevention education and intervention services.

Janet Perreault, a survivor of her teenage son's suicide and her ex-husband (her son's father) contacted me to learn about HEARTBEAT meetings and inquire about local suicide prevention services. Janet had moved to Colorado from California where she held an administrative position in a psychiatric facility and had become well-informed of suicide dynamics and depression treatment. She asked to join Susan and me in our work. Another prayer answered! Janet's mind was like an idea fountain, constantly bubbling possibilities, and her energy seemed inexhaustible. Encouraged because she, too, felt strongly about the need for a local suicide prevention center, we met with local mental health agencies, the county health department director, and county coroner, with our concern and proposal. Commitments from several agency administrators to support our endeavor encouraged the three of us to donate $20 each to open a bank account and rent a post office box. In May 1993, after months of laborious meetings to write by-laws, objectives, our mission, to develop an action plan, and assemble a Board of Directors, we applied for and received the IRS non-profit status as the Suicide Prevention Partnership of the Pikes Peak Region.

I wrote my first grant proposal for start-up funds to a local foundation that miraculously resulted in a $5,000 check. The owner of an office building provided us a small two-room office space, various agencies donated office furniture, we applied for a telephone number, and as an unemployed SPP director on the board, I volunteered as office manager and we were officially in the suicide prevention business.

A grant from the county government funded the initial major project of the Suicide Prevention Partnership–development of the community's first suicide hotline. With Susan's previous hotline training experience and guidance, we wrote a training manual, screened and trained volunteer respondents, and hired a clinical supervisor. This hotline, though considerably modernized, continues to extend help to hurting people in the Pikes Peak Region.

An Air Force acquaintance of Susan's, a Greek Orthodox priest, Father Frank Meyernick, was very interested in suicide prevention among Air Force personnel. Upon Frank's recommendation Susan, Janet, and I were invited to meet with the Wing Commander of Schriever Air Force Base near Colorado Springs. During our meeting, the Commander asked what we thought would be helpful to distressed airmen and their families serving under his command. Almost in unison we answered, "crisis support teams" and described to him the role such teams would play, providing support benefit much like that relied upon in a close-knit civilian family or neighborhood. Each team would consist of two or three peer volunteers trained to compassionately respond to stressful situations among military, providing support where no family or friends were available to call upon.

Training would include suicide risk identification/intervention and encompass response to a range of stress-related events that could culminate in airmen being overwhelmed, hopeless, depressed, and suicidal (ie, incidents of family violence, child abuse, sexual assault, illness, injury or death of a family member, etc). The on-call team would be activated by base chaplains, the initial point of contact in crisis situations. The Commander asked us, "Can you develop and train these teams?"

We assembled military-sensitive, suicide-aware, first-response-experienced experts to plan, research, and edit a training manual. We wrote a training contract proposal to the United States Air Force that was accepted and a proposal to the Colorado Health Department to research and print training manuals. The initial Crisis Response Team development/training took place in the spring of 1994 at Schriever AFB. It was very well received and we contracted to repeat the training to in-coming airmen volunteers the following April 19 and 20, 1995.

The simple concept of peers-helping-peers through Crisis Response Teams won attention on other bases. Father Meyernick was transferred to USAFE, Ramstein, Germany, where he convinced the Commander of Crisis Support Team value. Susan and I traveled to Ramstein three consecutive years to develop and train teams and a crisis line. The success of this program was promising but the CST concept was soon replaced by more sophisticated military suicide prevention programs.

Confronting suicide and the issues surrounding these tragedies always will be a part of my life. It is gratifying to see new survivors joining forces with veteran survivors, lending their passion to increase awareness and activism across the country. The support group movement has grown from three or four in 1980 when

HEARTBEAT began, to hundreds and in every state and some in foreign lands. Most states and many cities have offices or centers specifically for the purpose of directing suicide prevention efforts. Postvention is a credible and permanent component of the suicide prevention triad (prevention, interevention, postvention). I am proud to have had a role in helping some of it happen.

Suicide is a tragedy of immeasurable proportion. The grief of those who survive these tragedies is indefinable. The all-consuming anguish we experience in the early days, weeks, and months of our loss eventually gentles into manageable sorrow. Although we never "get over it," we do "get on with it" and find a new normal in our forever-changed life. Around the world, suicide bereaved are gaining strength and healing from putting their grief to work. Giving solace to others, fighting stigma, changing attitudes toward mental illness, creating suicide-informed communities–saving lives. We make a difference!

If I have comforted another wounded like me, if I have encouraged just one who has lost hope, if I have offered peace of mind to someone tormented by guilt, if I have soothed a broken heart or strengthened a doubting soul, then I have given meaning and purpose to my son's death. What greater tribute to his life than this?

Losing My Mother, Finding Myself

By Nicole Masco Morton
Wisconsin, USA

My last memory of my mother being alive was when she dropped me off at a sleepover party with my girlfriends. I was thirteen years old– old enough to understand what it meant that my parents' marriage was over, yet, looking back, I don't know what possessed me to initiate our last conversation. As I was grabbing my things, I looked back at her in the driver's seat and asked, "Do you want me to call you later?" As if I, a young teenager, could provide the emotional support that she, a grown woman, needed from a peer or girlfriend. "No," she said, "I'm fine."

My mother was born into an extremely dysfunctional, dirt-poor family. She was the middle of three children, and the only daughter. She was abandoned by her father as a child, and had a very difficult upbringing. I never knew many details about her childhood– she never told stories about when she was a little girl. I know that she wasn't much for school, that it was a struggle to get her to earn her diploma. It always seemed to me that her story started when she met my father. I loved hearing about the two of them meeting in a phone booth during a rainstorm. I don't know what she did before she became a mother, but I do know that when my sister and I were born, we were her whole life. We were absolutely spoiled rotten. We had more toys that any child could possibly play with in one lifetime. We had the best of everything an upper-middle class income could buy. We were shielded from any unpleasantness– poverty, discrimination, conflict. We had it all, short of the white picket fence. My childhood was glorious and perfect.

My parents hid their decaying relationship well. I don't ever remember them fighting. At the beginning of spring break of my eighth grade year, when my mom announced that my dad was moving out and had gotten his own apartment not far from our house, I could feel the rug being pulled out from underneath me. The rest of that week was a blur. I don't remember seeing my dad at all. One of the very few memories I have during that time is of my mom taking my sister and me shopping. If there was anything my mother was good at besides raising children, it was retail therapy. I joke that most of my formative years were spent at JCPenney, Sears, and Marshall Fields. On that particular shopping trip, my sister and I, as typical tweens, were asking to buy this or that, and my mom's response to each request was, "No, your father will buy it for you when he moves out." Thinking back on it now as a grown woman I wonder, was she worried that she would be penniless when he was gone? Was she afraid of living out her mother's, my grandmother's, reality of poverty and struggle? Didn't she know that couldn't possibly happen, because my dad was a real stand-up guy?

My father is a smart, hard-working man. He is charming and a real people-person, which led to a career in sales and management and played to his strengths. He is physically handicapped, having survived a bout of polio when he was five years old. A few years ago, when my husband and I announced that we were expecting his first grandchild, he completely broke down emotionally and confessed that he never thought he would have children of his own, let alone a grandchild. Such was the impact that his disability has had on his sense of self-worth. I have a vague memory of him recounting his relationship with my mother, and describing how he married her because he thought no one else would have him. Not an auspicious start for a relationship, to be sure. He supported my mother's family financially as well as emotionally, standing in as something of a surrogate father figure when my mother's older brother was serving overseas in the military. As much as my mother defined herself by her abilities as a homemaker, my father defined himself by his abilities as a patriarch and a breadwinner.

Was it his sense of obligation that kept them together? A level of comfortablity? A desire not to rock the boat? Ironically, it was when they each found a measure of self-awareness that the bottom fell out. For my mother, it was a trip to Europe. She had never been anywhere or done anything that wasn't within the framework of family. A few years before she died, my mother went with her best friend on a tour of England and France. I think it was the only thing that she had ever done for herself and herself alone in her entire adult life. I have seen the pictures of her at all of the usual tourist traps– the changing of the guard, Big Ben, the Eiffel Tower. She is positively radiant. She met distant relations of her best friend's family. She drank wine and shopped to her heart's content.

When she returned, it was like a light bulb had gone off in her head– that there was more to the world than her little domestic nest. I don't think she ever mentally came home. In a self-indulgent fit of pique, I snottily asked her, "Do you wish you were still there instead of home with us?" Without missing a beat, she said, "yes." She had never worked a day in my life, and suddenly she was doing freelance interior design for my father's boss. She wanted to work as a volunteer librarian at my school. She signed up at the community college to take elementary French classes. Who was this woman?

For my father, it was losing his younger brother. A radiant free spirit, my uncle was eight years younger than my father. Handsome, extroverted, doted upon; he was the apple of everyone's eye. In his very early thirties, my uncle died after having asphyxiated on his own vomit in a kiddy pool after a raucous summer party with friends. His death was completely senseless, and utterly destroyed my father's family. Later, my dad told me that it was a wake-up call for him: that if someone who was as exuberant and loved life as much as my uncle could be snuffed out like a candle in an instant, shouldn't he be taking measures to live his own life to the fullest; to be fulfilled in every way possible? If this meant being completely honest about a stagnant and loveless marriage, so be it. It took a few years, during which time my sister and I were totally oblivious, but then came the announcement.

Hindsight is indeed 20-20 when it comes to things like this. It is so obvious now what my mother was doing during that week of spring break. I have two other vivid memories of that week. One was when she left the house under the guise that she had to retrieve a lost pair of sunglasses from some place, when in reality she went to go to church for emergency counseling. Another was when my mother's best friend came by the house, worried that my mother had been incommunicado for several days, bearing a bunch of yellow daffodils to cheer her up. My mother refused to come downstairs to see her, and used the excuse that she was on the phone with our parish priest. She never did come down until after her best friend had gone. I know beyond a shadow of a doubt that my mother would have been busted if she had. She gave things away. She hardly ate. She had always been a fad, yo-yo dieter, but by the end of the week she was fitting into my clothes. So obvious. The Friday of spring break, a friend of mine was having a sleepover birthday party. I was going to be out of the house for the whole night, and my mother made arrangements for my sister to sleep at a friend's house as well. Sometime during the evening, before my father got home from work, she got ahold of one of my father's guns, loaded it, hid in their walk-in closet, and shot herself in the head. She left no note. She made absolutely sure that my father would be the one to find her. The next morning, I was surprised to see my father's car in the driveway to pick me up. I asked him on the way home how Mom was doing. He didn't answer. About a block from our house, my dad pulled over to the side of the road and told me that Mom had died during the night. It was the first time I remember ever seeing him cry.

In the span of time between finding her body and retrieving us from our sleepovers the next morning, my dad had had his parents come to our house from the city, spoken with the police, had her body removed, and the evidence of her demise taken care of. I don't know when he decided not to tell us the truth about her death. In keeping with our having been shielded from life's unpleasantness, my sister and I were told that our mother overdosed on sleeping pills. I suppose it was thought to be more humane than the grisly reality that confronted my father upon going to bed the night before, but the truth would come out eventually. I know that my family meant well, but you only can put off the inevitable for so long.

The next several days after my mother's death would be a blur of neighbors and family friends stopping by, fretting over my sister and me; delicately questioning my father about what had happened. It was an endless stream of people coming and going, hugging us, then leaving with empty promises to help with whatever we needed. Some of those people I don't ever remember seeing again. I knew I was going to miss a few days of school after the weekend due to the funeral and whatnot, and I also knew that my friends would wonder what was happening, so I contacted a few of them. Now, granted, I shouldn't have had very high expectations of support from my peers, but with every phone call, things became more strained and awkward. One of my friends never even said, "I'm sorry for your loss," not even in the years that followed. One friend got so hysterical on the phone that I ended up consoling her by the end of our call. By the end, I felt like I was being more of a burden by trying to reach out to my friends.

The funeral came and family drove in from all parts of the city and suburbs. I remember the scent of lilies, and the pianist singing Bette Midler's "The Rose," both of which I hate with a passion to this day. Then, as the evening drew to a close, and I was upstairs with my sister and cousins, my grandfather approached me. The moment he spoke to me became one of the defining points of my life. He took me aside and said, "You're the lady of the house now." He intimated that I had new responsibilities as the oldest daughter. I don't think he ever realized the impact that his statement had on me, on how I viewed myself from then on out. Looking back on it, I don't even know if he meant it in the context of anything other than me having to accompany him to drive an elderly aunt back home that evening. All I know is that that moment has shaped my personality, perhaps even more than the loss itself.

Her pictures were taken down, her side of the closet emptied, her jewelry put away. We did not speak of her. We did not have any context of a memorial other than the funeral service. We were not taken to her gravesite on her birthday or Mother's Day. Someone suggested that my father take us to a psychologist to make sure that we were adjusting well. The doctor that my father found was absolutely horrible, to the point that I have completely blocked out anything that occurred during the one and only session we were forced to sit with him. Dad didn't make us go back. From then on, it was like nothing had happened, and things were left to fester and percolate under the surface. For reasons too numerous and too entwined with other people's history for me to ever fully understand, we were abandoned by my mother's side of the family. My aunts, uncles, cousins, and grandmother, with whom we shared every holiday and birthday from the time I was born, became complete strangers. We were utterly cut off from my mother's history and a big part of my childhood past. People whispered about us. Kids gossiped at school. We were like social pariahs in the neighborhood.

One afternoon, my sister and me had gotten home from school and the telephone rang. My sister answered, and a woman's voice on the other end of the line started to say, "The reason your mother killed herself is because..." My sister got so scared that she hung up. We never found out who it was on the phone, or what "secret" she was prepared to reveal. Shortly thereafter, my grandmother slipped up and mentioned "the gun" in conversation relating to my mother's death. These two incidents motivated my sister and I to confront my father to find out what really happened the night she died. He chose to tell us the truth about my mother's death, by a self-inflicted gunshot wound rather than ingesting pills, so that there would be no more secrets between us. It forced me to mourn her loss all over again, because it was an enticing fantasy to think that maybe, just maybe, she had overdosed on pills by accident, especially since she didn't leave a suicide note. The fact that she was an active participant in her own death was concrete proof that she chose to leave me and my family behind to end her pain, and I was devastated all over again.

The loss of my mother had become a focal point of my identity in a number of ways. My mothering instinct, which had kicked in after that fateful discussion with my grandfather, may have been a nascent part of my personality, but became one of my defining characteristics. I parented my friends. I was the Peacemaker, the Arbiter, the Listener, the Kisser of Figurative Boo-boos. When one of my best friends confided in me that he had lost his virginity, I cried. I literally mourned the loss of his innocence as if I were his parent. I suppose that I should be proud that this facet of my personality has evolved into empathy and compassion, but for the most part it just made me emotionally exhausted and wondering who was going to take care of me. I cultivated a strong sense of overachievement. I was obsessed with structuring my life in ways that it would be impossible for me to repeat the mistakes my mother made. Literally obsessed.

She was not a good student; I was a natural learner. But I took that several degrees further by going to college and immediately to graduate school, and then continuing education beyond that. She never traveled; I jumped at the chance to take a tour of Italy my senior year of high school. She was not a confident driver; I trekked back and forth four hours each way to and from college on a regular basis for years. For almost the whole time I knew her, she didn't have a job; she was completely financially dependent on my father. I was determined to have a job upon finishing graduate school. I wanted my own apartment, my own bills, my own credit, my own car. My poor boyfriend (now my husband) lamented the fact that I didn't need him. I couldn't figure out why he didn't understand that that was the whole point.

It wasn't until a few years after my mother's suicide that I was getting ready to go to college and, for some reason, my dad had gotten it into his brain that he wasn't going to let me leave until he was sure that I had dealt with the loss and was ready to move on. He forced me to go and see a different therapist that he had found. I was stubborn. I was ornery. I was unaware that I was about to meet the woman who would save my life on more than one occasion. She was, and is, the most gifted healer on the face of the planet, as far as I'm concerned. I joke that everybody needs to be in therapy, but not just in therapy, in therapy with my therapist. I mentioned that hindsight is 20-20 with situations like mine, but I didn't realize until I started on my healing journey that I blamed myself for my mother's death. I thought that I should have been able to see the signs of her depression and her suicidal tendencies. That my thirteen-year-old self should have intervened. That I should have recognized the signs of her clinical depression. That I should have been able to save her. It was my therapist who was able to help me realize that it was not my fault and set me on the path to forgiveness. I literally had an experience, not unlike the scene between Robin Williams and Matt Damon in "Good Will Hunting", of a dawning of realization, and a lifting of a tremendous weight that I was not even aware that I had been bearing.

Not only was I coping with the guilt of not having been able to "save" my mother, my father was struggling as well. During the police investigation after my mother's death, my mother's family was pushing to have my father imprisoned for murder because she didn't leave a suicide note, and because no one could believe that she knew how to load and use a gun. (My family doesn't know of any instance where she could have ever come in contact with one prior to that.) My father failed three polygraph tests until a very smart forensic psychologist figured out that my dad had been asked, "Did you kill your wife?" (which, because he was wracked with guilt, he felt that he was responsible), instead of being asked, "Did you shoot your wife?" At which point, he was able to pass the test and all charges were dropped.

I coped with my loss by exerting an extreme amount of control over every facet of my life. I was terrified by the thought of being abandoned again, so I never allowed myself to be put in a situation where I couldn't exit gracefully and painlessly. But, ironically, I didn't truly begin to heal until I was able to let a measure of vulnerability into my life. You can't build a life partnership with someone when you have to be the one holding the reins all of the time. And, yes, it was scary, but when I let myself give up a measure of control, the world did not come to a screeching halt. In fact, it was quite pleasant to be helped by others, to be pampered, to be nurtured.

Finally, as things always tend to do, everything came full circle when I started a family of my own. Becoming a mother to my son has given me a whole new appreciation for my upbringing and the gifts that my mother had in terms of child rearing. It cuts both ways, though. I look at my little boy and I can't imagine having gotten to a place that ending a life was more preferable to struggling through hardship; that a swift and brutal end was more appealing than being around for all the major milestones. I think about the things my mother has missed: my prom; my high school, college, and graduate school graduations; my wedding; the birth of her grandson. My heart breaks for her and for me. But such is the reality of depression. I can never approach her decision as having been made from a rational place. As I look forward, I am nearing the age that my mother was when she died by suicide. As with all of the significant turning points in my life to date, I expect that there will be something of an emotional earthquake. But lately, I have been feeling less that

I will be lost without a blueprint of my mother's experience for me to follow, than liberated that I will be able to make my own way.

For families today going what I went through, I feel fortunate for them that there is so much more awareness about mental illness. That is not to say that the stigmatization of depression is gone by any means, but I feel like at this time people at least are more likely to realize when something is going horribly wrong and that there are resources available. Since suicide is so much easier to see in hindsight, it is easy to blame oneself for not interpreting the signs and intervening, but I have learned through my journey of healing that there is no blame to be laid at the feet of the survivors. I, myself, was not able to fully begin healing until I released myself from that blame. I think my family would have been quicker to heal and build a newer, healthier foundation by being open about my mother's death.

We never were given an opportunity to speak freely about her, to ask questions about her death, or to ask questions about her life, for that matter. It wasn't that we were discouraged from doing so, or that there were repercussions had we tried; it was more like it was like the hesitation to pick at the scab that was healing over the wound of her loss. In reality, it would have been so much more useful for us to be open in our discussion. For that matter, it would have been helpful to have an outlet for our frustration and anger. To have been given permission to be angry with her and her decision to take her life would have been extremely cathartic.

Taking advantage of the resources available in the mental health profession is huge. For me, finding a therapist who had a profound understanding of my story and my experience was a significant portion of my healing process. I don't know the extent to which support groups were available twenty-five years ago, but that would have been extremely helpful for me. If nothing else, to be able to be with others who shared my experience, to know that I was not alone in my grief, would have been so gratifying.

I would suggest to families not only to seek out professional support, but that they should read everything they can get their hands on. One book that resonated so profoundly for me was, *Motherless Daughters,* by Hope Edelman. Though the book was written with an eye toward all different types of loss (sudden death, prolonged illness, suicide, abandonment, etc.) it allowed me to understand from a clinical point of view how my mother's death has affected my personality and my life choices. My favorite advice from that book is to live with your grief, not under it. It is true that time eventually takes the sting out of the loss, but if it is not dealt with, the emotional aftermath of the grief comes out in the strangest of ways, and in the most unexpected of places. I had significant postpartum issues after the birth of my son, and it was through several therapy sessions that I realized that I was carrying the loss of my mother and my subsequent issues of abandonment through to that time in my life. Since my mother had not stuck around for me, I wondered how I could possibly be worthy enough to take care of this tiny, new, precious life. I had to release myself from blame all over again, learn to grieve the loss of my mother as a role model for parenting, and begin to see that my choices of how to parent my own child were my own and not defined by her history.

There is hope. There is healing. There does come a time when the grief becomes a small and quiet part of you, rather than an overwhelming tempest. It doesn't happen all at once, but it does happen. You may have to revisit your grief again and again as life's circumstances change and examine a different facet of it from a different angle. But deep within, there is a reservoir of strength that you may have never known that you possessed. You will survive this, and come out on the other side stronger, wiser, and intact. Most importantly, you don't have to make the journey alone.

What Nelson's Suicide Taught Me

By Buddy Knox
Louisiana, USA

When I was asked if I was interested in contributing a chapter to *Seeking Hope*, I immediately replied that I would. I then began thinking about what I could contribute that would be helpful to other survivors and decided that I would write about my journey from being a victim to being altruistic. It is my understanding that a general definition of "victim" is a person destroyed by or suffering grievous injury from another, or one who suffers some loss.

I have experienced the loss of two family members to suicide. On November 11, 1988, my sixty-nine-year-old uncle, Hays Town Schmidt, or "Unc" as he was affectionately known, completed suicide by purposely taking an overdose of prescription drugs. On August 11, 1994, my twenty-nine-year-old son, James Nelson Knox, Sr., completed suicide with a gunshot wound to the right temple.

Unc's suicide was painful and shocking to my family and me. Unc was more like a dad to me than an uncle; my dad died when I was twenty years old and Unc became a father figure for me when I needed male parental guidance. My wife often described Unc as "one of the last true southern gentlemen." Unc was in good health, had an excellent retirement, nice home and a new car. He was an old bachelor, and was very lonely so my wife, Betty, and I tried to get Unc to move in with us. He was a very independent person and refused to, saying he didn't want to invade our privacy. Unc's suicide was a great loss for me and my family and we worked through the grief without professional help. We had great support from friends, co-workers, and our church family, and even though it was tough going at times, we managed to survive the loss.

Things changed on August 11, 1994, when my son Nelson completed suicide. He had just been through a bitter divorce and had recently resigned from his job as deputy sheriff in East Baton Rouge Parish, LA. He did so because of financial concerns. Being a law enforcement officer does not pay well and even though it was a job that Nelson loved, he realized that he needed more income now that his family was divided. I knew he had been experiencing some depression, but things seemed to be getting better for him. Nelson let us see only what he wanted us to see.

Before I continue, I'd like to tell you about Nelson. He was born on a crisp cold morning on January 31, 1965. He was a beautiful baby... he had his mother's blonde hair and bright blue eyes. As Nelson grew older, he displayed the wonderful loving and caring characteristics of his mother's personality. Nelson was about three years old when he became a country music fan. His favorite artists were Johnny Cash and John Denver. Santa Claus brought Nelson a 45-RPM phonograph and a little red rocking chair for Christmas that year. He would sit in that little red rocker for hours, rocking away and playing his few Cash and Denver records over and over again.

When Nelson was four years old, I became a deputy sheriff with the East Baton Rouge Parish Sheriff's Department. He said then that he also wanted to be a deputy sheriff when he grew up. Nelson became a "Junior Deputy" at age ten and continued in the program until he began high school. As a small child when Nelson got a new toy, he would take it apart to see what made it work. He always put the toys back together and darned if they didn't seem to work better than before. During high school, Nelson worked at a service station after school. He learned quickly and was soon doing mechanic's work. Nelson was a good mechanic and always would volunteer to fix cars, lawnmowers, weed eaters, and other mechanical items that belonged to family and friends. But he would never take any compensation from them.

While in high school, Nelson began to use poor judgment at times. He and his girlfriend had a baby daughter, Rachel, when they were sixteen years old. Nelson married the mother of his child at age seventeen and two more children were born from the marriage, another daughter, Ashley, and a son, James, Jr.

At the time of his death, Rachel was thirteen years old, Ashley was nine years old and James was seven years old. All three have ultimately done well in the years without their dad. Rachel was very mature and had to assume a lot of responsibility for her younger siblings because their mother is an alcoholic and was absent from the home frequently. In fact, for the next several months Rachel practically had to raise her little sister and brother. Rachel did a very good job of holding the three of them together even though Betty and I frequently had to bring food to the home, see that they had school supplies, take them to school and provide emotional support for them. This greatly increased he amount of stress, grief, and anger that Betty and I were experiencing which hindered our own recovery.

James began to experience separation anxiety and displaying oppositional/defiant behavior. About six months after Nelson's death, James came to live with Betty and me, and Rachel continued to look after her little sister. Why was this? Was their mother not able to care for them? Because of the difficulties that James was experiencing, Betty and I decided that she would retire early to focus on James and the girls. The early retirement resulted in substantial financial loss for us; however, we have never regretted that decision. With Betty at home and with the counseling that she arranged for the three of us, James' behavior began to improve.

Nelson shot and killed himself while sitting in his car in his ex-wife's driveway. A delivery man had noticed Nelson in the front seat of his car and notified Nelson's ex-wife of the situation. When she learned of this, she sent Rachel outside to verify the situation and then to the next-door neighbor's residence to call 911. I never did understand this; first of all, because she was the adult in the household, and because there was a working telephone in her residence. Rachel continued to live with her mom and had to assume a lot of responsibility for her younger siblings. At age sixteen, she finally dropped out of high school, got her GED and enrolled at Southeastern Louisiana University (SLU) in Hammond, Louisiana, about forty miles east of Baton Rouge. After a couple of years, she dropped out of SLU, moved back to Baton Rouge and partied for a year or so. She then enrolled in Louisiana State University and graduated in Fashion Design and Merchandising and is now employed by a large department store in New York City.

Shortly after Rachel enrolled at SLU, I purchased her a car, a used Toyota Camry that was her first car. While she and I were driving the car home she looked at me and sadly said that she sure wished her dad were here to see her first car. That ripped my heart out. Rachel accepted her dad's death and would frequently talk about it with Betty and me. She had actually observed Nelson's body in his car and spoke of dreaming about this for several years afterward. We would sit and talk and cry about Nelson's death.

At age nineteen, Rachel asked me if I thought she could join our SOS (Survivors of Suicide) group. Of course I encouraged her to do so, but was puzzled as to why she wanted to do so at this time. I later learned that she had a history of ending relationships with boyfriends that she really cared for and for no apparent reason. She told me that she had finally rationalized in her own mind that she felt abandoned by her dad and that she would end relationships because she was afraid her boyfriend would break up with her and give her that sense of abandonment again. She attended group for a couple of years and really was helped by doing so.

Ashley was nine years old at the time of Nelson's death. Until recently, I never heard her even mention that her dad was dead and it has been almost sixteen years since he died. The kids seldom spoke of Nelson's death because their mom constantly told them not to think about Nelson or to talk about him. Ashley was a very obedient child and tried to do as her mother wished.

Ashley's home life was often very chaotic and she would just go into her room, close the door, and study her schoolwork or do some of her artwork. She was very quiet and seemed to be distant at times. Ashley is a talented artist and had some of her work displayed in the children's section at the Louisiana State Archives building.

As I stated previously, Ashley just did not talk about her dad, much less talk about his death. However, a few months after Nelson's death, she wrote a poem that I feel is about Nelson although she denies it. Remember, she was only nine years old.

The poem is entitled "Oh Bird!" and says:

OH BIRD!
Oh bird, way up in the sky,
Could you tell me, "How do you fly?"
Your big broad wings, your sweet smile,
Could you come sit with me for a while?
Flying higher, and higher and higher,
WATCH OUT! OH NO, GUNFIRE!
Goodbye sweet bird.
You can't leave me.
Oh, please fly free.
My dear sweet bird, tell me,
Who will sing to me?

All that studying paid off for Ashley. She graduated from an honors high school in Baton Rouge and received a four-year scholarship to Tulane University in New Orleans where she received a degree in microbiology. She then enrolled at Louisiana State University and received a master's degree in philosophy.

While in school, Ashley worked along with her sister Rachel in the fashion business in Baton Rouge. She now is also living and working in New York City and her goal is to become a writer for one of the national fashion magazines. Knowing Ashley's tenacity, she will most surely achieve her goal.

James, who was seven years old at the time of Nelson's death, began to have the serious behavioral problems that I previously mentioned. Within a few months of his dad's death, his mother agreed to let him come live with Betty and me. He did so until age twelve when his mom rushed into our house one day and snatched him up and brought him to live with her. That was a disaster. He stayed with his mom until he was fifteen years old and then returned to live with Betty and me until he was twenty-two years old. During the time James lived with his mom she did not send him to school, but said she was "home schooling" him.

By the time James came back to live with Betty and me he was far behind in schoolwork. He tried very hard to catch up but just couldn't. He dropped out of high school and got his GED. James always has been very interested in computer technology and we encouraged him to attend one of the schools in the area that specialize in computer training. He did very well and has recently been hired by the state of Louisiana as a "computer guru" with the Department of Revenue in a very good job with a promising future.

Seeing Nelson's children mature and begin to achieve their goals brings back the memory of Nelson at age twenty, when he realized his lifelong ambition and was hired by the local sheriff's office. Within two years, Nelson was promoted to the rank of sergeant and seemed really happy with his life. Then things began to fall apart. Nelson's wife began to drink excessively and to gamble frequently. This led to family problems and financial difficulties. After six years as a deputy sheriff, Nelson decided to resign and take a job as a private investigator. This broke his heart. He was not happy in this job, but the family simply needed the additional money that he earned as a P.I.

Things then began to spiral downward; Nelson was deeply in debt, his divorce was finalized, he became severely depressed, sought medical help, and was prescribed Prozac. He seemed to be much better when he took his medication. However, his ex-wife still influenced Nelson and convinced him that he should stop taking his Prozac. She told him that he shouldn't get his feelings from a bottle. (This advice was coming from an alcoholic.)

My wife and I met with Nelson at our home on the evening of Tuesday, August 9, 1994, and made arrangements to take care of his financial concerns. On August 10, he and my wife went to our credit union to obtain the necessary cashier's check for Nelson to pay off all his debts. Later that day, Nelson and his children, along with a family friend, went swimming, had a picnic, and later that night ordered pizza and watched videos at the friend's home. When Nelson took his children home that night, one of his ex-wife's boyfriends was at their home. Nelson's ex-wife and the man were intoxicated and there was a big argument between all of them. Nelson left and went to his apartment. The next morning at approximately 7:00 a.m. Nelson drove to the home of his ex-wife, parked in the driveway and shot himself in the right temple. Nelson had never mailed the cashier's checks; they were still in his wallet. This leads me to believe that even when Nelson was with my wife at the credit union, he knew what he was going to do.

After Nelson's suicide, I became a victim in every sense of the word. It was a great loss and as each day passed I felt as if I were being destroyed. I certainly suffered grievous injury from his actions and I had no input into the decision that was causing me this great pain. The emotional pain was so great that it caused me to experience physical pain deep down in the center of my chest. It felt like someone had put a knife in me and was twisting it. The journey I've taken over the last fifteen years spans periods of total disbelief, hopelessness, denial, despair, depression, anger, fear, guilt, and sadness to periods of acceptance, joy, contentment, happiness, and optimism. The first two-and-a-half or three years were mostly filled with the former and the last twelve years or so have been filled with ever increasing periods of the latter. I will never heal completely and I am very aware of that, but life is so well worth living. That is something I did not believe for several years after Nelson's suicide.

The world I had lived in for fifty-seven plus years was full of belief in God and in Jesus Christ as my Savior. In my new world, I had great doubts. If there is truly a

God in Heaven who gave his only begotten Son for the sake of mankind, then how could this God, if He truly loved me, take away my precious son? Surely if there is a God, He understood just how painful the death of a son is. If there is a God, where was He when my son was in such great pain and depression? I truly had doubts of the existence of God. I was not able to recognize it as such at the time, but if there was a God, I was extremely angry with Him. I found that I was not able to attend services at my church but would not admit to myself that I was mad at God. Shortly before Nelson's suicide, he came to church with us and during the service I looked over and saw tears streaming down his cheeks. It was heartbreaking for me. I kept telling myself that it would make me too sad to go to church and recall that memory. I now realize that the real reason I didn't go to church was because I was mad at God.

When I would see another young man my son's age, I would question God as to why that young man was still alive and my precious son was dead. I would ask God that if He really exists, then prove it to me by making the other young man dead and my son alive again. I think the term mental health professionals use is "bargaining." Well, I certainly did my share of bargaining even though I would not wish for my pain to be transferred to anyone else. I would not want their world, as they know it, to be ok.

During the many months before I began healing, I was terrorized by the thought that I could lose my dear wife Betty. She seemed to have been totally destroyed by our son's completion of suicide. She also experienced great pain deep inside her chest. She described her pain as being like a cold, black hole where her heart was supposed to be. I have heard other mothers describe their pain with the very same words. I was truly fearful that I would lose her to a broken heart. Yes, a broken heart. Twice during the first few months she had to be rushed to the hospital with symptoms of a heart attack. Upon being examined by doctors, they could find nothing wrong with her heart. I suppose that doctors have yet to become able to diagnose a broken heart. Maybe this is justly so.

For approximately five months after Nelson's death, my wife, our three surviving children, Nelson's children, and I went to a local grief counselor. She was a very nice and compassionate lady, but she was not helping us get through our grief. In January 1995 our counselor suggested that we try the Baton Rouge Crisis Intervention Center (BRCIC) and Survivors of Suicide (SOS) support group. Betty and I began attending the Tuesday night support group that month.

The BRCIC requires that survivors come to the center for an intake interview before joining the group. This is to establish whether or not a survivor is appropriate for group and also if the survivor is at a place in their grief recovery process that would be conducive to a group setting. As I sat there during my intake, I struggled to survive. The agonizing pain was as bad as the day Nelson died. And that Frank

Campbell (Dr. Campbell was Executive Director of the BRCIC at the time) had the insensitivity to actually try to get me to talk about Nelson's suicide! Well, he did get me to talk about it and before I completed my intake, I knew I was in the right place. Frank asked me to sign an agreement that I would attend at least twelve weekly meetings of the SOS group. I thought it sounded excessive, but I agreed to sign the document. I mean, after all, if I didn't keep my commitment, what was Frank going to do - end out the support group police to get me? Well, that was in January 1995, and here it is mid 2010, and until a couple of months ago I missed very few weekly meetings.

I credit the SOS group with much of the success I've had in rebuilding my life after having to survive the suicide deaths of two of my closest loved ones. During my first night in group, I was sitting there with so much pain and anxiety that I thought I would die. When it was my time to introduce myself during the "go around," the pain, anxiety, and fear I was feeling were indescribable. I finally finished my introduction, "My name is Buddy Knox and on August 11, 1994, my twenty-nine-year-old son Nelson shot himself in the right temple and died." I was so overcome with grief that I could not even acknowledge "Unc's" suicide. It was over a year before I could acknowledge both during the "go around."

Then my dear wife Betty had to do her introduction. It ripped me apart to hear her struggle to do so. At the time I felt I would not be able to fulfill my twelve-week commitment. Then, an elderly and very wise gentleman who was in group did his introduction. He said "My name is Jim Moore and on January 4, 1971, my son Jimmy shot himself in the head with my revolver. It was just before his twenty-sixth birthday," I didn't hear much that night, but I did hear what Jim said. I looked at Jim– his hair was combed, his shoes were shined, his socks matched and he talked making complete sentences. I thought to myself that here is a man who has been through the exact same thing that I am now going through and he seems to be normal in every way. I decided at that moment that I was going to work extremely hard getting through my grief and try to become an instillation of hope to others like Jim was to me. You might notice that I said "work through my grief." That is because grieving is really hard work and will leave you totally exhausted.

As a side note, Jim Moore founded our support group about thirty years ago. At the time, Jim was a crisis counselor on The Phone, the BRCIC's crisis hot line. A lady who lost her son to suicide came to the center seeking help. Jim met with the lady and from that beginning came our current SOS group. Jim and his wife Edith have been involved in many survivor activities and in 2004 Jim and Edith were honored with the American Association of Suicidology Survivor of the Year Award at the annual conference in Miami, Fla.

Nelson was one of four children that Betty and I have. Our daughter Robin was the oldest and then came Nathan, Nelson, and David. I love all my kids, but Nelson and I shared more common interests and we spent a lot of time together. We both loved fast cars, fast boats, LSU athletics, fishing, hunting, and anything mechanical. (Nelson used to say, "We both love fast cars, fast boats, and fast women, but not necessarily in that order.")

Nelson was sitting in the driver's seat of his car when he shot himself. A good friend of mine had the car taken to a detail shop to clean the interior. Friends strongly suggested to me that I get rid of the car, but I absolutely refused to do so and kept the car for about a year and a half and drove it on weekends. I felt very close to Nelson and would drive around having conversations with Nelson. I eventually gave the car to one of my granddaughters, Miranda, who was my daughter's first born. Miranda really loved Nelson, and was hesitant to accept the car, but did so and got several years of use from it.

I was at work when I learned of Nelson's suicide. It was around noon and I was leaving my office to attend a business luncheon. My supervisor came running across the parking lot, flagging me down, and simply said, "Buddy, I've got bad news for you, your son killed himself this morning." Even though I have three sons, I knew it was Nelson. My first thought was that I needed to go to Betty's office and tell her. I could not let anyone else tell her because I knew the news would devastate her. It was about a fifteen-minute drive from my office to Betty's office and all the way there I was trying to decide in my own mind how we were going to get through this without me telling Betty that our precious son was dead. How foolish a thought! But, that is the kind of thing I had to deal with. From listening to other survivors, I am not the only one to have ridiculous thoughts.

When I got to Betty's office she was out to lunch, so I had to sit for about forty-five minutes waiting for her. Thankfully, I wasn't alone. My brother Nathan worked in the same building and when he saw me he could sense that something was wrong and I told him about Nelson. My brother Nathan and my best friend "Tank" (who had come after he heard about Nelson's death) came to Betty's office and sat and waited with me. When Betty came back from lunch I sat her down and told her what had happened. The only way I can describe her reaction was that she let out a primal scream. Betty worked on the second floor of a six-story building. People all over that building said they heard Betty's scream.

But let me get back to the healing process. As I said earlier, I continued to participate in the weekly SOS group, I read every book I could find on surviving suicide, and I did an awful lot of journaling. Fortunately for me, the BRCIC has a very good lending library and I was able to easily obtain books such as Iris Bolton's *My Son, My Son*, Carla Fine's *No Time to Say Goodbye*, and others such as *After Suicide Loss; Coping with Your Grief*, *Suicide and its Aftermath*, and *Swallowed by the Snake*. These are just a few of the many that I have read.

In early 1996 some group members formed the SSS group. SSS (Survivors Supporting Survivors) is a group of survivors that act independently from the BRCIC. The purpose of the group is to conduct survivor-related events such as an annual memorial event, Christmas parties, swimming parties, and other social events for survivors who had difficulty in participating in any social setting since their losses. SSS held its First Annual Memorial Event in May 1996 and I was asked to be a speaker. I accepted the invitation and was absolutely scared out of my wits every time I thought of getting in front of 100 or more people and telling my story. But I did it.

I told my story to all those people. I choked up a few times, but I made it through my talk. Afterwards, several men approached me and told me how much it helped them to hear what I had to say. They had been like I was in the early days after my loss, too macho to show their feelings. I then knew that I have the ability to help survivors through their grief process. I dedicated the rest of my life to helping survivors, doing this in memory of my son Nelson.

Another very healing thing for me was journaling. I would sit at a nearby coffee shop almost every Saturday morning and write in my journal and can now look back at the journal and see just how much pain and anguish I was in and how far I have come since then. The next year or so I spent learning all that I could about survivors by reading, watching TV documentaries, attending conferences, and talking with knowledgeable people in the field of suicidology. I attended the AAS and SPAN conference in Bethesda, Maryland, and met many survivors from around the United States and from around the world. I learned that regardless of where you are from, we survivors have a lot more in common than we have differences. We all have the pain, the guilt, the fears, and all of the "maybes" and "what ifs" that seem to haunt us. In 1997, I joined the first group of survivors on the LOSS Team. The LOSS (Local Outreach to Suicide Survivors) Team is a concept of Dr. Frank Campbell (who was Executive Director of the BRCIC at the time). The same Frank I met for my assessment. The LOSS Team is made up of highly-trained survivors and BRCIC staff members who go as first responders to the scene of each suicide in East Baton Rouge Parish (county).

After responding to several suicide scenes, I soon learned that not only could I provide support to others, but also that I could benefit personally from being a team member. About one week after my first outreach, I was called to the scene of a suicide on the LSU campus. A young man shot himself in the head while driving across campus. While at the scene, I observed the law enforcement officers, EMT personnel, coroner's investigators, and funeral home personnel and saw how they all treated the young man's body with dignity and respect. This took away some of the anguish I had about how my son's body might have been treated.

The LOSS team was asked to provide a panel for presentations on being a survivor to various groups and agencies. We spoke to a class of LSU students in the Masters of Social Work program; we spoke with a group of third-year medical interns at a local hospital, and spoke to a statewide group of morticians. I served on the panel and found that the more I participated and the more prestigious and educated the group was, the more confident and comfortable I was as a speaker on this subject.

Each year from 1998 until 2002, I attended the AAS annual conference where I spent time attending sessions and learning everything I could about survivors and how I could help support them. I also served on the BRCIC Board of Directors from 1998 until 2003, serving as President of the board in 2001 and 2002. I resigned from the board in early 2003 when I became a paid, part time staff member. In 2002, I became a member of the Capital Area United Way Agency's speaker's bureau. For several years, I gave presentations at some of the area's large businesses during the United Way Campaign. During these presentations I told about our agency and would tell my story about how the BRCIC was responsible for my ability to realize that my life was well worth living even after suffering my two losses. Almost every time I gave a presentation, there was at least one survivor in the audience. That person would approach me after my presentation and reveal his loss to me and tell me how glad he was to have heard my presentation and to see how open I am about my feelings. What they didn't know is that I had usually picked them out as a survivor while giving my presentation. We seem to have a certain body language during discussions about suicide.

In the next several years, I accepted invitations to give presentations in Houston; Louisville; Augusta, Maine; and New Orleans, just to name a few. I also travelled to Northern Ireland on two occasions and gave presentations in Downpatrick, Belfast, Londonderry, and Armagh.

Something that I learned the hard way is that each person grieves in his or her own way and on his or her own timetable. Betty and I were very fortunate in that after the first few weeks, if she was having a really bad day, that I seemed to have been okay that day and vice versa. Our children really grieved differently.

Our daughter Robin, our first born, was obviously visibly shaken early on. However, Robin is an academic and seemed to logically accept what had happened without any counseling. For the last four years Robin has lived in Maui and on the infrequent visits that we now have with her, I detect a bit of sadness. I don't know if it has anything to do with Nelson's death, but I often think that it does. I hope to address the issue with her at sometime in the future.

Nathan, our oldest son, is very macho. He's a blue-collar worker, a motorcycle rider, and an outdoorsman. He continues to believe as I once did that real men don't show their emotions, seek counseling, or take anti-depressant medication. I really worry about him at times especially when life deals him an unkind blow. At times,

Nathan will do something that takes some of the worry out of me. During one of the memorial events at the BRCIC we did a balloon release. Everyone wrote a note to their loved one, tied the note to a string attached to a helium-filled balloon and we all released our balloons at the same time. When Nathan released his balloon, I thought I detected a cigarette attached to the string so I asked him about it. He said that, yes, it was a cigarette, that he had bummed many cigarettes from Nelson during his life and that maybe it is time for him to start paying him back. It was a very light moment and came at a good time.

Our youngest son David had the hardest time with Nelson's death. We should have expected it because David is our most sensitive child. He gets that from his mother. David did not seek counseling either. For two or three years after Nelson's death, David would get up and leave if a conversation came up about Nelson. It didn't have to be about Nelson's death; even if it was about some fond memory the family had, David would just walk away. David just didn't seem to care.

In 1997, Betty was asked to speak at the BRCIC Memorial Event. She gave one of the most powerful talks about losing a loved one to suicide that I have ever heard. The 100 or so people at the event were so quiet that you could have heard a pin drop. They wanted to hear every word. The talk was recorded on videotape so I gave David a copy of the tape and asked him to watch it. Several days later I asked him what he thought about the tape. He said he hadn't watched it yet and seemed totally unconcerned. Over the next week or ten days I asked David about the tape and he continued to tell me that he hadn't watched it yet. I was on the phone with David that last time I asked him and when he said he still had not watched the tape I lit into him and said some very cruel and unkind things to him about not caring that his brother was dead and slammed the phone down. I still regret that conversation.

Within ten minutes, David's wife Dawn was at my door. She chastised me for fussing at David. She said that David had tried to watch the tape numerous times but the most he could watch was his mother saying "My name is Betty Knox and on August 11, 1994, my son Nelson shot himself in the right temple and died." Dawn told me that when David would hear that, that he would start crying and that he often cried himself to sleep at night. I later apologized to David and haven't mentioned the tape again. I truly regret the way I talked to David that day and even though it has been thirteen years since the incident, I still think about it often. I did learn a very good lesson from this and always let new survivors know about it so they won't make the same insensitive mistake that I made. Just because someone doesn't want to talk about the person who died or about their suicide, doesn't mean they aren't thinking about it. Some people need their space and just need to know you are there for them if they ever need to talk.

Another painful aspect my family had to cope with in association with Nelson and Unc's deaths was the social stigma of death by suicide. I personally never felt much of the stigma and have never been embarrassed by the fact that my loved ones died by suicide. I know that in some societies, suicide is an honorable means of death. I can't say that I endorse that concept, but I don't feel that death by suicide should be looked down on or demeaned.

Shortly after Unc's death, Betty and I were having dinner at a local cafeteria. One of Unc's friends was there and he approached me, asking what had caused Unc's death, that he had seen Unc recently and he seemed very healthy. When I told the man that Unc had died by suicide, he immediately started to shush me and began whispering about keeping it quiet. I then told the man that it was not a secret and I had no intention of trying to make it a secret. He got angry with me and walked off.

We also had to deal with the belief that many people have that if a person dies by suicide they immediately go to hell. I had heard that belief for many years but don't know if I really believed it. To me, my God is a loving God and I don't believe He would condemn my son to hell because he died from an illness. Yes, an illness. Nelson suffered from clinical depression and would not take his medication as prescribed by his doctor. The result was Nelson's death. My two surviving sons suffer from Type 1 diabetes, and they have to take insulin injections twice a day. This also is a disease. If my sons refuse to take their medication, they will die. I have offered this analogy to many people over the last sixteen years and most have agreed with me after thinking about it. I don't want survivors to feel embarrassed by the fact that their loved ones died by suicide. It should not be a secret. To the contrary, I want survivors to talk about their loved ones, talk about their lives and deaths and reach the point where they can recall the many fond memories of their loved ones' lives.

I like the person I am now more than I liked the person I was before Nelson's death. Before, I had the typical male ego: I knew everything, I could do anything and others who showed their feelings or needed help were weak and soft and needed to take control of their own life. Squirrels in my backyard were a nuisance and made a mess just to annoy me; small children in a restaurant were there for the sole purpose of annoying me and ruining my meal; birds and other wildlife were put on the earth so that I would have something to hunt and kill (and being from Louisiana, to cook in a gumbo or a jambalaya). I had been able to fix everything in my life. But I couldn't fix this.

I am now a totally different person. I had a lot to learn and spent several years doing so. In fact, I am continuing to learn and it has been almost sixteen years since Nelson's death. I realized that I needed help and I don't consider myself soft or weak. Squirrels and other wildlife are beautiful and it's very peaceful for me to just sit on my patio and watch them although I reserve the right to put a few of them in a good Cajun dish from time to time. Small children are wonderful. When I see a young couple with their children in a restaurant or other public place I almost always tell them how beautiful their babies are and I mean it.

I don't think I was ever suicidal, but I do know that the thought of dying didn't seem so bad to me. Prior to coming to the BRCIC for help, I think that had I been at home and had a heart attack I would not have called 911. I think I would have just sat there and died. That's how bad the pain was; that's how much I missed my son; that's how hopeless my future seemed to me.

All the activities I discussed in this chapter have really helped me heal from my losses. Now I'm so glad to be alive. I can enjoy doing things that I enjoyed prior to Nelson's death. I can go fishing, attend an LSU athletic event, or work on an old car without the excruciating pain that I had in the beginning. I still miss my son, I miss him dearly, but life is good and I am so glad to be alive.

Finding My Way After Kent's Suicide

By Janet Schnell, MSW
Indiana, USA

I am the middle child in a family of five children. I have two older brothers, Allan and Chris, one younger brother, Kent, and one sister, Denise. We were born about one year apart from each other. My siblings and I grew up in rural southern Indiana, in a time when the simple joys of making mud pies in the front yard was our favorite form of entertainment. Bike rides and rambles through the woods were a regular occurrence. We relied upon each other for entertainment and support. In 1995, when our brother Kent died by suicide, we would need to draw upon each other for support and strength.

Kent was one year and four months younger than I. Growing up I remember him as being quiet and small in stature. He liked to follow his bigger siblings and we always tried to protect him. Kent loved to make people laugh and enjoyed being with his family. He found enjoyment in backyard ball games. Our family had the perfect yard to gather the neighborhood kids for quick summer play.

Living in a rural area we seemed to spend a lot of time outside. We also were mischievous. I can remember a summer when our mother warned us against eating "poison grapes," or at least that's what we called it. One day my older brother Chris and I decided to try this forbidden fruit, already knowing it would get us into trouble if we were caught. When Kent discovered what we were doing he wanted us to share. Since we had been warned they were poison grapes (and not wanting to share them) we told him he could eat the leaves. Of course our mother caught us. I don't remember what punishment was dealt out, but I do remember being forced to drink syrup of ipecac. Chris and Kent escaped the dreadful fate as mom determined I had eaten the most. The "poison grapes" left a stain around my mouth.

Being a quiet child, Kent never liked having attention drawn to him. I remember a time of playing hide-and-seek. Kent was hiding but ready to pounce and scare me if I found him. Instead I had given up because he had hidden so well. I yelled out I was not going to look any longer. Suddenly I heard what sounded like a half laugh, half cry. I thought it was a distraction to get me to come find him, only to discover he had actually cut his foot. Kent had to be taken to the hospital; he needed stitches to repair the cut. I felt guilty for not continuing to play the game and save him from injury. As his big sister I could have prevented him from being hurt.

Our family attended two different elementary schools. Allan, Kent, and Denise needed help with speech development. This was the first time we were separated by schooling. We rejoined each other in high school. I remember our drives to and from school. Kent and I sat in the back seat of our brother Allan's car. We always joked about his driving inabilities. Kent and I thought we were more cautious drivers. I bought my first car from Kent. He sold me his old Dodge Dart for the price of the new tires he had recently put on it. Kent always was generous with his family.

I met my future husband, Jerry, after high school graduation. He and Kent became fast friends. They would do things together even though I was not in favor of the activities such as going to bars. I always felt I would marry Jerry because my family approved of him. When Kent graduated from high school I remember him as being unfocused. I don't think he had a direction in his life at that time. He wasn't going to college and he wasn't happy living in Indiana. Kent seemed to hate the cold and the Midwest winters. Once he decided to move to Florida he was a much happier person.

Kent waited for Jerry and me to get married before moving away. We celebrated the beginning of our new life together as a family. Not long after the wedding, Kent decided to move to Florida. He really liked the sunshine and the general atmosphere; he just seemed to like everything about living in the South. This was before the age of the Internet, so when we would talk, it was by telephone and did not happen regularly. I was involved in learning to become a new wife and Kent to live independently of family. We did manage to visit Kent a few times while he lived in Florida. He liked introducing us to his co-workers and spending time together.

Unfortunately, a negative turning point in Kent's life came when a car hit our youngest cousin, Nathaniel. This was a hard time for our whole family. We were all very close to Nathaniel and his brothers' Dion and Brandon. Of course, we had to call Kent and tell him of the accident. The news devastated him. Kent had such fear Nathaniel would die, he stopped answering his phone. We were finally able to get in touch with him with an update Nathaniel was doing better and on the road to healing.

Another life altering event took place while Kent lived in Florida. I became pregnant with his first and only nephew. My pregnancy was very difficult with my hormones changing so quickly, I was constantly ill. I withdrew into myself and had thoughts of suicide. The ill effects caused me to lose so much weight. I weighed less at full term than when I had first gotten pregnant. I never shared that information with Kent. No matter how close we were, I didn't think he would understand what I was going through. I now regret not talking to more people during this difficult time. I'm sure everyone in the family knew something was going on because of my behavior change, but no one knew how to talk to me. Not even my doctor who asked if I needed help for depression. I always had the canned response, "I do not need help."

It was immediately upon giving birth that the depression was gone. I now believe it was the hormonal imbalance that caused the depression. Kent planned a vacation to be home when I gave birth. He was excited about becoming an uncle for the first time. After Kevin's birth at 1:40 a.m., Kent waited at the hospital to hold his new nephew. Chris and Kent developed a friendly rivalry as to who was the most important uncle. Chris called himself the No. 1 Uncle, but Kent said that he was the 110-percent Uncle because 100 percent wasn't good enough.

These events began changing Kent's mind about living so far away. My husband and his brother drove to Florida to help him move back. Kent found a job in Louisville, Kentucky, as a representative in a rental car agency. He loved his job and co-workers. We would spend endless nights discussing his job responsibilities. Kent was in his mid-twenties at this time and single. Looking back, this really seemed to be a turning point for him, a time when he began to focus more on his future as a single or married man with a career he loved.

Even though Kent liked living closer to his family he still hated the cold winters. He loved spending time with my son, taking him to the park to play, taking him to the zoo to see the animals, and playing video games with him. Kevin would run to Kent, as he always was willing to pick him up and throw him in the air. My son began spending the night with his uncle two hours from home because they loved the close connection. Kent had a lot of joy being Kevin's 110-percent Uncle.

Soon our little sister Denise was pregnant with her first child. I remember Kent being there when she gave birth. It seemed to be a really proud moment in his life that he was included in the birthing ritual. He was so happy being uncle to his nephew and niece. Kent would hold Natasha with tenderness a princess deserved. Natasha loved to make him laugh with her whimsy attitude. We loved Kent living so close and being able to come home for important events. Our last time together as a family was to celebrate our mother's birthday.

In the days before Kent's suicide, our mother, my son, and I were planning a visit to Louisville. At that time Kent and Chris lived near each other. Kent, Chris, and I had a three-way telephone call to discuss when we would arrive at his house. Kent also talked about a recent conversation with his girlfriend. She was encouraging him to start dating others because of their long-distance relationship. This seemed to bother Kent but he was more interested in what I had to say. As a lot of people who know us, you never ask a woman in our family for an opinion, because we always have one. One of my biggest regrets was not listening to what Kent had to say. I had to voice my opinion. Why-oh-why did I not just shut my mouth and listen with my ears? Maybe then I could have heard Kent talk about depression.

Weeks earlier, he made an appointment with two different doctors because he was having constant ringing in his ears and pain in his knee. Both doctors said he would have to live with the sound and discomfort. Neither asked him if he was depressed. Not knowing this could be a sign of depression, I did not know to ask. I wish I had listened to what Kent had to say, or more importantly what he was not saying. At the time, I thought we had a great conversation discussing future plans. Looking back, I realize that phone conversation may have been his way of saying he had thoughts of suicide.

We made the trip to Louisville two days after the phone call. Plans were for me to drop off a delivery I had for Kent. Chris, Mom, Kevin, and I stopped by his place. We knew Kent was home because his car was parked in front. When we knocked on his door there was no answer. Chris had the key, but the deadbolt was set so we could not get in. Chris knew when the deadbolt was set, it was Kent's way of saying 'do not disturb' because he was sleeping. Mom, Kevin, and I were staying at Chris's condominium nearby so we left. Later we telephoned Kent, but he didn't answer. We thought he had gone to work for the evening. The next day, Monday morning, Kent's boss called Chris to say that Kent had not come into work that morning, which was unlike him.

We didn't want to worry our mother without knowing all the facts, but we needed to go check on Kent so we made an excuse we needed to leave and get doughnuts. We asked if Kevin could stay with her as we ran the errand. I remember telling Chris as we were driving to Kent's apartment, "He has done something really stupid, I just know it."

There was something within me that was sure something was wrong, but I wasn't going to panic, at least not at this point.

When we returned to the apartment, it was just as we had left it the day before. The chain lock was still engaged. We had to contact the apartment manager to get inside. He in turn had to call the police department, because in the state of Kentucky the laws are such that the police are the only ones who can force an entrance into a locked apartment. Two police officers arrived, a man and a woman. When they forced the door open it made a very loud sound as it bounced against the back wall. Kent lived in a second story apartment. We waited on the ground floor and noticed his home was dark because all the curtains were closed. The female police officer exited the apartment to find a flashlight before going back in. A few minutes later she came back out and said, "I'm sorry your brother is asleep." I remember saying in disbelief, "He would have woken when the door slammed open." I was not prepared for her next reply, "I'm sorry, he is asleep and is not going to wake up." We knew immediately that she meant that Kent was dead. I remember sinking to my knees and just screaming as my brother Chris was hugging me and crying. I was frozen and not able to breath, move, or comprehend my life without my baby brother.

We did not know how Kent died. Kentucky law treats every death as a homicide until that possibility is ruled out. The apartment manager took us to his office for the police to process the scene. They asked us to wait until a determination was made. All I could think was, "I need to call people. I've got to let them know something has happened." It was a Monday morning and most of our family members and friends were at work. One of my first calls was to Kent's girlfriend. I knew she lived far away and it would take a lot for her to be able to be come back to Louisville. I called my husband's boss to get in contact with Jerry to come home immediately. At that time, he was an over-the-road truck driver far from home. Next I called my sister without thinking she was home with her one-year-old baby. She could hear it in my voice immediately something was wrong. Denise pleaded with me to tell her. I broke into tears and told her, "Kent is dead." I still remember her wailing, "No!" Our dad arrived at Denise's soon after. Because Dad and Denise were in Indiana and we were in Kentucky it was difficult to console each other. Chris called our mother's cousin, who lived in Louisville, to be with her until we knew the details about Kent's death.

The police notified us once they had investigated and found Kent's death to be a suicide. It was the longest ninety minutes of my life. They took his body away and cleaned the apartment for us to go in and get some of his belongings. I felt so confused and sad discussing a funeral for my baby brother. Why did Chris and I have to pick out clothes for him to wear in his casket? We were the older siblings and should not have been burying our brother. As I was reaching inside his closet to pick out Kent's sports t-shirt and suit, I noticed his blood soak out of the carpet around my shoes because it had not dried from the cleanup yet. All I could think of was that it was Kent's blood. It was all so horribly real. I wanted the weekend to start over and to hear his voice once again. Maybe I could have changed Kent's mind of wanting to die. When we walked out the door of his apartment I saw his winter coat. I could still smell Kent in it, so I took it with me.

As Chris and I drove back to the condo we decided I would talk to my son and he would talk to our mother. We did not know how to tell them but knew we had to. Chris went to our mother in the living room and I took Kevin into a bedroom. As I was explaining to him that his uncle had died, Kevin took Kent's coat and wrapped it tightly around himself. It was really important to him to have his uncle's coat. My little four-year-old son wrapped in a giant blue winter coat from his 110-percent Uncle. It was a very difficult time for Kevin and me. A mother never wants to see her child in pain. Especially when the hurt was caused by an uncle he adored. I don't think Kent ever intended to hurt his family. He did not realize how much his death would affect the rest of our lives.

A friend drove us back to our home in Southern Indiana to make the funeral arrangements. Mom and Dad's house was packed with family members, neighbors, and friends, all to support us. It was a good friend I remember hugging and wailing in disbelief, telling her Kent was dead. She helped me so much by listening and holding me when I felt so weak. At this point, I wanted the world to know I was hurting and everything needed to stop. The inevitable question of "Why?" kept resurfacing. No one saw the signs of depression. No one we knew could explain why this happened to our family. Suicide crosses all boundaries, even in closely connected families.

From what we've been able to piece together, a recent ice storm must have severely affected Kent. Not being able to get out of his apartment and the dreary days must have made an impact on him. But he did not tell anyone. He had begun enquiring about a gun. Kent asked a friend about the best one for self-defense and the time limit of purchase. In my eyes this would have been a clear indicator something was wrong. Kent was so opposed to having a gun in his house for the safety of his nephew and niece. He would not even allow the fake gun that went with his video game. Kent must have found out the wait period for a gun permit was up to the day before our visit. My family and I believe he went to work and on the way home picked up the gun. Kent had circled March 4 on his calendar and wrote, "Starting a new life."

I suspect Kent may have believed in reincarnation. He didn't like his life and wanted to start over. My little brother thought that death would give him a fresh start. In his last note to us, he said we should not blame ourselves. My thought was, "Yeah. Right! Easy for you to say as all I can do is blame myself for not listening." Kent left me, losing his right to tell me how to grieve.

When I saw him for the first time, lying there in that casket, it was very emotional. I hit his wooden box with my palm as hard as I could because he shouldn't have been there. My baby brother could not be dead. As I stood there in the funeral home looking at him, the devastating realization set in. My fantasy of growing old with my brother and me sitting on the front porch watching our grandbabies play was taken away by him. What was he thinking? Who was he thinking of as he loaded the gun? Why would he leave me in so much pain? I wanted to die myself. Kent made the decision to change my life forever without consulting me. I felt so abandoned by my little brother with whom I had made mud pies, rode bikes, and played in the woods. Why, Kent, would you leave me? I knew this question could never be answered.

The funeral home director needed Kent's information on how he died to publish in the local newspaper. We knew the stigma of suicide in the community where we lived. Not wanting people to think badly of Kent or to blame us for his death, we withheld this information. The funeral home warned my family and me that the local newspaper was likely to request information from the coroner in Kentucky. He was right. The newspaper found out the cause of death through the public record. A follow-up article was printed after Kent's obituary identifying his cause of death as a suicide. I felt humiliated that people in the community needed to know how Kent died. To whose benefit was this for? Granted it wasn't a big article, but it was too big for me. I was very tender and raw emotionally. The comments that were made to me and behind my back were very hurtful. Even the people who thought they had my best interests at heart made comments that hurt me deeply. I needed people to just say they were sorry and hug me, not tell me how to grieve or how to live without Kent.

The same friend who came to support my family and me set up a family counseling session for us. She may have no idea how this simple act saved my life. Our family learned how to support each other in sadness and take care of ourselves. Grief is very different for each person. Personally, I went through some very difficult times in the days, weeks, months, and years afterward. I didn't know what I was feeling. I just knew that I hurt immensely.

My mother, Denise, and I began attending a Survivors of Suicide support group in Louisville. We drove two hours to attend because in our area the only other group offered was for parents who lost a child. Nothing for siblings or specific to suicide deaths was available. I knew I needed someone to understand my anger and grief. As I said before, we each grieve differently. I was the angry survivor who wanted to yell at others and lash out. My mother and sister were the forgivers. One of my goals in the beginning was to get through a meeting without breaking into uncontrollable crying. It took a long time, but eventually I was able to talk about Kent without the tears.

The support group was not enough. It was my husband's push that helped me understand I needed a personal counselor. I knew I found the right person when I felt like a huge weight was lifted off my shoulders after talking with her. She let me cry and talk about Kent's death. My counselor offered guidance and helped me identify my feelings of abandonment. I still had a lot of feelings of guilt to work through.

My family began feeling stronger. We did not want another family member or friend to feel alone after the death of a loved one by suicide. About eighteen months after Kent's death, we began research about starting a Survivors of Suicide support group in our local area. My mother, sister, and I went to many churches and organizations looking for guidance and support. Many turned us away because they did not believe there was a need or we were not long-term committed to a group. We had found the benefits of a Survivors of Suicide group and thought others would agree. Finally, a Protestant Church opened its doors to us to facilitate a support group for family members and friends who lost a loved one to a suicide. We found a counselor to volunteer leading the support group, bought a few books, and created a pamphlet to introduce Survivors of Suicide of Dubois County.

Attendance fluctuated over time. We definitely fit a need in our community by the reaction people had after attending the once-a-month meetings. I took the initiative to take the group into a sustainable long-lasting support group. My mother and I sought other survivors who would be willing to commit to the group and become board members. I applied for grants on behalf of Survivors of Suicide of Dubois County. Each step of the way I found people willing to offer me help and assistance. Even the federal government was kind when I applied for the non-profit status recognition. A community lawyer helped our group with the legal wording. Through the inspiration of others, my mother and I attended a training class to learn how to facilitate Survivors of Suicide Support groups. The stigma I felt from the community lessened through education and understanding. Our family led the way in hope and healing after a suicide death. We still grieved the loss of Kent and that would never change, but we did not need to be alone in our grief.

Once Survivors of Suicide was established, I turned my interest to suicide prevention. We had many speakers come to our community to talk about suicide prevention. They would talk about the warning signs and their opinion why our community had a high suicide rate. I felt frustrated because Kent did not show the obvious warning signs. There was no information on how to talk to someone who may be experiencing suicidal depression. It became heartbreaking and frustrating to me. But, as a door shuts, a new one opens. I attended a meeting to listen to a national speaker from Washington State discussing QPR (Question, Persuade, Refer). Dr. Paul Quinnett reviewed the warning signs. He also talked about what to do when you see those signs and how to talk to someone who has thoughts of suicide.

I became inspired to share what I had learned with more people. The very same person who was there to support my family after Kent's death encouraged me to talk to the area schools about implementing suicide prevention. I became certified to teach others the QPR model. With Dr. Quinnett's help, I co-developed a QPR school-based suicide prevention program. A school corporation would select two people from each school, elementary through high school, to become trained in suicide prevention. They would in turn teach administration, teachers, aides, janitors, cafeteria staff, and more, the QPR model. Once adults have been trained, the program would be offered in the youth health classes. I wanted adults to be trained first so if a child or teen came to them needing help, the adults understood suicide prevention and how to provide assistance.

It took one school in the community to begin the training before the word spread. Soon the other three schools in my county asked for the suicide prevention training. We began to watch our suicide statistics drop. I knew the program was working to help save lives. Since the beginning of the first training, I have taught suicide prevention in the four county school corporations, two other counties in Indiana, to law enforcement, faith leaders, business human resource departments, and more. Before I begin training I can feel Kent's warm touch on my left shoulder. I know he is with me encouraging me to spread the word and letting me know he is proud.

I became an advocate with the Suicide Prevention Action Network USA (SPAN USA) in the federal government with suicide awareness. For over ten years, I met with the Indiana legislators to discuss suicide in our state. Advocacy became my passion as I felt legislatures needed to hear a voice from the field. I was no longer ashamed to tell the public who my brother was and how he died. Along the way I made many new friends who were survivors. We are friends to this day. I believed in the SPAN USA mission of awareness and became a two-term board member.

But for each success I still found those who doubted who I was or my passion. The negative responses only compelled me to further my education. Before I turned forty, and with my husband and son's support, I began college. I started part time at a local college to build up my self-confidence. Not sure what I wanted to major in besides something helping people, I found compassionate professors who were interested in me and what I wanted to do. I needed to rely upon these same caring professionals when my father died from congestive heart failure. His death was almost one month before Kent would have turned thirty-nine. It was hard to say goodbye to a man who was always my biggest cheerleader in life. But there was a part of me that found joy Kent would have our father with him to celebrate his birthday.

My first mentor helped me define who and what I wanted to become. Social work seemed to be the right fit for me. After two and half years, I was ready to transfer to a larger university. I became identified as the "suicide person." And I was okay with that title because fellow students came to me when they needed help. During my third year in college though, tragedy struck for me. And again it was after an ice storm. My son Kevin was in his last semester of high school when he was involved in a single-person car accident. He had gone to a friend's house and was returning home.

At 12:30 a.m., the phone rang with a first responder on the line. He told me Kevin had been involved in an accident and was on his way by ambulance to a local hospital. My only child had hit a patch of ice on the road that was hidden by the crest of a hill. My husband and I rushed to the hospital as the emergency crew was stabilizing Kevin. After x-rays to determine his level of injuries it became apparent to the emergency medical doctor that Kevin needed to be transferred to a trauma care unit. Jerry and I were present as Kevin had a chest tube inserted in his left lung so he could be life-flighted to a larger hospital. My son suffered eight broken ribs, a punctured left lung, an injured spleen, and broken collarbone. He had two surgeries to repair the damage inflicted to his body by a tree. Kevin spent twenty-seven days in the hospital. Ironically, enough he was released on the thirteen-year anniversary of Kent's death. I felt my baby brother had a hand in giving my son back to me and letting me know he would be okay. I believe Kent wanted me to remember March 4 as the day Kevin was on the road to recovery and not his anniversary death date.

Finding My Way After Kent's Suicide

I was able to graduate with my class with a bachelor's degree in social work. I received the National Association of Social Workers Bachelors Student Award. Professionals were taking notice of my accomplishments. A few months later, I was accepted into the one-year fast-track graduate program. I strived for a specialized field in social work with my emphasis in suicide prevention, intervention, and postvention. My graduate research paper was on suicide postvention titled "Understanding the Label Survivors of Suicide." I researched what survivors of suicide would like to be called. The reasoning behind research is if you can identify with someone and create a commonality, a better understanding can develop. Understanding the needs of family members and friends who lost a loved one by suicide can help professionals in the treatment process. I asked family members and friends who lost a loved one by suicide: How would you like to be identified?

The family and friends left behind after a suicide call themselves survivors of suicide, but people who had attempted suicide and lived also call themselves survivors of suicide. This can lead to a lot of confusion. The grief process is very different, along with the healing process, for those who have lost someone to suicide. Identification is important. While doing research, I had to reach outside my university for additional resources. I knew I wanted my paper to be accessible to the professionals helping family members and friends who lost a loved one by suicide. Through the help of a good friend I made contact with a postvention suicide researcher in another state. With help from this specialized research professor, I submitted my graduate paper to present at the American Association of Suicidology Annual Conference in 2011.

College life was not easy for me. I struggled with algebra and accepting I would not be the perfect A student. There were challenges along the way with skeptical students and professors who objected to my knowledge in suicide. I always had presumed well-educated people would know about suicide awareness. I assumed if I knew it, professionals and peers would know the information, too. I had to take a step back and realize that I had been trained outside of a university setting. Soon I learned when talking about suicide prevention, intervention, and postvention I needed to be specific with details. Many people were going to need the very basics from the beginning. Even though I had naysayers who questioned if I would hold true to suicide education when I first began college, I can now say my passion only increased.

As a result I have had many people seek my help over the years. I get calls because someone was worried about a loved one or they wanted to talk about a suicide, death. But for every person who wanted to talk about suicide there were those unwilling to address the "S" word. I am not sure if there is a fear that discussing suicide would plant the idea in others' heads. Some professionals may be afraid that open dialog will cause others to feel uncomfortable talking about suicidal depression. I have learned that no matter where you are in life, you always will run across people who are afraid to talk about suicide. Education doesn't change that, but people do. We have to be persistent and yet know how to be tactful and offer people a place where they are comfortable to talk about suicide. I am very comfortable identifying myself as a survivor of my brother's suicide. My hope is to show others they also can survive.

When my brother died, I knew I had two choices in life. I could either follow him in death, becoming suicidally depressed from missing him. Or I could make a difference. And now you know I have chosen to make a difference. Before I begin any training program, I identify myself as a survivor of suicide. It is who I am and I am okay with that title. My family and friends have helped me along my journey by offering love and encouragement. I have met caring people who have lost a loved one by suicide and talented professionals who offered support. Many times it was their kind word or warm touch that helped me accomplish the difficult tasks. Without a doubt, I would give up all my education and friends I have met to have Kent back in a second. I still want to have the dream of sitting on the front porchwith my little brother, watching our grandbabies play with my little brother. But reality is I lost that dream. My way of coping is by helping others. Knowing I might help prevent suicide or offer my assistance to a family member or friend who lost a loved one by suicide, gives me hope. Every time I can teach someone what to say or how to listen, I'm providing hope. I know my family and I have changed lives within our community. I couldn't help my brother because I didn't know how, but now I am able to help others and that brings me immense comfort.

Beyond Surviving

By Doreen S. Marshall, Ph.D.
Georgia, USA

I met Chris early in the summer of 1993 at the Meadowlands fair, a local state fair with amusement rides that my hometown hosted for a few weeks each year. I was twenty-one years old at the time and about to start my senior year of college. Our meeting was completely by chance; I was home for a few weeks before returning to a summer job at the college I was attending, and went to the fair after other plans had been cancelled suddenly. Chris was convinced this was fate's intervention, that we were meant to meet that night for some bigger reason. Our relationship progressed quickly after spending an intense summer together and we were engaged to be married by year's end.

There are many things I could tell you about Chris. He had a sweet tooth and a raspy voice. He played guitar by ear. He knew football stats better than most sports announcers, and often scheduled his life around Monday night football. He smoked Marlboro lights and tried to quit at least once a month. His favorite television shows were "Quantum Leap" and "Unsolved Mysteries." He usually slept well and snored when he did. Springsteen's "Thunder Road" was his favorite song.

He approached life the way children naturally do, with a sense of wonder and compassion toward others. He thought Golden Retrievers were kinder than most people. He was broad-shouldered and had a fragile heart. He believed in God, questioned his faith often, and prayed frequently. He was distant and passionate, hopeful, and hopeless at the same time. He came from a family who loved him and he had longtime friends. He was the kind of friend that if you told him you needed to be across the country with a thousand dollars by midnight tomorrow, he'd say, "Get in my car" with no questions asked.

He believed in the permanence of things, of love, life, and the fateful bonds that connect you to others. When he said something, he meant it. He dreamed big dreams and was frequently disappointed, but believed in the importance of dreaming anyway. He was easily social, funny, and, yet, one of the loneliest people I knew.

On September 19, 1995, after balancing his checkbook, he called me at my graduate apartment, put down the phone on his dresser with me still on the line, and hanged himself. I did not know what was happening at the other end of the phone. To this day, and with everything I know about suicide, I still wonder if I should have known what was happening on the other end of the phone. He did not say goodbye, make a big announcement about his plans, or leave a note. We did not argue that night, nor was he angry. He just sounded tired, the way most of us would sound at 1:30 am on a Tuesday.

His last words to me were, "Tell me about your day– I'm just going to listen." As I spoke (about nothing, I am sure), I remember hearing his dogs barking loudly in the background. At some point, I asked him, "Chris, what's going on with the dogs?" and he did not answer me, though the barking stopped. I would later learn he was moving furniture around to create a blockade to entering his home and had put the dogs in a crate in another room. After a few minutes of calling his name and receiving no response, I figured he had fallen asleep. I remember feeling both annoyed and amused by that, said goodnight, and hung up the phone. I would call his phone back twice that night (receiving a busy signal) and go to bed, telling myself I would call him again in the morning.

The next morning, I called him as I got ready for work and school and the phone line was still busy. This was before cell phones were popular and there was no alternate number for me to call. I went to work that day at my internship site (a counseling center) and figured I would speak with him later that day. I had no idea our last conversation had already occurred.

There are three things I remember vividly about the hours of that day before I would learn he was dead. First, that morning, I was awoken from sleep with a shake so strong I would have sworn someone was in my apartment. I was alone, but it unnerved me. Second, as I went through my day, I found myself looking at a picture of us on my desk for a long time, almost as if I was seeing it for the first time. I remember focusing on the nuances of the picture– the expression on Chris' face in particular. Third, I recalled the night before that he had asked me if I was going to be in his area of town the next day (I was living in graduate housing about forty miles away) and I said, "No, do you need me to do something for you?" I was thinking, "Maybe pick up dry cleaning or run an errand?" He said, "No" and that felt unusual to me, as he wasn't typically elusive and would have let me know if he needed me to assist him with something. He also didn't typically ask about my whereabouts on school/work days.

I would learn about his suicide about sixteen hours after our last conversation, after repeated attempts to reach him on the phone that day and after learning that he was late in meeting his mother to make dinner for her and a friend. She indicated that if she didn't hear from him soon, she would ask his brother, a volunteer firefighter, to take a ride to his house to see if he was there. I confided in a co-worker that I was worried, that it was not like him to not call me all day or not show up for a commitment, and that I was leaving work to go to his house. When I called his mother back to see if she had heard from him, a friend of hers took the phone and I asked, "Where's Chris? Did you find him?" She responded, "Yes, he's outside with his brother. You should come here, though, instead of going to Chris' house. But don't drive– can someone drive you?" By the tone of her voice, I knew at that moment something terrible had occurred. A co-worker offered to drive me to Chris' mother's home. I recall sitting in the passenger seat of my co-worker's car, white-knuckled, gripping the plastic door handle the entire 45-minute drive. I still wasn't thinking suicide at that point, but I remember praying that he was not hurt. When I arrived at her home, Chris' brother greeted me on the front porch while my co-worker waited in the car. "Where's Chris?" I asked. His brother shook his head, said, "He's dead," and then he grabbed me, as my knees were buckling beneath me. The other events of that night I barely recall, but they sent my life on a trajectory that could not be altered. Nine months shy of our wedding, and three months before his twenty-fourth birthday, Chris had ended his life.

Many survivors talk about being plagued by the why of suicide. I believe that you never know the full why of the person who has died by suicide, but you come to your own understanding of why this has happened. Also, the why changes. The why I have now differs from the why of fourteen, ten, or even two years ago. It evolves and changes as my understanding of life, of death, and of suicide, changes. Figuring out the why of suicide is like putting together a puzzle when you are a child and realizing at some point, you have lost some of the pieces and will never fully know what the picture looked like. You have enough of the picture to imagine what it was, and at some point, you realize you probably are never going to find those missing pieces, but that you know enough to understand what it could have been.

I believe Chris lost his life at the hands of a terrible and debilitating illness called clinical depression. I believe he had been depressed since childhood and that his depression was treated ineffectively. In my opinion, this is no one's fault; our understanding of mental illness is still very far behind our understanding of physical illness, and in 1995, this was no different.

I believe that many ordinary life stressors were too much for Chris to endure when he was depressed, and they sent him to a place of despair frequently. I believe that he did not respond well to the medication he was given and that he took it somewhat inconsistently. I believe that some hurts he had experienced in life he couldn't put into words, even with those to whom he was closest. I believe that a prior suicide attempt provided some sense of relief for him from the difficulties of life and that he would occasionally return to thoughts of that attempt, sometimes briefly, sometimes longer, for that relief. I believe that he erroneously thought that sharing thoughts of wanting to die with those who loved him would have sent them away forever. I believe that he missed his father terribly, having lost him to cancer when Chris was very young. I believe the notion that someone you love could be taken away from you no matter how much you protested created a fear in him that was soothed, at best, only temporarily.

I also believe that he had moments of extreme clarity, where his ambivalence toward life was absent, and during which he fully intended to live until old age. I believe that when we discussed Kurt Cobain's death a year prior and he told me he didn't understand why people killed themselves, he meant it. I believe the night he told me about a previous suicide attempt and promised me he would never again attempt to end his life, at that moment, he fully intended on keeping that promise. That, to me, is the insidious nature of suicidal thoughts. These thoughts manifest in moments where your connection to life is at its weakest and, against all instincts of survival, you become convinced that dying is your best option to end the pain you are experiencing. Those same thoughts also convince you that if you did die, the world would go on unaltered without you, or in your darkest moments, that the world would be better without you. For me, this is one of the biggest tragedies of suicide; those dying have no idea how the world they leave behind is altered immeasurably for those who loved them.

The aftermath, for me, involved spending years struggling with the memories of him tainted by his suicide death. There are times when I still feel confused by what happened to his life and how it could have ended this way. I have wrestled with hating him, with loving him, with understanding his pain yet being traumatized by his actions at the same time. I have felt tremendous sadness at losing him and for the pain he experienced in this life. I have felt left by him and also felt I must have abandoned him in my ignorance of just how depressed he was. I have imagined his soul leaving his body dancing, knowing how frustrated he was in this life and how uncomfortable he felt in his skin. I have replayed what I have said and what I didn't say, and felt regret for both. There have been so many complex, contradictory feelings in this journey of surviving his suicide, all against the dim backdrop of losing one of the best people I will ever know.

Hindsight can be very difficult for the survivor, because after the suicide, events that seemed insignificant prior to the death suddenly hold great meaning as you try to make sense of what has happened. A few days before Chris's death, I became lost after driving home from a friend's house and ended up in an area of town that was unfamiliar and somewhat unsafe. When later that night I told Chris about getting lost, he said, "You know, wouldn't it be great if I could be with you all the time. I could watch over you and make sure you never got lost." At the time, I didn't think much of the comment, but after his death, it meant something very different to me. Now I believe that he was sharing with me his image of what he believed would happen after he died, or perhaps letting me know that although he was leaving, he would always be with me. When I decided to return to graduate school to study counseling, Chris said to me, "I think it's great that you want to help people who are depressed, people like me." I heard his support for the decision to return to school, but not the rest. Several months before his death, he told me that, "if anything should happen," to him, he wanted to be buried with his guitar and with pictures of the people he loved in his pockets. I remember saying to him, "Don't say that–nothing's going to happen to you." I didn't even remember this statement until after he died, but hindsight sometimes brings things into a different focus.

Suicide grief also can have a traumatic component for some survivors. Though I did not discover Chris's body, I have closed my eyes and seen him, both in a death pose and vibrantly alive. I have dreamed of him and believed in those dreams that if I could just find him, he wouldn't be dead. I have mistaken others for him in a crowd and rushed toward them, only to greet a surprised look that was not his. I have worried that others in my life will die suddenly and that tragedy is just around the corner. I have shuddered at depictions of hangings, in everything from movies to Halloween decorations. While such worries and sensitivities do not continue to disturb me on a daily, or even monthly basis, they exist in the quiet spaces of my mind and can be easily conjured when I am feeling particularly vulnerable. Counseling helped tremendously with these concerns, but even today, I have an increased sensitivity to the pain of those around me. Not a bad quality for the psychologist I have since become, but difficult nonetheless.

At the time of Chris's death, I knew very little about suicide. This is still shameful to me, knowing what I know now about suicide. When Chris died, the only person I had known who had completed suicide was an acquaintance at my high school. (I had never even had a conversation with him, but I remember the look on my English teacher's face when she heard of his death and then left school suddenly that day). I would learn in the days following Chris's death that suicide was all around me: Carol, the counselor whose office was next to mine at the time, lost her mother to suicide as a teen. My own father later confided in me that his maternal grandfather had ended his life when my father was a boy. How could it be that the experience of suicide was around me and I was unaware of it?

Carol was also the first person to have a discussion with me about suicide grief. In hindsight, I think it was important for her to discuss losing her mother in this way with me, as society (and her family) clearly censored her in sharing her grief. We ate apple pancakes in her kitchen one morning and she told me what it was like to grow up knowing her mother had killed herself. There were some odd similarities in the death method chosen by Chris and her mother, and I remember thinking that it was an unusual way for us to feel bonded. Though our losses were different, her feelings of loneliness, shame, and isolation resonated with me. She understood what it felt like not to have answers or words when someone asked, "What happened?" and to have to pretend that you were coping just fine and that the usual cares were your usual worries. She understood the "elephant in the room of suicide," how it felt like you were wearing a neon sign that flashed suicide when you went to the grocery store, and how friends became strangers when this happens. She was unafraid to listen to and to talk with me, a fellow survivor, and for this, I am eternally grateful.

While Carol was the first person I knew who talked to me about the suicide of someone she loved. She also was the first person to introduce me to someone who was helping other survivors. I am sure she had no idea how this single action would change my life, my healing, and my future clinical work. She handed me an index card one day with the name "Karen" and a phone number. She did not know Karen and to this day, I do not know how she knew of Karen's work. She said, "You might want to call her– she does a group or something." That Karen was Karen Dunne-Maxim, survivor of her brother Tim's suicide, advocate for survivors, and now Past-President of the American Association of Suicidology. She also was the facilitator of a support group for survivors of suicide that I would later attend.

My experiences with her survivor of suicide support group helped me learn how to cope with Chris's death. I don't believe that groups are for everyone, but the group gave me a place where, for two hours a month, I could share the burden of losing someone I loved to suicide and know that it would be held by others. I would hold their burden, too, and that would give me a sense of community that was non-existent in other parts of my life regarding Chris's death. There was no pressure to feel better, to pretend my heart wasn't broken, to be strong for the comfort of those around me. The group, for me, became one of the safest places to sit with the horror of what Chris had done. Hearing of the stories of others helped me find the strength to give words to what had been lost.

Karen would ultimately connect me to a larger community of survivors and professionals helping survivors across the country. Through Karen I would later become connected with Iris Bolton at The Link in Atlanta. Iris, survivor of her son Mitch's suicide, is the author of the book, *My Son, My Son*, and a pioneer in the suicide bereavement movement. My daily work with Iris helped me to understand what it means to be an advocate for other survivors. She taught me that, in advocacy, sadness can give way to strength and that by speaking openly about suicide, I could help to end the secrecy in which our loved ones ended their pain. If suicide were an illness of isolation, then maybe encouraging those in pain to reach out for support would prevent other suicides from occurring.

In 2000, I became the Associate Director for The Link's National Resource Center for Suicide Prevention and Aftercare. In this role, I came into daily contact with survivors on their grief journeys. It was there that I began facilitating support groups for survivors of suicide, not dissimilar from the one I had attended years earlier. Over the years that followed, I would talk to hundreds of survivors, eventually completing a doctoral degree in Counseling Psychology. I would complete dissertation research involving survivors in an attempt to impact services they receive. The work in suicide prevention, intervention, and postvention would add an unbelievable richness to my life both personally and professionally. It also launched my involvement in other organizations such as the American Association of Suicidology and the American Foundation for Suicide Prevention. The survivors and professionals I have met through these organizations inspire me with their courage in surviving and their dedication to helping those affected by suicide. The work I have done with these organizations helps to make meaning of Chris's life and his untimely death. Iris once called finding meaning in a suicide loss the gift of suicide, though I would label it the consolation prize, one I would quickly forfeit to have Chris still alive.

These days, fifteen years later, I am still left with a deep sadness when I think about Chris' life and his suicide. In Chris's death, I feel the world has missed out on knowing one of its better members. The world was a better place with him in it, and I am saddened that others will not know him as I did. I grieve that he will always be twenty-three in my mind. He would have turned forty next year, and I occasionally imagine what he would look like with graying hair and laugh lines. I wonder if he would be smiling. Despite the sadness these images bring, I always will be grateful for the brief time I had him in my life.

For those surviving a loss by suicide, I don't have any magic words to help your healing, but I will share with you what I have learned through my journey. You will grieve this in both public and private moments. Try not to judge your actions in those moments or decide for the rest of your life how you will feel about this loss. Take each day as it comes and give yourself permission to do what you need to in those moments to survive. You will be surprised by your sorrow and your strength. Over time, you will find that the intensity of the grief changes and your wisdom as to how to go on living emerges and, ultimately, you will learn to live with what has happened. You will spend the rest of your life wishing it had been different, that you could have changed it, but that wish doesn't prevent you from surviving.

Decide that you will survive, even if in this moment, you have no idea how. Engage the support of those who are willing to listen to you talk about the suicide, whether it is a support group, a good friend, a good therapist, or all three. Learn about suicide if you find that to be helpful in understanding your loved one's death. Learn about grief if you find it helps you better understand yourself.

Know that everyone who finds his or her way through suicide grief finds a unique path; there is no right or wrong way to grieve this loss and you will do it differently from others grieving the same loss. You are not alone in this journey; there are millions of survivors on the path with you. Allow yourself to have regrets but not responsibility for the suicide. You would have stopped this from happening if you could have; try to forgive yourself for what you did or didn't do. Above all, be gentle with yourself as you grieve. Ask for what you need as you make your way through your grief; you will never have a better reason to take care of yourself or to rely on the support of those willing to help.

Fifteen years later, I have since married a wonderful man, had a daughter, and experienced many joyful moments in my life since the suicide. I did not believe I would ever have another joyful moment after Chris' death. Joy does return, gradually, slowly, and with time– don't ever give up hope that it will return. You will find that sadness and joy can coexist in the same heart, as they do in mine, when I think about losing Chris and the blessings I have experienced in life since losing him. I have learned that staying engaged in life is a way to honor life, and that there is as much honor in laughter as there is in tears. The choice to keep going is the toughest choice in life, though it is a choice we all face every day, often in the face of immeasurable challenges and pain. I pray for those who will struggle with that choice as I am writing this and hope, as you read this, you find courage in your choice to survive.

A Man's Experience of Grief

By Adrian Hill,
Canada

In 1994, I attended my first suicide prevention conference with my wife, a noted psychologist with considerable expertise in suicide prevention and bereavement programs. Traveling to Canada's arctic, we visited Iqaluit in Nunavut, a community of 3,000 people, the only city in a vast region. I had no idea, no way of guessing, that five years later my family would join with so many others in suffering a suicide death.

Organized by the Canadian Association for Suicide Prevention, there were keynote addresses, workshops, seminars, and meetings with speakers from around the world. I volunteered to help out and immersed myself in the conference. I experienced firsthand the anguish and grief of the local community that has been ravaged by suicide deaths for the past twenty years. Knowing next to nothing about suicide, prevention, and bereavement, there was much to learn, absorb, and take to heart.

This first conference experience for me started an educational process that quickly accelerated in 1996 when I became executive director of the national Lawyers' Assistance Program in Canada. While I had helped found the program in 1990, I was now responsible for developing Health, Wellness and Recovery materials for 70,000 lawyers and judges across Canada. To me, it had become natural to include suicide prevention in the new materials I was creating.

Our interest in suicide prevention and bereavement services accelerated when our Lawyers' Assistance Program received an urgent call for help from the Province of Nova Scotia after a series of lawyer suicides in the city of Halifax. The Barristers' Society, the Nova Scotia Branch of the Canadian Bar Association, and the entire legal community were in distress. The economic downturn of the 1990s seemed to have triggered an epidemic of suicide deaths among older lawyers in particular. No one knew what to do or what to expect next.

Having an entrepreneur's approach to problem solving, I initiated what I hoped would be a comprehensive and integrated response to the situation. First, I undertook research, which included an attempt to research and to understand the scope of the problem. The LPAC 1997 Lawyer Suicide Study identified suicide as the third leading cause of death for lawyers and established an approximate suicide rate of 69.3 suicide deaths per 100,000 population, **nearly six times the general population.**

The original LPAC 1997 Lawyer Suicide Study was the first reported investigation of lawyer suicide in Canada and the data has been widely reported and quoted in research papers and in professional articles around the world. It appears to be the first time anywhere that lawyer suicide had been studied.

The LPAC Suicide Prevention Program

In response to the situation in Nova Scotia, LPAC began a nationwide suicide prevention and bereavement support-training program for lawyers and judges and for Lawyer Assistance Programs in 1997. LPAC consulted with Dr. Brian Tanney and Dr. Roger Tierney of the Canadian Association for Suicide Prevention (CASP) and with Dr. Lanny Berman and Dr. Morton Silverman of the American Association of Suicidology (AAS) for ideas and direction. We accessed information, data, and materials from the Suicide Information and Education Centre in Calgary, the leading suicide library facility in the world. We enlisted the support and expertise of my spouse, Dr. Heather Fiske, a clinical psychologist with expertise in hospital and community-based suicide prevention programs and strategies whose innovations have enjoyed strong peer support and approval within both CASP and AAS.

LPAC presented a half-day suicide prevention program at the 1997 National Workshop for the American Bar Association Commission on Lawyer Assistance Programs (CoLAP) in Washington, D.C., featuring Dr. Fiske and Dr. Berman, executive director of AAS. This was the first time that suicide prevention was addressed at any CoLAP Workshop and it appears to have been the first such program in the world. This was a remarkable accomplishment for a fledgling program.

LPAC and Dr. Fiske created the Suicide Prevention Education Manual with teacher and student materials for LPAC's Health, Wellness, and Recovery Education Series in 1999, the most comprehensive lawyer wellness materials available anywhere.

Awareness of suicide risk in the legal profession has been greatly improved by the CBA and its LPAC programs. Suicide prevention is now an accepted part of the mandates of assistance programs for law students and lawyers and judges. A cluster of lawyer suicides has not occurred again in Canada, but if it should occur, a program has been left in place to offer support.

In every year since 1999, we provided suicide prevention programs for the Canadian Bar Association, and for many provincial and state Lawyer Assistance Programs and Bar Associations in Canada and the United States. In 2001, LPAC presented its course materials for peer review at a major medical conference for addiction physicians.

In 2002, our website was expanded to include all of the twenty-five courses in the Health, Wellness and Recovery Education Series. These courses could then be read, downloaded, and printed without charge by anyone in the world. They have been translated into four languages for use by bar associations in Canada, the United States, Europe, New Zealand, and Australia.

A Men's Panel on Suicide Grief

In 2003, my wife and I again traveled to Iqaluit, Nunavut, for the annual CASP suicide prevention conference. She was to chair a panel of men speaking on our experience of grief and the panelists included me and two of our friends, Hugh and David. The panel presentation was dramatic, emotional, and very revealing.

Heather addressed seven questions to each of us:

1. How has your grief been expressed?
2. What steps or stages can you see in your healing?
3. What has helped your healing? Specifically, what have other people done or said that made a difference?
4. What has hindered it? And what do you think can or could have made a difference with the hindrances?
5. How do you think that your experience as a survivor has been the same as or different from that of women survivors in your life? What has been more or less challenging?
6. What have you learned in your journey so far that you want to tell others?
7. What gives you hope?

We learned that both Hugh and David had been stuck in their grief and confusion for nearly ten years. Each had lost a son in his twenties and the loss had been devastating.

Hugh told us that he had been angry, frustrated, confused and bewildered. While his wife investigated survivor groups and then busied herself in starting bereavement support groups and teaching at conferences, Hugh had been on the sidelines. His pain was so deep and so repressed that he had no means of understanding or accepting his loss, much less letting go or moving on. In addition to anger, Hugh felt overwhelming guilt and remorse, even though he fully understood that there was nothing further he could have done to prevent his son's death by suicide.

Slowly, over a period of more than ten years, little by little, cracks began to appear in Hugh's impervious shell. As Leonard Cohen wrote, cracks are how the light begins to get in. Hugh met other men and this allowed for quiet and private sharing so that little by little, Hugh began to experience progress.

The culmination of Hugh's growing understanding and acceptance was his participation on the panel in Iqaluit. For the first time in his life, he shared openly and publicly in a room full of suicide survivors. Tears flowed, anguish was evident, and they were joined by love, support and acceptance. At the end of the session, every man and woman in the room lined up to hug Hugh.

For Hugh, his healing was finally well under way.

David's story was remarkably similar but his approach had been very different. Rather than accompany his wife to suicide prevention and bereavement events and stand in the background as Hugh had done, David had stayed away all together. On his own, he had searched and researched with an engineer's zeal to find out and to understand why his son had died by suicide. He believed that if he could understand the reasons, he could come to understand and accept his son's death.

While telling no one about his search and his research, he studied the investigative file on his son's death, including the autopsy report and the coroner's report, difficult, even dreadful reading for anyone. David maintained a dispassionate and professional approach as a coping mechanism. His research led him to studies and to reports, which added to his general knowledge but gave him little insight into his son's death.

Like Hugh, cracks slowly began to appear in David's thick skin and slowly and gradually the light filtered through.

It now appears likely, these many years later, that both of these young men had died by suicide as a result of an undiagnosed and untreated bipolar disorder. While both had been treated for clinical depression, the medications they were prescribed would be useless or even harmful to someone who's true or correct diagnosis is bipolar disorder. This appears to be plainly established by research done in Canada by leading psychiatrists and psychologists and it is confirmed by similar research done elsewhere.

Hugh and David teach us that men can find the pain of a death by suicide, especially the loss of a child, overwhelmingly painful. It may be that our skills as men are limited in this area and that our ability to seek help is limited as well, perhaps by custom, training or habit. While Hugh and David's respective wives had turned their bereavement and suffering into a loving involvement in suicide prevention and bereavement support, Hugh and David's inability to step outside their intolerable pain left them locked in isolation.

For those of us who work in suicide prevention and bereavement support, the experience of Hugh and David is not unusual. For many men, the stereotype appears to fit.

Now, some of you may have noticed that I have neatly avoided my own participation in the panel. It's time to fill in my story.

As you now know, I became seriously involved in suicide prevention work in the mid 1990s and, by 1999, I was the author of a major study, the creator of a national program and I was someone who came to and presented at suicide prevention and bereavement support conferences. I helped set up chairs, take registrations, moderate educational programs, and I attended the bereavement services with my friends. Every now and then, a stranger would cry on my shoulder and I would provide the natural support we learn in our role as parents and as friends. I thought I understood.

My story continues in 1999. In addition to running my federal Lawyer Assistance Program, I was still practicing law and everything was moving along nicely. In fact, I was having a great year professionally and personally. My law practice was going very, very well and I felt honored to be chosen to represent a regional police service at a Public Inquiry. My wife Heather and my two children were doing well in their chosen fields. As an alcoholic in recovery, I had been sober more than ten years and I felt great.

Nonetheless, as the year developed, events began to overtake me. In September, a very close family friend died in my arms and taught me, for the first time in my life, to truly grieve. As it turned out, this was a new skill I would soon need in quantity.

The Public

Inquiry into police conduct in the death of a young criminal turned ugly when fundamentalist radicals became active and threats by fundamentalist terrorists became focused on me as the voice of the police detective who had fired the fatal shot. So now, I was going to work in body armor, protected by an armed tactical police team. As an aside, I must tell you that it is difficult to express the shame a man feels at bringing the risk of terrorism into his home and to his wife and children. As you can sense, things were beginning to get more than a little difficult.

In my recovery program, we have a tradition of mentoring called a "sponsor," and my sponsor was an elderly man who I love dearly. A survivor of lung cancer some fifteen years earlier, he learned that fall that his remaining lung was cancerous and he quickly became seriously ill. So in this setting and at this time in late October, I received a telephone call telling me that my mother had died by suicide in her retirement home in the South of England. My parents, immigrants to Canada in 1948, had retired to England in 1988. Using a combination of pills and alcohol, my mother had suffocated herself with a plastic bag after carefully researching the most lethal and reliable methods. She had sent my father out of town so that he could not be implicated in her death.

My mother, Francis, had been unable to walk, using a wheelchair for more than a dozen years. A fiercely independent woman, she had died by suicide rather than face the fear of being institutionalized with the loss of autonomy and dignity she believed that would bring. She had planned her death very carefully and packages with her suicide note were sent by courier.

I had no idea how to feel. I carried on with my work feeling numb and little else. I spoke with my father by overseas telephone, and he appeared to be frightened, confused, and uncertain. As is often the case in families when there is a death by suicide, people can act poorly. The results were hard to bear.

The funeral planning was delayed for a time as the police made their inquiries and the county coroner conducted a full investigative autopsy. I was asked not to come to England until those enquiries were completed. So, I waited for word and tried to keep in touch.

The funeral was finally scheduled for two weeks later but I was not notified of the arrangements until just hours beforehand. My father and two of our brothers had avoided telling me and another of my brothers about the arrangements for our mother's funeral so that with us in Canada, and my dad in the South of England, we were effectively kept away.

Many of our friends asked me why my father and brothers would do such a thing. I have no real idea but I now suspect that the fear and anger that are so often part of the family landscape after a suicide death were the cause. Anger that our mother betrayed life and killed herself. Fear of stigma, the shame that our family had a mom who chose to kill herself. In truth, I cannot explain further.

I was deeply hurt, confused and even shocked. I felt stuck. When I confronted my father about his conduct, he blamed the situation on me. He soon became ill and he, too, died a little over a year later. This is often the case when a couple has been married more than fifty years. When one spouse dies, the other often follows not long after. With both my parents dead, I was even more confused and stuck. But I was lucky. Things happened that brought me progress and peace.

First, I attended the Annual American Association of Suicidology Conference in Los Angeles in 2000. While I had planned to go to the conference anyway, what I discovered when I arrived was a revelation. For me, everything was different. Every poster, every bulletin and book, every presentation, speech and seminar, every face-to-face contact. I was pretty well known at the event and had dozens of friends and several hundred acquaintances in attendance. I had a good reputation as a hard worker, a friendly individual, and a kindly man. Word spread quickly and I was to receive hundreds of pats and hugs and words of comfort. During the survivors' portion of the conference, we had the usual candle lighting ceremony. The organizers asked me to light the candle during the service as a survivor who lost a parent. As a trial lawyer, I had thirty years experience in performing in public, even when I felt poorly. I walked to the front with my candle, lit it, and confidently placed it in the holder. My task complete, I turned to walk the twenty paces back to my seat in front of the crowded auditorium. It was the longest walk of my life. Safely seated, I cried on the shoulder of a stranger.

That stranger is now a good friend and colleague and, earlier this year, he and I were on a new panel, describing the experience of men's grief.

So, I will now fill in the answers to the questions that were posed to me in these panels:

1. **How has your grief been expressed?**
   I was bewildered, sad, confused and angry. At the same time, I felt a peacefulness in my relationship with my mother who is no longer in pain and distress. This leads me to an observation I feel compelled to make. While the experts will tell us that we should not compare our losses, I am most firmly of the view that there is a huge difference between the loss of an aged parent, disabled or otherwise, and the loss of a spouse or the unspeakable suffering of the loss of a child. While my mother's death by suicide opened my mind, my heart, and my eyes in a way I had never anticipated or expected, I have been spared the profound and complex grief that you and many of my friends have experienced. Quite frankly, your loss and pain to me appears intolerable.

2. **What steps or stages can you see in your healing?**
   From numbness, to hurt and loss, to anger and to peaceful resolution. I remember each of these stages with clarity.

3. **What has helped your healing? Specifically, what have other people done or said that made a difference?**
   I was so lucky in three different ways. Firstly, my wife and two children held me, comforted me, and loved me. This made all the difference. Secondly, I put the word out to my friends, colleagues, and associates and the results were truly astonishing. I received notes, cards, e-mails, flowers, and phone calls from over 200 people and I was completely overwhelmed with this support. From the janitor and the security guard in my office building, to friends and professional colleagues, to a former president of the United States. They all took time to get in touch. This outpouring of support was as humbling as it was healing. Finally, I had your help. I was already a part of the suicide prevention and bereavement support world and you all came to my rescue. At conferences and at meetings, from that day until this day, you all have had your hand in keeping me safe.

4. **What has hindered it? What do you think can or could have made a difference with the hindrances?**
   Clearly, my family and our dysfunctional history. I needed a chance to grieve at my mother's funeral and I needed an opportunity to comfort my father and be comforted by him. None of this was possible.

5. **How do you think that your experience as a survivor has been the same as or different from that of women survivors in your life? What has been more or less challenging?**
   Strangely, the stereotypes all apply. As a man, I was quick to shut down and shut off. On the other hand, I had the support of my family and my friends and I took their advice to reach out for help. They were smarter than I could be at that time and I was lucky to have their advice and even luckier to be able to take it. As I have told you, the support I received was truly astonishing.

6. **What have you learned in your journey so far that you want to tell others?**

7. **What gives you hope?**
   I'll answer these two questions together in a minute, but first I have to give you the final chapter of my story.

After my father died, I felt trapped in an issue I could never resolve. With my sister and brothers, I did attend his funeral and for me it was a ceremony for both of my parents. I taped letters from me and from my children to my dad's coffin with the goal of burying my hurt and anger with him. It only helped a little. One last event came to pass that made me whole again.

You remember my sponsor Clive and the reoccurrence of his cancer. As time went by, he grew more and more ill. He was in and out of the hospital and I visited him often, sometimes with my security detail in tow after my daily work at the Public Inquiry. One Sunday morning in February I realized that it had been several weeks since I had called Clive and when I did telephone I learned that he was back in the hospital and very, very ill. I drove to the hospital that day and learned that it was his seventy-fifth birthday. He wanted pizza for lunch and this became my birthday gift to him. He entertained his family, including his grandchild, and had a wonderful day. Yet, it was clear to me that his hours were numbered. With his family's permission, I let a number of our joint friends know and quite a few of them dropped by to see him the next morning. That evening I went back to the hospital to attend a meeting of Alcoholics Anonymous with my three closest friends and our plan was to drop by and see Clive, go to the AA meeting, then say goodnight to Clive. If he was well enough, we'd take him to the meeting as well.

When we arrived at the hospital, Clive's daughters were in great distress. Clearly, he was dying and he was very, very uncomfortable. We stayed for a few minutes and then went to the meeting as planned. We left the meting early, going back to his room before visiting hours closed. The scene in Clive's room was awful. He was semi-conscious and in great agitation and picking at his skin. His daughters were very upset. I looked at Clive closely and realized that his oxygen tube was behind his head and I replaced it in its proper place, with the canula into his nose. This is rather a personal thing to do for another man but as soon as I did it, Clive calmed right down and became relaxed. I realized that he had been suffocating without the oxygen, causing the behavior and symptoms we had seen.

With their father relaxed and comfortable, his daughters calmed down and together we watched Clive slip off into death.

For me, this experience with Clive healed the loss I had felt from my absence at the deaths of my own parents. While I truly regret that my mother died alone and at her own hand, I am now at peace with it. While I still regret my father's conduct at the time of her death and after, I am at peace with it. By being able to care for Clive and to comfort his widow and his daughters and to stand as his pallbearer, I found peace and serenity. In dying, Clive gave me what I needed to move on. There is a saying in AA, Doing for us what we cannot do for ourselves.

To answer questions 6 and 7, let me say this.

If there was one thing by way of experience or advice I would want to pass on to you all here today, it is this: Men need your support, love and experience every bit as much as women and children. For many of us, we also need your guidance and your ability to reach out even when we as men do not have the common sense to reach back and take your hand. We are teachable, if a little slow.

Have patience.

We, too, have much to offer.

Hope, Healing...Surviving

By Lois Two Bears
North Dakota, USA

I am a Native American woman from a small community located in North Dakota. My family and I live on the Standing Rock Sioux Reservation, which is located in South Central North Dakota and North Central South Dakota. We are of the Yanktonai Sioux Band of Indians. We come from a very large Tiospaye which in our language means "Family." I am married to my loving husband, Tony, and we have two surviving children, Richard, twenty-six years old, and Margaret, twenty-eight years old. We also have six wonderful grandchildren; five grandsons, and one granddaughter. This is my story, a story about our son– Brad Leigh Two Bears.

Brad was sixteen years old at the time of his death, a death by suicide. He was my youngest child of four children. His Dakota Indian name was "Hehaka Mani" meaning "Walking Elk" named after one of his grandfathers. He was shy, but yet he was very artistic, intelligent, and he was a handsome young man. He was not into alcohol or drugs and he was not a troublemaker. Brad could be comical at times but yet he had a serious side to him. I really loved that part of his personality, his comical side. He loved to draw and write poems and I still have his artwork and poems. At the time of his death, Brad was a sophomore in high school and he was going to graduate from high school early, at the age of seventeen. He had decided to join the military and "get away" from the Reservation. I believe he would have made a career out of the military, the Army, specifically. He knew what he wanted in life as far as his future was concerned.

And then there was Anne. She was fourteen years old, she was very pretty, and she was Brad's first girlfriend. They met the summer before entering his sophomore year of school. Brad asked Tony and me if he could transfer to the school Anne was attending. We hesitated at first and we asked him if he was sure that's what he wanted because he had attended his current school from Kindergarten to his current grade (tenth). He told us that was what he wanted and so we let Brad transfer to Anne's school at the end of the first quarter. They wanted to spend more time together. I knew Anne's home life was not perfect. I now know Anne was hurting inside, but no one knew how much. Her father had died and she missed him terribly. She was living with an aunt, but she wanted so much to live with her mother. Yet because of circumstances she had no control of, living with her mother was not possible. I invited her to our home numerous times and made her feel welcome. The more time Brad and Anne spent time together, the more intense their relationship became. I suppose they talked about things that were important to them, things they felt they couldn't talk to anyone else about. Things were going good as far as I knew.

But November 24, 2001, would change Brad's outlook on life forever and it also would change our lives in a way we did not expect. That's the day Anne died by suicide. She was on life-support at a hospital and was declared brain dead. On that morning my friend and coworker, Margaret, came to our home and told us about Anne being in the hospital. She told us to check on Brad to see if he was alright because she had been told that Anne and Brad were supposedly going to suicide together. I went to check on Brad and he was sleeping. I woke him up and told him about Anne being in the hospital and that she was not doing too well. I asked him if wanted to go see her and he said he did. I told him to get ready and that we were going to leave shortly. I called the hospital and talked to a family member of Anne. I asked her if it was okay for us to bring Brad to see Anne and she said it was okay. So Tony, Brad, and I made the trip to the hospital to see Anne.

At the hospital, there were numerous friends and family members of Anne, a team made up of school personnel and hospital and school social workers. It was then that Tony, my husband, and I learned of a "suicide pact" made up of seventeen young people, including Anne and Brad. I couldn't believe Brad would be a part of a pact because as far as I knew, he was doing just fine and he had everything going for him. To think that he wanted to die was shocking. We also learned of the "note" Anne left behind; an individual read the note aloud. One part of the note that stands out in my mind and I always will remember was to Brad. Anne had written to Brad specifically to remember how much she loved him and "To be sure and tell your mom I love her and I wish she was my mom." When I heard that, I broke down and cried, thinking "Why did this happen? "The school social worker asked Tony and me if she could talk to Brad alone and we consented to that. I had never been in a situation such as this and I wanted to do what was best for all those involved, including my son.

Later, the same school social worker took Tony and me aside and told us that she had talked to Brad and she felt that it was a good idea for him to be admitted to the hospital mental health unit. She had asked me if I agreed. I told her I didn't think that it was necessary. I informed her that I could keep an eye on him at home and do what I thought is best for him. She continued to tell me that it was better for him to be in the hospital. She also told me that I needed my rest and I could not watch him twenty-four hours a day. Eventually, Tony and I agreed with her.

We sat down with Brad and told him of the plans for him to be admitted. I said to Brad, "You know Brad, Dad and I love you very much. Even though we are your parents, we are not social workers or counselors. If you stay here (at the hospital), they can help you whenever you need to talk." He agreed to be admitted to the hospital and I have to acknowledge that I was relieved. When we were in the unit doing all the necessary paperwork, I looked at my baby, my Brad, and he looked so sad. I put my arm around him and said, "Brad, its okay to cry. You have people here you can talk to twenty-four hours a day, whenever you need to talk. They can help you." And that's when the tears started flowing, like a waterfall.

I wanted so much to take his pain away, his hurt. But how could I? I didn't have the training as a counselor to help him so I relied on the professionals. We visited him every day and my Aunt Vicki prayed with him and for him. I thought everything was going to be all right. Brad was released after a four-day hospital stay. After Anne's death and her funeral, it seemed Brad was coping with his loss the best way he could. I guess I took it for granted he was okay and doing fine.

But, in the end, Brad felt he had no choice but to "join" Anne. His suicide note explained how he felt and how he was so sorry for hurting us. The night before he died, we all were sitting in the living room watching television. I asked Richard and Brad what they wanted for Christmas. Koltyn was already sleeping, as it was a school night, a Monday night. Richard, being the cowboy he is, said he wanted cowboy boots, a hat, etc., all the things a cowboy needs. Brad was not a cowboy, he was not that type. Brad said, "What I want will never fit under the Christmas tree." I replied, "Well, you never know, it might be there Christmas morning!" You see Tony and I were planning on getting him an electric keyboard because he loved music. I don't know what he meant with his answer. Later that evening, around 10:30, Richard told Tony that Brad wanted to go to the local gas station, which was about five miles away. So, all three of them went. Later, Tony told me Brad bought the following items: one sandwich, a bag of potato chips, his favorite soda, his favorite candy bar, and his favorite chewing gum. Tony didn't think about what Brad purchased, he just thought he wanted a late night snack. Thinking about this now, I ask myself "Could this have been his last supper?" Again, we will never know.

When they returned from the gas station, Brad went into his bedroom. I knocked on his door and he was sitting on his bed, writing. I told him not to stay up too late and to go to bed because he had to go to school the next day. He replied, "Okay, after I finish writing this." I thought he was writing a letter to one of his friends who lived in South Dakota because he received a letter from her a couple of days before. I said goodnight to him and closed the door. I never once thought that would be the last time we would speak to each other and I never, ever thought that would be the last time I would see him alive. When Brad died, a part of me died, too.

December 18, 2001, seems like it was yesterday. I thought that day was going to be just another day, but it all changed in an instant when I opened his bedroom door that morning. My life would never ever be the same. A lot of things surfaced after Brad's suicide and a lot of his friends came to us and told us things that Brad had said to them. If only we knew then what we know now, but then again, I suppose a lot of parents say that after their child has died. There are always the "if only," "I should have" after a suicide completion. I had the same thoughts after Brad's suicide. Today, as I look back on certain things that happened, I realized Brad and Anne did have a plan. A plan that involved both of them completing suicide together.

As a mother, I wanted to do all I could for my children. I tried to give them the best and provide for them the best way I knew how. I disciplined my children in a positive way and I praised them for the good things they accomplished. They were never afraid to ask questions if they needed to. A few months after Brad's death, I realized I was angry with both him and Anne. I blamed Anne for taking my son away. I was angry at Brad for not talking to us, for not telling us how much he was hurting, and for not telling us how much he missed Anne. Eventually, I accepted his death and my anger towards the both of them went away.

I waited about six weeks after Brad's death before I attended a support group for survivors of suicide. After the first meeting, I couldn't wait until the next one because I found people who knew what I was going through. They had the same questions I had– questions that had no answers. I knew I could count on them to help me if I was having a bad day. I will forever be grateful to these people. I also did a lot of journaling then. I found that writing was a release that helped me heal. In my journal, I could talk to my son and I could tell him my feelings. I cried many times when I wrote in my journal because I missed my son so much. I also did a lot of reading. Before I knew it, I had many books on death and dying, including suicide. I also read books written by individuals who had near-death experiences. As I look back on those days, I realize I was trying to find an answer to my son's death and I also was trying to get closer to him.

I went back to work after two weeks off and that helped ease the pain. But eventually I had to take another week off because there were days that I could not handle it. I had to drive thirty-six miles round trip to and from work. Some days, when driving home after work, I would cry so hard, I had to pull over alongside the road and get myself together. Then there would be times when I would get home, pull into the garage, walk into the house, look at Tony, and start to cry. Tony would put his arms around me and comfort me. I also began seeing a counselor because it helped me talk about my son, his death and how I was coping. I am not ashamed to let people know that I needed help emotionally and mentally. Without the counselor's help, my life would probably have taken a different route. A route that probably would have led to destruction, but I'm glad it didn't turn out that way.

After Brad died, I watched my surviving children very closely, including my grandson, Koltyn. I always checked on them when they were sleeping and I made it a point to check to see if they were breathing. I never wanted to go through a loss like this ever again. I recall one incident about four months after Brad died. Tony and I came home and Richard, our son, was supposed to be home. We walked in the house and called his name. He didn't answer. I asked Tony, "Where do you think he is?" Tony then began to go from room to room, checking the closets. I stood in the middle of the living room, beginning to relive the morning of December 18th. I started to cry and said, "I don't wanna go through this again!" Tony said, "He's not here. I think I know where he might be. He said he was going to help tear down the old rodeo grounds." So he drove to the old rodeo grounds and there he was. Tony came back to the house and told me Richard was there helping and he would be home when they were finished. When Richard finally did come home, I told him to be sure and leave a note next time, telling us where he will be or where he's going. I told him I didn't know where he was and I was really scared. He said, "Mom, I was okay. I was just helping at the rodeo grounds." I'm glad he was okay, but today, I still have that fear.

The death of my son devastated me so much I didn't realize what I was doing at times. I wanted so much for Brad to be alive, to be home. I wanted things to go back to the way they used to be, normal. I wanted so much for him to be beside me so I could hold him in my arms. When I was alone I used to sit on my bed in my bedroom, holding his picture, and I would cry my heart out. I knew he died and that his body was buried, but I still had the question, "Are you okay? Please give me a sign just to let me know you're okay!" I desperately wanted to know if he was really okay. Then one night I truly believe he came to visit me in a dream. In my dream he asked, "Mom, why are you always crying? Please don't cry anymore." And in my dream I was surrounded by people, family members, and Brad had a blanket. We were facing each other and the look on his face was contentment. He looked happy and not sad. He then took this blanket and wrapped it around me and said, "Remember Mom, I will always love you." Then I woke up. I remembered instantly what I dreamt. Then I realized and understood he was definitely okay. It was me that needed to be okay.

In September 2003, a group of five people, including Tony and me, flew from North Dakota to Atlanta, Georgia, for an SOS Support Group Training held Friday through Sunday. The day we left for Atlanta I was on the plane, and as were flying, I looked out the window, looked at the clouds and I remember thinking, "So this is what Heaven looks like." I continued to stare out the window, looking at the clouds, hoping to get a glimpse of an angel, a glimpse of my son. I closed my eyes and pictured him smiling; I was content with that.

This particular training also just so happened to be held the weekend of Brad's birthday, which had been September 20, 1985. We had previously met Iris Bolton at another seminar and it was good to see her again and meet Jack, her husband. Jack and Iris were two of the facilitators for the meeting, as well as other individuals. Saturday, September 20, is a day I will not forget because I believe Brad came to me that day. Let me go back one day, to Friday evening, September 19, 2003, when Tony had mentioned to Jack and the other men attending that the next day, Saturday, would have been Brad's eighteenth birthday. So when we arrived at the meeting on

Saturday morning, one of the men gave me a white rose and I was surprised because I didn't expect that. I really loved and appreciated the gesture. He also gave Tony and me some words of encouragement, to remember Brad.

When it was time for lunch, Iris told all participants to go out to the garden or wherever we were comfortable and have our lunch. We sat on the porch, the five of us from North Dakota, enjoying our lunch and the beautiful day. I noticed this butterfly kept flying around me and I kept chasing it away but it would always come back. It would fly around me and then it landed on my knee. I chased it away again and it came back again! I looked back at Tony and my friends. I said, "This butterfly keeps flying around me!" Tony looked at me and said, "That's your son. Today's his birthday and he came to visit you to let you know he's okay!" I looked at the butterfly and watched it as it flew away and I turned to Tony and my friends and as tears were flowing down my face, I said, "Now I know Brad is okay!" What a beautiful day that was! Tony and my friends all had tears in their eyes. My friend, Margaret, was crying and laughing at the same time because she could not believe what had just happened, what she had witnessed!

My wonderful friend, Margaret, is an individual who has helped me heal tremendously. She has a heart of gold and truly is a helper. She has never lost a loved one to suicide, but when Brad died, she was there to comfort us. She is a former co-worker and it seemed she always knew when I was having a bad day. All she had to do was look at me and say, "Sit down, Lois, and tell me what's going on." She would then sit with me, let me talk, and listen. She didn't have to say a word, she would just listen. Oh, how I needed that so much in those days. She always would lend me her shoulder to lean on and to cry on. We need so many more people like her.

And many times after a suicide, the siblings are forgotten about. It seems like they are pushed aside, not literally, but they are taken by an aunt, uncle, or friends and all the comfort is given to the parents, the adults. But the siblings are grieving, too. I know this happens because my now thirteen-year-old Grandson, Koltyn, had just turned four years old when Brad died. He and Brad were very close, like brothers, even though there was a twelve-year difference between their ages. Brad loved Koltyn very much and Koltyn loved Brad very much. Koltyn knew something terrible happened to his Uncle Brad, but Tony and I, especially me, were in no condition, emotionally, to tell Koltyn what happened. All I remember was that I was very hysterical. Tony remembers when the funeral home came to take Brad's body away, Koltyn was hitting the dining room window, crying and shouting, "Where they taking my Uncle Brad?!? Where they taking my Uncle Brad?!?" Tears were falling all the while he was shouting.

One of my nieces was at our home that morning and she took Koltyn to go be with his cousins. For about two to four months after Brad died, Koltyn would often ask Tony or myself, "Where's Uncle Brad?" We would tell him that he was "in

Heaven singing with the angels." One day he asked where his Uncle Brad was and we answered, "He is in heaven." With an innocent look, Koltyn said to us, "I wanna go to heaven so I can see Uncle Brad." His reply shocked us and then we knew we had to explain to Koltyn how Brad died. We told him his Uncle Brad died because his brain was sick and his brain (meaning Koltyn's brain) was not sick. We also told him "sooner or later there comes a time that we all die. When the time comes, you will see your Uncle Brad again but not just yet." We felt he was satisfied with what we told him, but he did continue to ask other questions such as, "Did Uncle Brad do this? Did Uncle Brad like this?" We would answer his questions the best we could.

When Koltyn was in the fourth grade, he began to have problems. He would act up in school and make remarks like, "I'm gonna kill myself!" Although I don't think he really understood what he was saying, the principal and his teacher didn't know what to do about his behavior. He was being labeled as a student with ADHD and/or a student with behavior problems when all the while he was just beginning to grieve the loss of his uncle. His feelings of sorrow and grief were kept inside for so long that he didn't know how to express himself. I went to the school and talked to the principal and told him my story and how close Koltyn was with Brad. I didn't know if he really understood the situation but at least he tried to. I immediately made an appointment for Koltyn to see a psychiatrist. At the first appointment, I once again told my story of Brad, how close Koltyn and Brad were, how Brad died, and what was happening with Koltyn in school. He talked to Koltyn alone and he began to see him on a regular basis. No one told me to take Koltyn to a psychiatrist. I did this on my own because I did not want to go through another devastating experience. Koltyn is now in the seventh grade, attending a different school, and this school provides him with what he needs and he really likes it. To this day, he still talks about Brad every now and then. I know he will not forget Brad because he loved his uncle so much.

Brad also left behind another individual who was not only his cousin, but also a best friend, Marcellus. They were like brothers. They attended school together, all the way from Head Start to the time Brad transferred schools. I can look at Marcellus today and I can see the hurt he still carries with him. He, too, misses Brad so much that at times I feel he's lost. They were constant companions. They would have graduated the same year from high school. When Marcellus graduated, Brad's classmates, at his former school before he transferred, wanted to have an empty chair representing him-- but no, oh no, the school administration didn't like it or want it. We were told by school administration that the students changed their minds. The students were told we didn't want that done.

At the graduation, two of Brad's classmates approached Tony and me and asked us why we didn't want the empty chair. We just looked at each other and informed them what we were told. We all went to the principal and the seniors more or less demanded what they wanted. In the end, there was an empty chair among the graduating seniors. I am so proud of the students for standing up for what they wanted and believed in. As you can see, it's the adults who don't want anything to do with suicide. We also gave a one-time scholarship to one of the graduating seniors. This was my mother's idea and I appreciate her for that. She wanted to do this because she said Brad was a smart student and she wanted to help another student the best way she could and I believe that was her way of healing. Towards the end of the graduation program, they have a rose ceremony. The seniors give roses to individuals who they feel helped them throughout their high school years. I was surprised and broke down in tears when Marcellus came up to me, handed me a rose and gave me a big hug. I could not help but think of Brad, this could've been him.

So many things I have to experience without my son, so many things he will not ever get the chance to experience. I remember how much I hurt from Brad's death. And then there were times I felt like I wanted to sleep, to be in a deep, deep sleep and not wake up for a long, long time. I didn't want to die, but I just wanted to sleep and not be bothered. Believe me, there were times when I did think about suicide, about dying, so I could be with my son, but I realized that suicide was not the answer. As I look back on those days, those feelings I had back then, I realized I was definitely depressed. I'm glad I had the courage to seek help before something terrible happened to me. What really helped me take the step in the right direction was my family: my husband, my surviving children, my grandchildren, and most definitely, the support group. Slowly, but surely, I became well, mentally and emotionally.

Brad died one week before Christmas and now the holiday season is not the same. If it weren't for my grandchildren, I would never celebrate Halloween, Thanksgiving, and other holidays, but especially Christmas. Those days would be just another day for me, but I see how excited and happy they get when those days are here and so I celebrate with them. I enjoy seeing their smiling faces but it sometimes make me wonder how many grandchildren Brad would have given me. But it's just a thought then it goes away. I think of Brad every day. I often wonder what his life would have been like. I had so many questions, so many unanswered questions back then. I still have those questions, but it's not as intense as it was in the beginning. Nine years have gone by since his death, but it seems like it just happened yesterday.

My mother and my sisters really tried their best to help me when I was feeling down and I know they were hurting, too. But they didn't really know how I felt because they didn't lose a child, especially by suicide. One day (it happened to be May 18th and Brad had died on December 18th) I was feeling lonely and sad because it had been five months since Brad died. My husband was on the ranch helping his brother brand calves and I didn't want to sit at home so I drove to my sister's home. I already was crying when I walked into her home. She asked what was wrong and I answered through my tears, "It's the eighteenth today!" and continued to cry. But she didn't understand how I was feeling. How could she? She didn't have a clue how I was feeling on that day. It seemed the eighteenth day of every month made me sad for about a year. That's something I know she didn't understand. Although my mother and sisters did not understand my feelings of sadness, they were there when I needed them or if I didn't want to be alone.

In another instance, I had an acquaintance who I met through work. Every time we would see each other, she would ask how I was doing and I would always give the same answer "Fine." But that was never the case because I was never fine. One day we saw each other at a meeting of some sort and she asked how I was doing. So instead of giving the same answer of "Fine," I said, "You know, I'm not doing so good. I feel like..." But before I could finish the sentence she said, "You know, I gotta go. I'll talk to you later." Off she went and there I stood! She really is a nice person and I know she meant well but that's an example of how people really don't know how to talk to you when your loved one dies, especially by suicide. I talked about my son's death publicly because I didn't want any mother to go through what I went through. I tried to help families deal with their loss if they experienced a suicide in their family, especially mothers. I wanted to connect with them, to make them realize they can heal from this terrible tragedy. It seems that people think of you in a different way after your child dies by suicide. I have had experiences where people did not want to pass me in the hallways at work or at a store and they would go out of their way to avoid me. I knew they were really uncomfortable being around me when we were in the same room. I could see their discomfort when I mentioned Brad's name.

As a Native American person, I turn to my Higher Power for help and guidance. In our Dakota Language, He is called Tunkasila, meaning Grandfather. Because Brad died in our home, we had a Spiritual Leader, sometimes referred to as a Medicine Man, come to our home and Smudge: meaning to purify. He prayed and smudged every room, to rid of evil spirits, if any, so that we, as a family, can continue to live in our home. We have turned to our Traditional Ways for healing, to help us deal with the loss of Brad, our loved one.

Tony and I try to continue to help people who have lost a loved one to suicide. We let them know we are there for them if they should ever feel the need to talk. We tell them that it's okay to cry because tears are healing. We also tell them to talk about their loved one that has died. He or she had a life and just because they are no longer with us on this earth doesn't mean they no longer exist. Their Spirit continues to be with us even though we can't see them. They are here. I personally have a conflict with individuals, specifically Native American people, who believe if a person commits suicide (their words, not mine), his or her soul wanders this earth forever. Or as another individual stated, "When you take your own life, you're stuck here until the time comes when you're supposed to leave this earth."

Now, how do they know that? I ask. The people who make these statements have never lost a loved to suicide so I don't understand how they can make these comments. My Uncle Richard also came to our home the day Brad died. He gave me some powerful words of encouragement and I will always remember them. He said, "My niece, we all have our lives laid out on a path for us by Tunkasila (God) even before we are born. Some paths may be short, some paths may be longer. Your son's path was made out to be short." His words comforted me, but still I had questions that no one could answer. Some religious people say suicide is a sin or suicide is something Native American people just don't do. I truly believe that Jesus died for our sins and if suicide is a sin, then my son, Brad, was forgiven the night he died by suicide. He was hurting so bad he felt that the only way to get rid of this hurt was to suicide. That's something none of us, who are alive, will ever understand.

The Standing Rock Sioux Reservation has a high rate of suicide, mostly young people. There have been clusters of suicides in recent years. There are people here, on Standing Rock, that are doing their best to prevent further suicide completions from happening. There are some parents who have not accepted their child's death, their child who died by suicide. And so they have anger towards suicide prevention programs or towards people who do work in suicide prevention. They just don't talk about their loved who died by suicide. They, too, believe talking about suicide will cause a suicide to happen. They need to understand that education and awareness on suicide is the key to prevent further suicides from happening.

Then there are some people who say talking about suicide is glorifying it. Some Native American people believe that it is taboo to talk about your loved one that has died by suicide or to even say their name. I believe that this is just part of the stigma many people have about suicide. There are even individuals who work in the field of suicide prevention who I believe have become enablers without realizing it themselves. The word suicide or suicide prevention is not mentioned at all in the work they claim to do. Why work in the field of suicide prevention and then don't even say the word "suicide" for fear of being yelled at? And then there are some people who have college degrees that say, "If you talk about suicide, you're going to cause it to happen!" or "Young people don't want to go to conferences about suicide."

This is certainly not true. Believe it or not, our young people do talk about suicide. The adultsare the ones who don't want to talk about it. We are the ones who need to take that first step and say the word "suicide." Tony was the strong one when Brad died. Two days after Brad died, Tony went to Brad's school and talked to his classmates and told them to seek help if they are thinking about suicide. And at Brad's funeral he spoke about suicide. He told the parents and grandparents to talk to their children. He said, "Tell your children you love them. Tell them every day because you never know what's going to happen." I don't know where he got the strength and courage to do that but he did. My husband and I survived Brad's death differently.

At first, he spoke to students and parents, but after the funeral he shut down and chose not to talk about Brad. I was the complete opposite. I couldn't get enough of talking about him. Whenever we had to go to town to get groceries or do errands, I always had a book with me. I always was reading. Then one day Tony said to me, in an angry tone, "Why do you do that? Just let him go! He isn't here anymore! He's gone!" I said, "No! Brad had a life and I am not going to forget about him!" Tony now admits he thought long and hard about what I said because after that he talked about Brad and he was not ashamed of the way he died. He later told me he realized I was right. After Tony accepted Brad's death and began to talk about it, he became stronger. He realized that talking about his death also helped him to heal. Tony and I are lucky because although we had our differences after Brad died, we remained together. We walked this path of grief together and supported one another and we continue to do so. I don't think I could have survived Brad's death without Tony. I couldn't even go in the room to pick out his coffin at the funeral home. I look back at all that happened and think to myself, "How did I ever get through that?"

When Tony and I became very active in suicide prevention and education, I wanted my surviving children to become involved, too, but they have not. I did ask my daughter, Margaret, if she was ready to speak publicly about her brother's death. She just shook her head no and I let it go at that. I feel she will talk about Brad's death when she is ready to and I will not force her to do something she is not yet comfortable with. Tony and I went to the communities and schools on our Reservation, and talked about our son's death. We told our "story." We hoped that the people, the young people, would learn from our story. We wanted them to know how much a suicide can hurt family members, what it does to all who knew the person who died by suicide, emotionally and physically. We wanted them to know that it is okay to ask for help. We told the young people to never keep it a secret if their friend tells them about a plan, if they plan on harming themselves. And that it's okay if that friend gets mad at you because it is better to have that friend be mad at you for a little while than to lose that friend forever. Suicide is forever. You can never take it back. We hoped they listened to us and learned from our experience.

I met a lot of wonderful people on this path to healing. People who have experienced what I had, suicide. Whether it was a brother, sister, mother, father, a child, a loved one, we met on this path of healing and have remained friends forever. There is a bond that cannot be broken. My life is not the same and it will never be the same because my children are not here to walk this path with me. I say "children" because in June 2008 my oldest son, Alden, was murdered. He was only thirty years old and left behind an eleven year old son, Dylan. The one thing that I never ever want to forget is the sound of my boys' voices. I still can hear them today, laughing and talking, enjoying themselves. And although their lives here on earth were short, their memories live on forever in my heart. I never knew how much losing my children would hurt. A hurt that, to me, is unexplainable. Some wonder how I am surviving with my youngest son taking his own life by suicide and with my oldest son having his life taken from him by murder. It seems, at times, my heart has been ripped out of me. I have come to realize death is a part of life and life does go on. My life today has changed tremendously and I have learned from my tragic and difficult experiences.

If a loved one of yours dies by suicide, don't be ashamed of how they died. Talk about your loved one; remember all the good things they did in their life. Get a journal and write about your feelings. Don't keep your feelings and tears inside. Remember tears are healing. And remember, there is hope, you will heal, and you will survive.

Mitakuye Owasin!
(We are all related)

When Frank Died

By Dottie Granger
Louisiana, USA

The Day He Died

My world exploded June 9, 2002. Events are now described as before my husband Frank died, or after Frank died. I am no longer the Dottie Granger I was the morning of June 9. I'm forever changed.

How am I going to pick up the pieces of my family's life together? Nothing prior has prepared me for this day...It's Sunday. Frank has gone to church at 6 a.m. He returns to drink coffee with me as I dress for church. We say our "I love you's" as I leave and he goes to visit with his mother. When I get home, I don't see him inside or outside yet his car is in the driveway. For the first time in my life I'm experiencing terror as I read a note he left on the counter and scream. "Where is he?" Screaming, I go again and again through the house and outside. I need help and no family or friends are answering their phones. In time, my sister and brother-in-law arrive and it is my brother-in-law who finds Frank. He is dead. He has shot himself. I scream more and throw my shoe at the door. Within minutes, our house is swarming with firemen, policemen, people from the coroner's office, and news media with cameras. For seventeen years, Frank was an elected public official in our parish; therefore, his suicide will be on television and in the newspaper. The coroner's office activated the LOSS Team (Local Outreach to Suicide Survivors). Three team members arrive to share with me their stories of losing their loved one to suicide. They give me information on a support group at the Baton Rouge Crisis Intervention Center, a book on suicide and survivors, tips to help me in the coming days, their phone numbers if I want to call them, and, most of all, hope that I can make it through this and I don't have to do it alone.

Suicide was a word I didn't think much about or understand. Now I'm consumed. How did this happen? Frank told me seven days ago he was depressed. Six days ago he saw his doctor. Today he killed himself. My brain will not wrap itself around this. I'm in shock and sense I'm having an out of body experience watching myself from far away.

Our girls, Melissa, age nineteen, and Lauren, age seventeen, have been out of town for the weekend and were on their way home. Am I going to be the person to shatter their lives as I tell them what their daddy did today? Am I sure this isn't a dream? Yet even the few nightmares I've had never included suicide. The Loss Team has left, but they assure me they will return to talk to the girls. I don't understand what has happened so how am I going to explain suicide to them. I want help. On my request, a member of the team does come back several hours later to share with the girls and extended family and I'm thankful they came back.

Before He Died

I had been out of town a week with Lauren for her senior trip two weeks prior to Frank's suicide. The night I returned, as we talked, he said he was depressed. There had been a lot going on in his life. He said he would talk to a doctor the following day and did. His discussion with the doctor sounded good to me and he was willing to do whatever it took to get better. On Wednesday, he talked to a close friend who was going to get him an appointment with a counselor because the doctor stated that would be the next step and Frank agreed to the counseling. Frank was a functional alcoholic, sober for four years. He was going to meetings, not drinking, and said he wasn't desiring alcohol. Because I saw his willingness and actions to receive help, I felt hopeful that with time he would be okay. I didn't consider him taking his life. Others have gone through the same or worse circumstances Frank had and continued to live. I didn't see signs of wanting to die and we were together all weekend except for the couple of hours going to church separately.

Frank was kind and a good-hearted man. The girls and I would tell him he "was our sunshine" which would make him grin. Frank was forty-three years old. We were married twenty-four years and looking forward to the next phase of our lives since both girls had now graduated from high school. The girls had a close relationship with their daddy. They would talk about sports, politics, play golf together, watch television, and go for snowballs (snow-cones). He was a daddy who was very proud of his girls. As a family we enjoyed football games, fishing, vacationing, and cooking seafood. What happened to his optimistic approach to life?

After He Died

Immediately, I blamed alcoholism for Frank taking his life. It was the only disease I knew he had that would kill. I didn't know much about depression other than antidepressant medication could help. Neither did I know depression and alcoholism can sometimes go hand and hand with both being treated. Could he always have been slightly depressed? Did he medicate depression with alcohol? Did his treatment for alcoholism not treat the depression? How long was he depressed? I only knew what I knew and only what he allowed me to know about him. I did not see signs of him wanting to take his life.

For a couple of years, I was drawn to reading many books on depression, suicide, and survivors. For me in my journey, I've come to believe just circumstances were not the reason Frank died. I believe clinical depression was the major force with its imbalance of brain chemicals. Nowhere did I find a reason for suicide in the note Frank wrote and, even if he did have a reason, it would not have been good enough.

I believe anything can be worked out in some way given time and at some point in the past he did, too.

Upon Frank's death, a special election was called in October 2002 to fill the position he held in our parish. In October 2003, the regular election was held. Anytime I would leave our home to meet friends and family, go the mall, or the grocery store, I would see the campaign signs in yards. They were a constant reminder he is no longer here and life goes on. Upon seeing the campaign signs, an internal battle would ensue to remember what was or to isolate. I struggled not to isolate. Tears streamed down my cheeks as I voted for another man to take my husband's job.

Immediately upon his death, I could not concentrate, would forget what I was saying in midsentence, rub my hands on my lap or move my feet, would at times lose track of time, and I became hypervigilant with Melissa and Lauren and, in return, they were with me. Both of them wanted me to be with them or to know where I was at all times. We were afraid something would happen to the other, which is understandable. We just lived through the realization of love not being enough to keep anyone alive. And Frank getting help and wanting help wasn't enough at the moment. I also continually went over the last week of Frank's life, trying in my mind to get him help in different ways. Then I'd remember he killed himself. I'd start the process over. Death by suicide wasn't computing in my brain. I desperately wanted a different ending. I couldn't stand the pain long before I would feel numb. I would say they forgot to give me anesthesia when my heart was ripped out. Then the cycle would repeat itself. This grief was unlike any I had experienced. I didn't know how to help myself. From the beginning, I said "We are going to get help" and the girls said, We would "stick together like Velcro." Our goal was to go through this tragic situation in a healthy manner so it would have the least possible effect on our future.

We went to a grief counselor who helped us one-on-one and the girls did a weekly group for teenagers who lost family members. That helped the girls start remembering the good times with their daddy by doing a collage. However, we really weren't addressing the suicide part of his death. The counselor thought we would do well in the SOS (Survivor of Suicide) group at the Baton Rouge Crisis Intervention Center. The counselor did tell me I had symptoms of Post Traumatic Stress Syndrome (PTSD). My response was: "So these symptoms I'm experiencing have a name!" I knew Frank had died and something had happened to me. Now I knew what that something was. But I wondered, what do I do about PTSD and will I have to live this way forever?

We went to the grief counselor first because I knew going to the SOS support group meant we would be facing not only the death, but also death by suicide. I wasn't ready; maybe he was on a golfing trip and would soon walk through the back door. How could this happen? We always discussed where to live, campaigning for office, his job, which car to buy, where the girls would go to school or camp, vacations, but not him killing himself. I didn't ask for this and didn't agree to this. I wanted no part in what the future would hold. I wanted our lives back, as I knew them. Reality slowly kept sinking in, as I would wake each morning with tears and without my husband beside me. Why and how did this happen? Same question and no answer. The end of August we walked into our first Survivors of Suicide support group meeting. I don't remember anything anyone said; yet I wanted to go back. And each week on Tuesday night we would return.

When my life blew apart June 9, suicide took my coping skills. They weren't working for me anymore or I couldn't find them. I wanted a new tool chest of skills and a manual to survive. I can follow directions. I was told there wasn't a manual but keep coming back. So I cried, talked, and asked questions. Each week after group I asked, "When will this pain stop?" I was told, "I can't tell you when, but I can tell you it will." Now I had hope I wouldn't always hurt this way. These people in group, sitting in a circle, knew what I was going through and I knew where they had been. They were a group I didn't want to be a part of, but a family I needed now.

I didn't trust my judgment anymore because I didn't see suicidal signs with Frank. This could happen again. I learned suicide survivors are at a higher risk for repeating suicide in their families without counseling. I was determined the girls and I were not going to go through this again if I could help it. We three would stay in SOS and/or counseling. I would ask girls, "Are you thinking of suicide?" in the same manner as I would ask, "Do you want fried shrimp for supper?" I believe it is a viable question for me to ask anyone now. Lauren continued in group and after a while Melissa chose one-on-one counseling. I did both. At one time, the three of us as a family saw a counselor for a few sessions. The three of us grieved differently and at different paces. For most of the first two years, I felt lost in the woods without a compass or lost in a fog. In my pain, I would forget how to help myself. The SOS group members would share their experiences and options for me and the girls to use between meetings. I found hope for us from the members who were at various stages in their grief. We could see members we wanted to be like in the future and our growth in listening to new members. We wanted healing and the group was a safe place to talk and listen, knowing others truly understood. And a place to learn to trust again. I didn't want surprises. I wanted to learn what we might experience in our grief and if we didn't experience the worst, I would be thankful. We also learned we didn't have to be strong for each other, we could stand together, support each other, and cry together.

The first year was hard with emotional and physical pain. For a few months, I could feel Frank's presence with me. Then one day the presence was gone and we started all the firsts– holidays and special days. Making a plan in advance for those days made them easier to get through. On his birthday, we wrote on balloons at the grave, released them, and watched until they were out of sight and went out for dinner. On Thanksgiving, I didn't feel very thankful, just sad and tearful. Our first Christmas was better than the three of us expected, because in SOS group, we made a plan and I felt we deserved a special Christmas this year so I asked my sister to help me with Christmas shopping. Frank loved the Christmas season and we missed him terribly. Picking out a tree had always been a family affair. This year we decided to do something different and cut ours at a tree farm instead of buying it off a tree lot. An employee wanted to chop the tree down for us. We said, "No, thank you!" We three got rid of stress that day by sawing the tree down and I began to feel anger. Not necessarily at Frank, but at the situation. Anger brings its own unique pain and comes suddenly out of nowhere.

I didn't want to stop wearing my wedding rings and since June 9 I also was wearing his. I decided after Christmas to have them melted down and made into another ring and a cross necklace. I did not want to take our rings off when the jeweler asked for them. Hot tears ran down my face. He returned one on Valentine's Day and the other a month later. I have our "rings" back and I can wear them every day in a different form.

Anticipation of the first year anniversary was worse than the actual day. It felt like a freight train was heading toward me. We made plans. The girls were with friends as was I. We chose to eat at a restaurant together for dinner. Having a plan helped us stay out of bed and occupied our minds. Not that Frank wasn't in our thoughts and conversation, but we actually made it through the first year.

The second year was harder in a different way. Shock was wearing off and reality was more real in my heart and brain. At times, I felt like I was watching a movie of my life with someone else as me. Journaling helped to ground me. I also threw ice against the brick wall outside and hit a punching bag to release my anger. This new normal is not what I wanted. I didn't want my one-day sons-in-law to not know their father-in-law. I didn't want people asking me why Frank took his life. I didn't want people shying away from me because they didn't know what to say. I didn't want to make decisions by myself as opposed to being part of a couple. I wondered how different life would be compared to now. In SOS group, one young girl bought herself presents from her dad. She said if he were alive, he would give her gifts. I did start buying myself gifts at times from Frank and it was a comfort to me. Before donating Frank's clothes, I made quilts for Melissa, Lauren, and me. Sewing the quilts made it easier to let go of his clothes. Now his shirts keep us warm as we wrap ourselves in them. I tried during the day to look for the good things that were in my life, things I could be thankful for, and wrote them down before going to sleep. Some things I was thankful for: tears when I needed to cry, a handkerchief, air to breathe, my family and friends, counselors, people who shared their story and hope with me.

When Frank Died

My brain still kept asking what happened. Frank prayed, went to church, read his bible, and was a Christian. Where was God for Frank? I can clearly see and recall His care, comfort, and protection for the girls and me on June 9. Where was He for Frank though? I asked God to help me see– to give me some puzzle pieces of what happened so I could one day find peace. Later anger, uncertainty, distrust, and who knows what else erupted like a volcano at God. The month before Frank's death, I had read the book of Job in the Old Testament. Well, if Job could question and be extremely frank with God, I could, too.

I cried, screamed, fussed, wailed, whispered, and looked up in the heavens as a broken person saying, "God, you have the power and could have stopped him. Where were you? I trusted you with my family!" Since Frank's death, others freely shared with me how close they or their family member came to taking their lives and didn't. God, You did nothing." On and on I railed and wailed until there was nothing left to say except, "Regardless of what I don't know, you are my God and I will trust you. You've said you would be the father to the fatherless and husband to the widow. We qualify now and I will continue to remind you of that promise." Oh, I felt better after getting all of it off my chest and I'm glad I didn't listen to the ones who suggested I should not get upset with God.

I found my God's shoulders were broad enough. He is sad, too. He cried at Lazarus's death. Psalms 56:8 told me He collects my tears. Deuteronomy 29:29 told me there are secret things that belong to the Lord our God...He says He will never leave or forsake us. That means God was with Frank. Wherever we go, we can't hide from God. That means God was with Frank. No pit is so deep that God is not deeper still. That means God was with Frank and was (and is) with me even when I felt I was in a pit. God's ways are not my ways though! His thoughts are higher than mine. God is merciful. God sees the whole parade of my family's life. I can only see through the knot hole in the fence board. No matter how far down we go Jesus is there to yank us up by His blood. For what seemed a long time, I read over and over the books of Job and Psalms. I found comfort and slowly could see a future. It was not the future I thought I'd have back on June 5, 6, 7, 8, and the morning of the 9th, But instead a different future, a fork in the road, with God going before me for I had not gone this way before. Job did have a good life after his fork in the road and he lost so much more than me. If Job could make it so could I! I experienced I can't always see God's hand clearly; however, I always can trust His heart. I know God loves Frank, Melissa, Lauren, and me for the Bible tells me so!

I'm thankful my anger with God was diminished with this explosion. It brought me relief by being honest although I honestly don't like what has happened and I don't have to like it. I still remind myself over and over what I know to be true of God. I still ask for peace and acceptance so I can have a healthy life with as few as possible lingering effects.

The LOSS Team, as previously mentioned from the day Frank died, was started in December 1998 by the Baton Rouge Crisis Intervention Center. Dr. Frank Campbell created an active postvention model program in addition to the SOS support group. Dr. Edwin Shneidman created the idea of postvention and taught that postvention is prevention for the next generation. Two years after Frank's death, I wanted to give back to others what had been given to me through the program. After discussing my desire to volunteer with staff, it was clear I had healed to the point where I could be a resource for others. I started going on LOSS calls as an observer along with other more experienced team members. I watched and learned how to be a help to the families. Even though I had received the help of the LOSS Team, I didn't remember much that they told me which is normal under such traumatic circumstances. I did remember they, too, had personally experienced the loss of a loved one to suicide and I remembered they were from the crisis center where help was available to us at no cost.

They also said I could call them personally if I wanted to and I did. Soon I was taking on– call time as a team member. Once newly bereaved family members know you have lost your loved one, a connection is made. I found it easy to talk to family members. Each call is different– different circumstances, different number of people to talk with, different questions people may ask, each showing different emotions. They may not understand what the police and coroner's office is doing. I can answer questions for them or find the answers. What is always the same: someone who found the deceased and someone is left behind hurting. After each call, the team members always debrief together. I have not found that going to the scene has had any adverse effect on me. In fact, I believe it helped my grieving.

I had one more possession of Frank's to deal with by this time – the gun. I didn't want it, I didn't want to leave it with the police, I didn't want to sell it, and I didn't want it to harm anyone again. I had heard two members of the SOS group say they had wind chimes made. After finding a metal smith, I decided I wanted the gun to be transformed into a candlestick. I told the metal smith to decide on the shape since he was the professional. When I returned for my candlestick, we both had tears as he explained the symbolism of the candlestick he fashioned. Free flowing upward toward healing, rough yet smooth lines as life is. For me, seeing the gun in an entirely different form also has helped in the healing process. I don't see a gun but a candle to be lit. The wood from the handles was carved into two small crosses, one I hang on the wall and the other on our Christmas tree.

I get nervous inside and the shock hits me in the chest when flashbacks reoccur. The pain goes past the bones into my marrow. I wonder how a person withstands this pain and I'm not considering suicide. I can't and don't want to fathom Frank's pain. I heard it said if people felt one half the pain that causes suicide then we'd all die. Suicide is like going over a waterfall and we and sometimes the victim can't see how close they are to the edge. The brain is so complex. I don't want to get to the edge so I'll keep reaching out and try doing what others say helped them to heal.

I continue to talk with people I trust and in the SOS group. Talking gets my thoughts out of my head. And as a friend once said, some things cannot be healed unless they are talked about. I have a picture of Frank when I know he was experiencing happiness that I look at often. I try to do something nice for myself daily. And check to be sure I am eating, sleeping, not isolating, and journaling. Journaling allowed me to free my mind of thoughts or events I don't want to forget. Perhaps by putting them on paper they won't continue to race around in my brain. I can let them go knowing I can read them anytime I want or need to. By journaling I can see how quickly my emotions can change back and forth and remind myself, this too shall pass. I wanted to get to a place where my heart and head matched. When I would say my husband died or I'm a widow, it wouldn't debilitate me. In time it did happen.

It is ingrained in my mind where I was (driving in traffic near my home) when I had a foreign thought: Today is a good day. The thought quickly passed but the feeling of hope lingered. And I did reach a plateau of feeling good for consecutive days. Then I'd feel guilty for feeling good. Grief is exhausting. Healing takes time and work. As I said before, I would look for things and people who were in my life and write a gratitude list. Reading over the list justified to me I didn't need to feel guilt for having happy days. It didn't mean I was forgetting Frank or not honoring him. I was thankful for the time Frank was in my life and because I loved deeply, I also hurt deeply. I could still miss Frank, cry, and have a good day. What a new concept!

I didn't like changes. I grieved for what could have been and what won't ever be. Yet everything has changed and our old ways of doing life wasn't working for me. A new normal set in. What is normal? What do I want to be normal? What do I like? What do I want to include in my life? What traditions do I want to stay the same or change? Who am I now that I'm no longer a wife? How do I parent solo? How do I accomplish the many man jobs Frank took care of like connecting the boat trailer to our automobile, starting a finicky lawnmower, or moving heavy objects? Initially the answer was "I don't know," to each question. Slowly, I would step out of my box and try something new. I learned to ask for suggestions, make mistakes and start over again, and even change my mind. I've come to embrace some change and I want to keep learning and growing.

At three years, I could see life a little clearer. I liken it to the fog lifting a little. My body was not as anxious. When I misplaced my keys or anything else I didn't fall apart. That was a trigger from not being able to find Frank. Flashbacks were not as numerous and racing thoughts weren't as often and severe. Sleep was a problem: too much, not enough, or at the wrong times. I used to say some days were meant to be slept through, although I recognize now I was using that as avoidance. Not a good thing in the long run. At times, medicine would help for a while, then for some unknown reason would stop. I tried lavender, new pillows, redecorating the bedroom, warm milk, etc. As of today, melatonin is working every night. Good sleep is an important part of me taking good care of myself. Without it I would be tired and my thinking could easily be distorted. I'm learning how to deal with hypervigilance for both girls. At times, it has manifested itself with me thinking they are not leaving town for a weekend with friends, but to kill themselves, or they would never come home again. When they were sleeping, I'd believe they'd stop breathing. I'm aware now that I'm hypervigilant and not losing my mind.

It's my problem to learn to handle. The girls don't need to change their ways for me. At the times I am hypervigilant, I calmly check with them to show myself they are okay and tell myself for what I've gone through this is understandable and it won't always be this way, but today it is. I talk about the experience at group and with trusted friends. I recognize triggers sometimes cause me to project anger at situations or people which I would ordinary not be upset about. Releasing anger through throwing ice is a visual help. I'm learning to recognize the signs of the triggers and look closely afterwards at my circumstances and my feelings at that time. Usually one of my five senses is involved. Perhaps there is a pattern. Awareness is the first step in helping myself, but triggers are unconscious. I know I'm now doing more than surviving day-to-day. I'm want to live and live a good life. I pray God help me, help you, help me.

Four years after Frank, died I was asked to be one of the peer facilitators in our survivor support group. The group has two professionals and three peer facilitators. I don't have a professional background with counseling, but I can give new survivors hope and information that was given to me by survivors when I started attending group. It has been a humbling experience to take what was freely given to me and pass it along. For me, this is good coming out of a tragic situation. I don't have answers for anyone else, yet new survivors can look at me today and know through their grief work they won't stay in the same emotional and physical spots because I didn't and others before me didn't. That's the hope all new survivors want and need regardless of who their love was, how they died, or the circumstances before and after the death. I have come full circle now: receiving the LOSS call, attending group, being a LOSS Team member and peer facilitator. I'm looking beyond myself. It's been baby steps in the right direction.

At five years the fog lifted more. I never want to forget 2002 and the subsequent years though. It's been a journey that has changed the core of my soul. I'm different: stronger, more compassionate, and empathetic, quicker to forgive myself, and others. Situations that used to bother me, no longer faze me. I have a different and deeper appreciation for life, I take more time to smell the roses, watch the moon and stars, and try things I would never have thought I would. I have a deeper relationship with God. I like the new me.

In 2008, both daughters married. Lauren and Cheyene started dating in 2003 and married in March. Melissa and Jason started dating in 2007 and married in August. When each son-in-law asked permission to marry my daughter, I said yes if– if they had a counseling session with the counselor the girls had been seeing for their loss. "Yes, ma'am," each said to me. Both of these men grew a foot taller in my estimation. They were good men before, but now great men in my eyes. I wanted them to understand what my daughters had gone through. I felt they needed to have a better understanding of depression, suicide, and the complicated grief which goes with it. At different milestones in Melissa's and Lauren's lives they will grieve again. I wanted their future husbands to know it is normal. Depression can, doesn't mean it will, run in families. I wanted them to know the signs, symptoms, and treatment. Then I could feel comfortable giving my daughters away in marriage.

Shortly after Frank died, both girls asked me who was going to give them away when they married. I said I would. And I did. I was concerned beforehand how I would feel doing another job for Frank he should have been doing. Both days were just as they should have been and I was so proud to place each daughter's hand in her almost husband's hand as I said "I do" in response to the minister asking, "Who gives this woman in marriage?" We had a large picture of Frank at the reception and the girls placed the handkerchief they used for the funeral in their bouquet. Both weddings were beautiful. I'm happy, in spite of my nest being empty, although a little sadness and tears roll down my cheeks again because Frank isn't here for the next part of our lives.

Throughout the years, I was not aware of the fogged state I was in until it lifted. Each time it lifted, I believed I was out of the fog completely. Not so. In the seventh year, it lifted again. This time I believe it is finally gone, as is the depression because my sleep is so much better. I haven't been hypervigilant since before the girls married because I now share responsibility for them with their husbands. Occasionally, triggers come out of nowhere. I may be sad and confused a few days. I bounce back quickly or I will start journaling, talking to trusted friends, and I always can bring it up in the SOS support group. I will do everything possible to help myself have a good life.

I'll never know why Frank took his life and today I don't have to know. I don't like it and never will like it. Ninety-Nine percent of the time I accept it. I'm beginning to understand now why Carla Fine author of *No Time To Say Goodbye* said something like the level of stress from the suicide of a loved one is catastrophic, the same as the experience of surviving a concentration camp, it never truly goes away. You incorporate it into your life. I'll continue working on the one percent. Sometime during the first year after Frank's death, standing on the side of his grave, I said

"Frank, I'm breathing so I have to go on living." I've chosen to go on living, and because of the past, I'll value each day. I will not let it destroy my family, or my future, or me. I never believed suicide could happen to my family. Suicide only happened in other families. I thought somehow we were protected. Not true. With a lot of hard work, I have a life I didn't believe was possible the night of June 9, 2002.

The Professional and Personal Intersect at Suicide

By Mary Chandler Bolin, Ph.D., Licensed Psychologist
Kentucky, USA

The American Psychological Association's "Ethical Principles of Psychologists and Code of Conduct" (3.05) states the following regarding 'multiple relationships': "Multiple relationships that would not reasonably be expected to cause impairment or risk exploitation or harm are not unethical."

* * *

Carol Graham is an attractive, petite, blonde woman who grew up less than an hour from my hometown, and one of her high school friends was my summer church camp counselor when I was in middle school. Carol is soft-spoken, belying an inner strength. Her smile is ready, and tears also may well over with no embarrassment. She is a woman of faith who built a beautiful family– a career-military husband (whose postings took them around the world and cultivated friendships on several continents) and three children who got along so well that they shared an apartment and wrote NCAA basketball tournament brackets on the walls each spring.

I would have wanted Carol Graham as a friend, particularly if that friendship could have begun without a tragedy. Our first contact was in June 2003 when I returned her phone call on a Friday night, after work, because waiting until after the weekend seemed unbearably cruel. Carol was calling in search of answers, any answer, any hint of an answer. She had found my business card in her son's wallet, and on a to-do list in his room, the entry, "Call Mary."

That son, Kevin Graham, had died by suicide earlier in the week, and I wept as I told Carol how sorry I was to have no answers, no information for her. I had never had the privilege of meeting her son. It was as though all the air had been sucked out of my living room, and out of wherever she grasped a phone, hoping for some hint to understand why Kevin chose to die. I could only offer the weak explanation that I do a lot of public speaking and perhaps Kevin, or one of his friends, had picked up my business card at a campus program. I offered my condolences and my wish that I had some way to make all this be different for her, for Kevin, for all who loved or shared friendship with him.

We talked for a long time, perhaps an hour or more. Carol explained that Kevin had participated in the National Depression Screening Day on-campus the previous October, and he'd called her in Korea to say that he finally knew why he had been feeling so bad. He was depressed. Kevin made arrangements to be seen at the university's student health service, where he was prescribed an anti-depressant.

During that academic year, Kevin also struggled with his career direction. He had always planned to be a physician, like his grandfather, but after his grades started to slip in a few pre-med courses, his academic advisor appropriately encouraged him to consider other options. Like many college students, Kevin's career aspirations were closely woven with his sense of self and identity development. He was not aware of the counseling center's resources to assist his search for a career that honored his intention to help others. He enjoyed German and philosophy, and considered becoming a foreign-language translator/interpreter. When he mentioned to his peers the idea of majoring in philosophy, there were jokes about smoking a pipe and "philosophizing" as a poor way to earn a living.

Because his older brother, Jeffrey, was about to complete ROTC and follow their father into a military career, Kevin decided to pursue that path as well. And he became aware of military restrictions related to being able to serve if prescribed particular medicines. Kevin was set to be the lead cadet at camp in the summer of 2003, and he did not want to face the embarrassment of telling the officers about his treatment for depression, nor to risk losing his ROTC scholarship and career. He did not explore the option of a medical waiver. Kevin decided to discontinue his medication, without monitoring by his provider or another physician. Within weeks, he was dead.

As with many suicides, it "made no sense"– at least on the surface. Kevin was smart, handsome, athletic, well-liked by friends, and loved by his family. He left no note, no indication as to the final breaking point. I could only say to his mother that he must have had an incredible internal pain and despair and hopelessness that he was not able or willing to let the outside world see, or see him through.

* * *

The first time that I met Carol Graham in person was in July 2003, at the home of the university president, who was friends with Carol's sister and brother-in-law. Our meeting was for the purpose of deciding how memorial funds dedicated to Kevin might be used to further suicide prevention on campus. I always will remember the incredible sadness in the room, and Carol turning to me to say, "What can we do with this money so that maybe some other family does not have to feel this kind of terrible loss?"

By random luck, or providence, or karma, or the stars in their courses, or whatever one believes in– I had become involved with state suicide prevention efforts the previous fall, after a friend expressed to me the concern that the university was not represented. I had previously provided trainings to faculty and staff, and had worked extensively with suicidal clients, but the state coalition was the first systematic prevention effort that I had joined. Rather than design a program unique to our institution, I suggested that we adopt the program that the state had researched and selected. I had met the program's developer and knew that the suicide prevention trainings could be adapted for everyone in the university– students, faculty, and staff.

By Fall 2003, I had become certified as a gatekeeper instructor for QPR: Question, Persuade, Refer– only the second person in the state to offer these layperson trainings to increase awareness of suicide risk, and information about how to intervene and refer appropriately. Within six months, we had trained several hundred individuals at the university. While this new initiative could never fully ease the pain of Kevin's death, his family seemed to take some comfort that perhaps another student's life– or anyone's life– might be saved if those nearby could recognize the warning signs and risk factors, and be bold enough to ask the hard question, "Are you thinking about killing yourself?"

* * *

At my office desk in mid-February 2004, I received a call from a university administrator alerting me to the fact that one of our students was about to receive word that her brother had been killed by a roadside bomb in Iraq. When I heard that the student was named Melanie and enrolled in nursing, I had a time-stands-still moment with my heart beating in my ears and my wondering if I would be able to not throw up. The student was Melanie Graham, and the dead soldier was Second Lieutenant Jeff Graham, her brother. After Kevin's suicide, Jeff was offered the opportunity to remain stateside, but chose to go to Iraq with his unit. He died warning others of the danger he had spotted.

"How much more can this family bear?" was my first thought. Within days, General Mark Graham, Carol, and Melanie were burying a second son and brother, in their hometown, next to Kevin's grave. With them was Jeff's fiancée, Stacey.

Melanie said she never imagined being an only child.

General Graham has talked openly about his two sons dying in different wars.

Today, Carol wears dog tags with the images of her two sons.

By the summer of 2004, the family had endowed the Jeffrey and Kevin Graham Memorial Fund, which continues to support suicide prevention at the university.

* * *

Since 2003, in suicide prevention trainings ranging in length from forty-five minutes to eight hours, I have shared at least a brief version of the Graham family's story of loss. I tear up and have to compose myself every time, even now– seven years since beginning this work.

This is how the professional became personal for me. I feel a deep commitment to this family that has allowed me to see and share their pain and their survival. I care deeply for Carol, Mark, Melanie, and their circle of family, friends, and suicidal persons they have helped keep alive.

Kevin was never my client, so I had no ethical requirement to protect confidentiality nor to keep a professional distance from the Grahams. I am not a direct survivor of Kevin's suicide. I am a mental health professional with a very personal connection to his family. I speak the truth of the Graham family's loss, grief, disbelief, crisis of faith, resilience, healing, strength, courage, advocacy. I speak in memory of all the "Kevins" we have lost.

* * *

The Graham family– Major General Mark Graham, wife Carol, and daughter Melanie– each have contributed significantly to an understanding of suicide and how survivors grieve and find ways to move forward, and have added their voices to the too-large chorus of those who have lost friends or loved ones to suicide.

In various public speeches or media interviews, Mark has referenced the two stars that rest on the shoulders of his Army uniform. Beneath one star is engraved the name "Kevin." Beneath the other is engraved "Jeff." Both died "fighting different enemies" before they could see their father pin on those stars as a Major General. His very personal experience of loss has informed his professional efforts, and he tackled head-on the rash of suicides that occurred at Ft. Carson (Colorado), amid criticisms starting in 2006 that wounded soldiers were not receiving adequate care. His efforts have been two-pronged– for the military to provide the best possible care, and for soldiers to seek the help they need (either on their own or with assistance and encouragement from a "buddy").

By March 2009, the Army had designed and distributed "ACE cards":

> **ASK** your buddy,
> **CARE** for your buddy,
> **ESCORT** your buddy.

Those familiar with traditional military culture will recognize that the ACE program is a dramatic departure from the stigma of seeking help for psychological/emotional concerns. Historically, troops were more likely to be directed to speak with the chaplain (who would have some clinical pastoral education but seldom be a credentialed mental health care provider) rather than to meet with a psychologist or psychiatrist who might be available to diagnose and treat very real and distressing conditions such as Post-Traumatic Stress Disorder (PTSD).

As a general, Mark has had access and influence which helped move forward military efforts to reduce help-seeking stigma, and to increase awareness and ability by officers and enlisted to appropriately refer those in need of care. He has appeared in Army training videos and been quoted widely in military and public media. While stationed at Ft. Carson (which has 21,000 employees), he regularly visited wounded soldiers in the Warrior Transition Unit. In November 2007 (just six weeks after his arrival at Ft. Carson), Mark invited local and national experts to provide guidance for the new Warrior and Family Community Partnership Program that he was announcing. Also during his command at Ft. Carson, he made sure that all soldiers– regardless of death in the field or by suicide– received the same full military funerals and memorial service. This had not previously been the case.

Maj. Gen. Mark Graham now has placed himself in the forefront of Army efforts to prevent soldier suicides. His journey is one from very private mourning and refusal of speaking invitations, to now setting an example of public acknowledgment of the incomparable pain of suicide loss. He understands the long military tradition of not speaking openly about suicide and its impacts, and also his potential to help break the stigma of help-seeking, at a time when an estimated 75 percent of the military still admit to a sense of stigma around mental health concerns. Historically, soldiers have feared losing their military careers, or at a minimum, being seen as weak if they sought psychological or psychiatric evaluation or treatment.

Beyond speaking of Kevin's death, Mark began an ambitious experiment at Ft. Carson – to mobilize mental health services and encourage access for depression, anxiety, PTSD and other invisible concerns– just as readily as a soldier would seek treatment for an obvious physical wound. He also describes his own transformation to being a much more physically expressive man. Now he hugs others. He did not used to do that, and recalled a friend hugging him after his elder son's death and offering to share some of the emotional burden. That offer clearly has shaped Mark's journey of healing and providing support to others.

* * *

Melanie Graham, while still a college student, turned to her grieving parents, and said, "I never thought I'd be an only child." As a psychologist and administrator of a university counseling center, I have sat quietly with students who have lost siblings to suicide. But never with a student who lost both her brothers less than year apart in tragedies so sudden that the entire world seemed to go dark. Melanie had found Kevin when he took his life by hanging, in June 2003. I first met her, soon after his funeral, during that first sad conversation about how the memorial funds might be used for university suicide prevention. I will always remember how sad and thin and fragile she looked.

Across years of conversations with Melanie's mother, it became obvious to me what a tight bond Melanie had shared with both her brothers. Melanie's sorority sisters thought that Kevin was her best friend (rather than her brother) because they spent so much time together. The Graham family lived around the world due to Mark's military career, so the three siblings were the constants in an often-changing equation. The family has photos of Melanie with Kevin and Jeff on the Great Wall of China, and on the golf course, and laughing together as toddlers. Her father has mentioned the shared language, "Grahamanese," that the kids shared.

Melanie now speaks openly about the loss of her brothers. She had noticed Kevin seeming sad during his junior year (when he had scored high on a free campus depression screening), but no one in the family recognized the depth of Kevin's distress. He always had been the high achiever and athlete, and even failing grades in chemistry and despondent comments did not sound an alarm that perhaps despair and hopelessness had clouded his thinking. Melanie and others never imagined that Kevin would even consider taking his own life.

Melanie took some time off from college, sought counseling, and enrolled in Cameron University. I had the privilege of helping Cameron establish a suicide prevention effort utilizing QPR gatekeeper trainings, funded by the Graham family. I remember being so mindful of Melanie's ability and willingness to learn about suicide risk factors and warning signs– fully aware that Kevin (in retrospect) had given signs of his depression that no one around him knew to recognize and address.

As with many suicide survivors who speak about their losses, Melanie has shared the normal, human regret that she lives with every day– that she wishes she had known the warning signs of depression, so that she could have tried to keep Kevin alive. She also heard me say how important it is not to become immobilized by the burden of what we did not know before and thus could not have acted upon. At the time, I was aware how hollow my words must have sounded, "We are responsible to act on that which we know at a particular point in time, not on what we will learn in the future."

Today, Melanie works as a nurse, dedicated to helping others. Along with her parents, she was honored in May 2010 with the public service award given by the American Foundation for Suicide Prevention (AFSP).

* * *

It is hard for me to imagine Carol Graham seeking any time in the public spotlight. Though I know her only through hundreds of e-mails and phone calls and a few in-person meetings, I have a sense of her deep faith and family commitment operating behind the scenes– and for much of her life being able to keep things running smoothly in support of others, and with no attention to herself. That came to a crashing halt with the news of Kevin's suicide, while Carol was in Korea anticipating a new military posting in Oklahoma, closer to her three children.

Carol has said to me "I didn't know you could die from depression." Only after Kevin's suicide did Carol learn that there was a multi-generational history of depression in family members. "Why did we keep secrets? Why were we afraid to speak the word 'depression' and admit that it runs in our family, and people had been treated? I don't blame that secrecy for Kevin's death, but maybe I would have been able to see past his 'together' exterior to realize his deep depression underneath, if I had known that at least part of the problem was probably brain chemistry imbalance that many of us may share. If he had had a heart problem, I would not have hesitated to drag him to the best cardiologist. But I did not have the pieces of this awful puzzle that might have looked different if Kevin had hope."

Carol has been central to that military culture change, aside her husband, the general. She describes her sons as both dying fighting their own battles. As a civilian, and as a mother who lost sons to suicide and in Iraq, Carol is uniquely positioned to confront the stigma of help-seeking, and to provide compassionate caring for other survivors of suicide– particularly the loved ones of troops who have died by suicide at home or while deployed.

Over the past seven years, I have had the privilege of witnessing Carol's journey from the early days of nearly-immobilizing grief and her predictable (to those working in this field of suicide prevention and postvention) questioning how she could not have known that Kevin was at risk. Her husband has echoed that question, "How did we not know?" She remembers Kevin's comments about his "brain not working" or how tired he was. But by May 2003, when his older brother graduated, Carol noted how good Kevin looked due to lifting weights and running. Carol had worked as a high school counselor, and still wonders how– as his mother– she could not read his underlying depression. A photo of Kevin and Melanie with Jeff at graduation is the last image of her three children together.

She shared with me how she had encouraged him to exercise, get enough sleep, continue eating well, and go to church. She prayed for Kevin, talked with him often by phone, and expected he would get through his period of stress just as he would have gotten over having strep throat. When her husband got the horrific news of Kevin's death, Carol's first move was to pick up her bible. Carol has credited her faith as key to moving through her shock, disbelief, sadness, anger, and despair into an emotional space where she can remember, smile, tell stories of Kevin's life, and focus her life's energy on helping other families faced with the crisis of suicide.

Carol now serves on the national board of SPAN USA, the Suicide Prevention Action Network, which has put her in contact with many of the preeminent researchers, speakers, and mental health professionals in the field of suicide prevention. She is in demand as a public speaker, and shares her family's painful story– but with an injection of hope for those facing their own despair or fearing for the welfare of a loved one. Within the military system, she has pressed for quality services for those struggling with PTSD, depression, and other mental health challenges, and for compassionate support for loved ones and caregivers.

I close this chapter with a statement from Mark and Carol Graham, which we use as part of our QPR suicide prevention gatekeeper trainings: "Following the deaths of our sons, my wife and I were together in a car in Kentucky. . . I looked at Carol and said, 'We can either allow the deaths of our boys to define our life and be the entire book of our life, or it can be a sad and tragic chapter in the book of our life.' We agreed then that it should be a chapter and not the entire book. Easier said than done, however, we are trying each and every day to help others and raise suicide awareness and to keep the book going in a positive direction. . . Now, when we speak out for mental health issues, we feel like we are helping all the 'Kevins' in the world that do not have a voice. Today, we thank all those at the University of Kentucky who are making a difference by becoming QPR gatekeepers, helping to create smaller communities of caring within the much larger institution that each of our three children had called their college home."

It is my deep privilege to know the Graham family, to count them as friends, to hold them as examples of resilience and healing, to honor their bringing hope out of despair. As a professional, I have deepened my understanding of survivors of suicide and my appreciation of the power of survivors to demand systemic attention to prevention, intervention, and postvention services. These are amazing human beings who will never know how many lives they have touched and perhaps saved, directly and indirectly. On the personal level, I have been blessed by their honesty, their genuine emotion, and the appropriate sharing of their pain in the service of helping others not to feel the same pain of loss. For me, this intersection of the personal and professional has been one of the richest and most rewarding experiences of my adult life. I encourage you, the reader, to learn how to honor the life of Kevin Graham– and all our world's "Kevins" – by joining the army of those working to reduce the tragedy of suicide.

Finding Hope After Zita

By Mark C. Wilson
New Zealand

The love of my life took her life in March 2006 when she was six months pregnant. I thought my life was over; what more did I have to live for given what we had to look forward to? But how wrong was I. As I write this toward the end of 2010, I am in a new relationship and am about to become a father again. The horror of my tragic loss has been replaced with pure joy, hope, and a future; all things that I believed were taken from me on March 5, 2006. I always have been an optimist, but I never imagined this to happen. I'm writing my story about losing a life partner to suicide in the hope that others who have lost a partner can see that there is hope, and there can be joy in your life again.

I met Zita over breakfast one Saturday morning not long after I moved to Wellington, the capital city of New Zealand, in 1992. I was part of a group of young twenty-somethings who met at the same café each Saturday morning for brunch, good talk, and friendship. I happened by chance to be seated next to Zita and was instantly taken by her charm, intelligence, looks, and style. How lucky was I– a slacker who was drifting a little with no clear direction to meet this smart intelligent lawyer who worked for the country's top legal firm. Our relationship developed over a period of months and soon we were well and truly in love. By mid 1994, we had made the commitment to marry and plan a future together. Zita had won a scholarship to study at NYU– to earn a masters degree in taxation law. We quickly organized a wedding (thanks in part to Zita's super organizational skills) and married in January 1995. In August of that year we took off to New York City as newlyweds full of the fresh optimism that living in a small country at the bottom of the world affords. In a way that year was our dream year. We made friends, Zita studied hard, achieved good results, and we embraced the challenges and wonders of the city. We traveled widely throughout the United States embracing the diversity, culture, and landscape. By mid-1996 New Zealand was calling and we returned to our normal lives.

Our dream year was over though. Prior to our return to New Zealand we were aware that life was becoming difficult for Zita's oldest sister Karen as Karen had been diagnosed with bipolar disorder a year or two before we had left for the US. There were sporadic episodes that saw her hospitalized due to extreme behavior. I guess when you're living half a world away, these sort of dramatic events are easy to push aside. It's the classic case of having to read between the lines to really find out what is happening and, frankly, sometimes family dramas mean you're not in the right space to pitch in– rather, leave it to another family member to sort out. We put Karen's issues in the "too hard basket to deal with" and continued to live our lives.

Zita's younger sister Megan also exhibited many similar behavioral traits which were generally put down to her being creative and free-spirited– which indeed she was. It is only in hindsight that I can now see that her behavior was also hell-bent on destruction. Meanwhile, Zita played the role of mentor and sensible sibling. The stereotype of a tax attorney is sensible, serious, and not overly creative. Zita's battles were played out internally as I was to find out. Returning to New Zealand was pretty easy, fitting back in with our friends and families, but it had made Zita and me aware of just how complex Karen's bipolar was. Hospitalizations were becoming more commonplace; we received numerous random aggressive phone calls. Megan, in her free-spirited way, didn't want to get involved and protected her older sister's behavior as not being out of the ordinary. They both were exasperating Zita.

By mid-1998, Karen was in a bad way, exhibiting suicidal behavior and causing a lot of stress within the family. It was while Karen had been hospitalized that she took her life. Zita and I had been on a six-week trip round the world and found out the terrible news at the Atlanta airport as we were heading home. It was to be a long, emotional flight from one side of the world to the other. The news of Karen's demise rocked Zita to the core. Zita's quest for a safe, stable world free of mental illness was ripped apart by this event. Her family's mental illness was exposed to the world, it seemed to her. I recall now, some twelve years after that event, how well Zita seemed to cope with the loss of her older sister. She loved Karen, but they weren't close in a way that she wished she was and perhaps observed longingly in other sisterly relationships that friends of hers had. Zita resolved to reconnect with her surviving sister, Megan, and to move closer to her mother who lived in a small settlement south of Auckland, New Zealand's largest city. We had never really given much thought to move from Wellington. We had a strong group of friends and a lifestyle that we liked. But soon after Karen's death, Zita thought it was time to move north, to Auckland. It's a sprawling city without the heart and soul of Wellington, a place we loved living in. Auckland was an hour from her mother's and a job opportunity for Zita at a multinational finance firm seemed the right move.

We began a new life. It was difficult, more difficult than we had ever imagined. By late 1999, Zita herself was experiencing self doubts about her immense abilities, she struggled with the pressure of work, began to lose a lot of weight and sleep became elusive. It was not long before we realized that she was exhibiting many of the classic signs of depression. We kept her condition to ourselves, not communicating it with family; rather we decided to rely on first-grade professional support. We retreated into our own world, avoiding friends and social functions, which Zita feared and became anxious about. Her internal battles overwhelmed her and it soon meant that Zita was unable to continue at her high-powered legal job. For someone who had excelled and achieved professionally all her working life, she took this as a failure. How could an honors student such as she fail? She took it very hard and fell into a deep depression.

Meanwhile the relationship she had tried to build with her younger sister Megan was strained. Both Zita and I felt that Megan was beginning to exhibit more obvious bipolar extremes with her behavior becoming more and more erratic. The free-spirited Megan was fast becoming erratic with violent outbursts when they met up for family functions. By 2002, they were mostly estranged, frustrated by each other's personalities– Zita's order and control and Megan's wild free-spirited ways. At one point in late 2002, Megan sent a text message to Zita that sounded desperate and a call for help. It frightened Zita enough to call me at work to express her concern. When she finally tracked Megan down, Megan berated Zita for being overly protective and controlling– she had sent the message to a number of her friends and none had reacted in the way Zita had. She said it wasn't a call for help, rather a call for friends to be there for her, not control her as she felt Zita was doing.

On April 1, 2003, we heard that Megan was missing from the school where she taught– and it was two days later that we found her dead in her car. She, too, had taken her life. How could suicide take the life of two siblings? Zita questioned life and the universe. She felt the loss hugely, despite the past two years of strained relations between the two of them. Zita was devastated that she hadn't listened to her own inner voice about Megan's behavior and our knowledge of suicidal behavior. Neither of us had believed that Megan was heading into the same dreadful path of suicidal behavior. Despite knowing so much about suicide, we didn't want to believe it could happen again, particularly when Megan had told us we were being overly protective and unnecessarily anxious. Despite our concerns, we had not followed up on them. We were devastated. It was a monumental tragedy, in many ways more devastating than Karen's loss. Megan's battle had exhausted her and medical specialists. Megan's death felt futile, a tragic call for help that she wasn't able to call for as openly as we imagined she was able to.

More and more Zita felt that suicide was her destiny. She felt terribly alone. Her two siblings gone to suicide. Instead of her family growing with nieces and nephews, it was now just me along with her mother. Zita felt the shame and stigma of suicide tremendously. It felt like the support that our wider friends and family had given when Karen died five years earlier had disappeared. We were both traumatized by finding Megan dead and constantly questioned our own judgment by not acting sooner in getting help for Megan. It was so unfair.

When we had arrived in Auckland three years earlier, Zita attended a peer support group. About a year into her attending the group it was placed into recess. Zita was aware enough that this sort of group needed to continue and was pivotal in setting up a new support group for people bereaved by suicide, the first group of its type in Auckland– a city of about one million people. Although I wasn't involved with this group, I helped out with candle-lighting and other administration tasks. After Megan's death, I began attending meetings to both support Zita and to process my own grief and shock at having found Megan.

Not long before Megan died, Zita had found a faith. It gave her strength and another outlet for her pain and a solution to many of the ills that she felt. She worked hard at keeping well and not succumb to the depression that she continued to struggle with. I did not want to join her church. I found it oppressive and too prescriptive for my thinking, but saw that it offered a vital support network and perhaps some of those answers about life and the universe that she was struggling to find herself. I felt I supported her the best way I knew how by providing a loving home environment. In the four years that she had been diagnosed with chronic depression, she had accessed some of the best medical and holistic care she could find. All this, combined with her faith and our love for each other, we fully believed that we could get through this tragedy and rebuild our lives and plan our own family that had always seemed so elusive in the ten years that we had been married.

It was in October 2005 that we found out that Zita was expecting our first child– a much cherished pregnancy. It symbolized a new beginning and a road to recovery. With the care of medical specialists, we knew that there were likely to be difficult times ahead following the arrival of the baby. We knew that this was the best thing for us to do. We felt truly blessed at this great opportunity. But by late summer 2006 (in New Zealand this is February), things were beginning to go terribly awry.

Sunday March 5, 2006, dawned. A late summer day with the first real hint of autumn in the air. It had been a hugely emotional weekend: we'd entertained her much-loved cousins for dinner, had been for walks, but she also had felt distant and distracted and not at all connected to the here and now. That Sunday morning I had felt the baby kick inside her– she was twenty-four weeks pregnant. She had said to me that she couldn't feel it.

Her vision seemed to fall away– into an abyss.

She had given up, exhausted with the fight to live. It was late on that Sunday evening after I had left the house for a couple of hours that she took her own life. She was six months pregnant and the last sister to go by suicide. All three, Karen, Megan, and finally Zita– all gone to suicide.

What hurt the most was not knowing what more I could do for Zita. We had an open and honest relationship. From time-to-time over the previous five years she had admitted to suicidal thoughts. One day she had rung me at work to say she'd contemplated killing herself, having gone near the train tracks that were close to our home. She had got through those tough times. I believed her and trusted her to be able to tell me when she was feeling that way. I never imagined during that Sunday evening that she would do what she did. We had discussed what she was going to have for dinner, the friends and family members that she was going to call and that I would be home by 9:00 pm. Alas, that belief and trust in her to be able to tell me when things were really bad was taken from her. Her depression had won.

As a forty-one-year-old male at the time, I had to come to terms with losing the love of my life. I had never pictured a life without Zita. Despite the despair of losing both Karen and Megan and Zita's own mental health battles, we remained strong and faithful to each other. In many ways I think that was what gave Zita the strength to do what she did. She believed that I could live my life without her. She had told me that a couple of months before she died. I dismissed it and said we would end up like the old couple that shuffled past us at that time. I think she knew that we never would be like that at all.

Zita knew that I had a resilience that she didn't have. She always knew that I had an emotional intuition and a laisse faire attitude to life that she envied in me. It is only now that I think those attributes are what have given me the strength to continue and flourish.

Despite spending time working with Solace (the support group that Zita helped create) and losing two sisters-in-law to suicide, the loss of my darling Zita was beyond description. Suddenly I was on my own without my rock beside me. The person who had been there for me unconditionally was gone and she had gone with our unborn child, something we had both cherished and had seen as our new beginning– where we could put suicide behind us and rebuild the family.

It was the undertaker that told me that the child that Zita was to have was a boy– a boy that Zita and I had so wanted. His name was to be Solomon Jay. I cried for his loss and for the loss of Zita. We suspected we were having a boy, and tragically it was confirmed to me. Now I cherish that they're together and will be together forever.

So here I was, alone, surrounded by love and support from family and friends. How was I to survive, let alone even contemplate rebuilding my life? It was hideous. The death of a loved one to suicide challenges everything that you stand for. I knew all too well the hurt and pain of suicide, as did Zita, now I had to live it directly. I was at the epicenter of the grief that I had so often talked with other people about in my support work. As sad as losing two sisters-in-law was, losing my life partner was achingly sad. It was beyond description.

My knowledge of grief and recovery weighed heavily. I knew eventually I would recover, but I also knew it would be a long difficult tortuous pathway to healing. I'd observed it in Zita with her losing Karen and Megan and in the support work I had done with Solace. I knew my life was changed forever and I knew there was going to be loneliness and heartache before light was to return into my life. I felt exhausted and burdened by this knowledge. Sometimes ignorance is bliss, particularly when it comes to grief. I knew too much about this experience.

Love of family and friends and an epic grief counselor got me through the remainder of 2006. I look back now and I know I functioned in some sort of suspended reality. I went to South America to explore Peru, Brazil, Bolivia, and Argentina for the first Christmas and cried every step through the Inca trail. I lit candles in centuries old cathedrals and called her name in the Andes and Amazon. I thought by running across the world I would forget the pain. I soon realized that you could never run from pain and loss. It is part of life and it is part of losing someone you love. But what it did do was make me see that life is rich, bountiful, and still full of joy. So it proved to be a monumental part of my recovery. I traveled foreign lands alone, as Mark. No longer Mark and Zita. Just Mark. I drew strength from the memories of Zita, from the positive things she said about me and about my ability to connect and form relationships, my compassion, and, most importantly, (as I was to find) my ability to connect with my own feelings.

My observations of male grief in New Zealand are probably quite similar to those of the US or other western nations. We are the ones that aren't meant to cry; we are meant to staunchly walk through this experience being the rock for others more vulnerable than ourselves. I knew this to be rubbish. There was no way I could support or engage in asking for support if I wasn't going to own up to my own grief and pain. I often envied Zita's female friends who had in-built networks of friends. They laughed and cried, talked, and laughed and cried some more. It appeared a good way to work through their own grief. Men so often retreat into their grief and other men tend to be uncomfortable around the physical expression of grief.

It was during the South America trip that I thought I could help myself by telling my story. I knew very few men shared their grief. It's not something that we are conditioned to do in our society, but I had found in our support group meetings that when men express their feelings they often had a lot to share. I work in the media. I understood the power of a story, and I realized that my life was suddenly one of those good stories. It had the dramatic elements that make people sit up and listen.

I wanted to respect Zita and her family's reputation. For many people they couldn't understand or comprehend how such an awful tragedy could strike one family. I soon realized that there always would be missing pieces in trying to find out why it happened to her family. The jigsaw puzzle of Zita's life and that of her family never will be completed. I accepted that I was never going to find out what happened in those final moments of Zita's life. I had to trust and respect that Zita was now at peace and that I had permission to progress with my life. Most importantly, there was a blank canvas in front of me and it was up to me to ensure that I painted the best possible future. What Zita and I had planned was over; rather it was up to me to create a new life. It had to be different to the way that I had planned to live with Zita. This doesn't mean that I had to forget, or push aside what Zita and I had, far from it. It actually was about living with her memory and our life experience, but engage in the here and now.

Man, it was hard. It meant going with my intuition that what I was doing was right for me. All I did now was for me. Zita couldn't guide me anymore. Weirdly though I often asked her advice, sometimes vocally asking her questions about the decisions I was making. I would then think, "What would she have wanted me to do?" Zita's legacy was in me and how I rebuilt and knowing that she would be proud of my choices, yet by making choices sometimes you make mistakes.

I can vividly remember one day when I was feeling particularly sorry for myself, sometime in the first half year after Zita's passing. I was walking to the letter box, tears rolling down my face and I thought, wait a minute, I can get through this, I can rebuild, I can do what I want and Zita couldn't alter that or determine what that was. I can go to afternoon movies rather than mow the lawns or clean the car. I can get a gardener in to do the yard work. It's all about doing the things that I needed to do for myself rather than worrying about what others might say. What a feeling that was. It meant me taking control of my destiny rather than having the guidance of someone else. It had become my responsibility and my doing. Suddenly life looked a little rosier. Rather than everything being a huge mountain to climb I saw it as being something like a blank canvas, The curtains had been pulled back and I was able to live and breathe again.

The weirdest things happen in life. Following Zita's death I would have attended the opening of an envelope. I was so desperate to get out and not be alone. I accepted every offer of dinner, babysitting, time at the pub, watching a rugby game with a mate, even joining a book club. It was at this book club that I met someone. Slowly at first, but I met someone that stirred a feeling in me that I thought I would never ever feel for anyone else again. Her name is Annabelle. She had been in a long-term relationship that had recently ended and we both felt those lonely Sunday afternoons the worst. We soon had "out-of-book club" experiences, meeting for coffee, going to movies. By late 2007, I realized that I had fallen for her. I felt so much guilt, I rushed back to my counselor confessing my sin of having met someone new! Was I being unfaithful? Was it too soon? How could I tell people without fear of their judgment? He laughed and reaffirmed to me that I have loved once and I was able to love again. Who would have thought? How could I balance the love I had for Zita with the burgeoning love I was beginning to have? I was torn.

Now we are expecting our first child. Five years on from Zita's death, I will become a father. I am truly the luckiest man in the world to have met someone who loves me. She is so understanding and respectful of my experience without really knowing what it's like. She's never lost someone to suicide (thankfully). I feel happy like I don't remember when. Every day I pinch myself that this is happening to me.

It is life I've realized. The worst that life can bring can be overcome. I've always been an optimist– a glass half full rather than half empty sort of person. Some days I say to myself that I don't deserve it, I should be unhappy, but then I go, "Wait a minute Mark! You're allowed this! In fact, I reckon you deserve it more so than many others." I know that Zita would be so proud of me for how I have rebuilt my life.

I talk on the phone with Zita's mother and we both pat ourselves on the back about how well our lives are going. I gain strength from her. I think my pain is terrible, but I also can't begin to imagine the pain of a mother losing her three children but she's a survivor and I'm a survivor, I've realized. She is very excited for me and what my new future is bringing. She has met Annabelle and likes her. Thankfully, Annabelle is fine about her being in my life as well.

I have grown as a man as a result of Zita. Her death could have destroyed me; I could quite easily have fallen into the world of alcohol and drugs to block the pain, but I chose to confront it. With the help of an inspirational counselor I was able to gain such an insight into my feelings and myself. There's nothing quite like being reassured that choices you're making are good ones. I knew that by seeing someone professional I was able to give my friends and family a break. I needed the honest truth about what choices I was making. As important as friends are, they often find it difficult to tell you the truth. They, too, were grieving the loss of Zita, but in a way that was different to mine.

If I had one recommendation to give any other man in my position: seek out professional help. Don't be shy, don't be scared. Embrace it, learn from it and share your feelings with those you trust. It was liberating for me letting go of my feelings. I actively sought to tell people about Zita and how she died, but in a way that encouraged engagement. Talking about suicide to those not affected by it is difficult, there's a natural tendency to run from it, particularly amongst men, but I strongly believe that by sharing I can learn more. My mates found it difficult at first seeing me in so much pain, but in time they came to accept that and provide an important help in my recovery. The world is full of such interesting people with a variety of experiences that you can gain new insights from.

Life is full of chapters. This is but one. I will never forget Zita, never. But I have learned that you can love again. It's different, so different, but it can be achieved. For the men who've lost the love of their life and are reading this, just know that there is hope, there is a future, that anything is possible. It is up to you and it is now in your control. You can live again. Give yourself permission to experience something new and you will be pleasantly surprised that you can love again. New love can sit alongside old love.

I wonder, as I head toward the fifth anniversary of Zita's passing, how I'll feel in five years time, or ten years time or thirty years time. Time has healed me (I hated that cliché when people told me that time is a healer), but I reckon it is one cliché that actually does make sense, but it only makes sense because of the work I have done to help myself.

In March 2011, I will become a father. I know that the most significant life event for me to date has been the death of Zita and that this will soon be replaced with the birth of a child. Life is both so beautiful and also so very cruel. Despite it all, I'm not sure I'd want it any other way. My experiences have prepared me for what is to come. I couldn't be more excited about my future. It's been a wild five years.

Be strong, or as Maori say in New Zealand, Kia Kaha!

Wrestling with Shadows: Losing a Patient to Suicide

Wayne A. Hankammer, MA, LPC
New Mexico, USA

I am no stranger to death. I've seen it as a cop in accident scenes and elsewhere. While I was the commander for an Air Force Security Police unit, one of our sergeants was murdered off duty. I have lost my father and dear friends, too. And I was a suicide hotline worker fielding a very lethal caller once. But nothing compares to the suicide death of a patient of mine (who will be referred to here as "Jordan") and how this suicide changed my life. Jordan was a chronically suicidal long-term patient of mine and when Jordan died, I had been working as a therapist for about eight years professionally. The review of Jordan's suicide with staff was painful and necessary, but the impact to me was delayed especially because I had been on vacation in Europe when he died. Perhaps it took that long for the reality to set in.

One morning, about a year after Jordan's death, I began to cry. Maybe the anniversary was upon me; I wasn't sure. As I felt myself heaving that particular morning, I withdrew to the guest bedroom for privacy, not wishing to wake my wife. I could see Jordan's face, I recalled what I learned of the death, and I remembered the nearly last thing Jordan said to me in that last appointment, "I think God is preparing me to die." This wasn't unusual because Jordan had said these kinds of things many times before. But the weird thing: I could NOT recall Jordan's actual name for some ten minutes.

Loss is a large factor in suicide. Its impact on the suicidal person is well documented as well as the devastation of loss from the actual suicide. Thus loss is a two-way street in suicidology: suicide, felt as loss, ends the life of one and changes forever the lives of others. Jordan's suicide was no exception to this.

"Loss of memory," I told myself is "a protective device against the pain." Then I realized the two-way nature of loss was to numb me, not shield me. Since this is a two-way street, did not Jordan's loss activate the same center of shame or pain in me that was also in Jordan's life? So to speak, like the wiring we all have deep within? That this loss through suicide also activated the same de-realized and dissociated memory? Could this be the link to the contagion of suicide or the personal nature of the pain of this loss being so profound, so devastating that the recoil of it touches my shame then cascades a series of thoughts, emotions, and behaviors that could lead to another suicide because this loss was still unresolved? I began to cry again... The answer is yes!

Intuitively, I know these are linked. That in the loss of Jordan and because I had a stake in Jordan's life indicated an intense bond. Our relationship had been fruitful, processing much traumatic memory, dissociative states, and Jordan's self-described "sinister" side. I think this was based on deep rapport and Jordan's acceptance of empathy that facilitated mutual trust. Literally, no conversation was taboo for us. Jordan and I had been to the brink and back before. Death was a frequent topic of discussion, delving deep into trauma and disowned aspects of personality conversations were often dark and each session searched for any hint if suicide was near or not. No amount of second-guessing can change the sorrowful end to Jordan's life. Although sometimes I think Jordan waited until I was away to die as–if that would shield me. If Jordan thought that, it didn't work. Time is an illusion, irrelevant when the connection between people is meaningful.

Death is profound for me, an awful loss and one I still struggle with today, over a year later. I am not the same as I was. I still hurt, but I'm better for the loss. There were so many possibilities at that point. Death was one; the thoughts were fleeting. I won't deny that...but the possibility to resolve this was (and still is) very strong which offset the reactive impulse. I use this energy today to delve into the morass of pain and ferret out through my subjective experience, unique to self as it is, to get into the core of the suicide dynamic and make Jordan's death meaningful again: a positive sublimation. Literally, the impacts I felt compel me to understand both the complexity of suicide as well as what may help me understand what links one suicide to another.

There in the core of my experience I recognized the face of chaos. That in the experience of learning of this death, imagining it, too, also was the splitting moment that caused the cascade of changes within me. It impacted my subjective experience with this universal concept of suicide and the realities of each life: death, uncertainty, and change. My assumption that Jordan was safe as long as we discussed those impulses and stayed in treatment was not correct. Nor could I guarantee safety to any degree. Those are realities now. The changes were heavy and stressful. But, I am stronger now and have redoubled my efforts to understand myself and the personal nature of suicide.

I actually had been writing my thoughts on Jordan's suicide for several weeks before the breakthrough event where I recognized the face of chaos. What follows are the characteristics I found in that relationship with Jordan that helped form my ability to cope with Jordan's loss. I examined my varied reactions. Introspection yielded some insights to Jordan's history, relationships between people, Carl Jung's concept of "shadow" toward Jordan's "sinister side," resiliency, being between life and death, addiction, the role of perception and humor, then some cathartic moments. Looking back or rather re-living those journal entries over the last fifteen months created a great synthesis, which resulted in calming me. I incorporated these hard lessons allowing the benefits to be reaped by others.

Jordan's History

Jordan's treatment spanned four-and-a-half years. Initially, Jordan presented with powerful detached and de-realized experiences. Jordan had avoided ever speaking of these experiences for fear of being judged. However, we developed a practical understanding of them as the mind escaping the torment of Jordan's traumas. Diagnosed with severe post-traumatic stress disorder, Jordan suffered depression and had severe guilt as well. Jordan reported, during an absence of over a year, attempting suicide twice with one attempt of a lethal intent through an overdose of stockpiled medications. Jordan returned with the goal to "get life back into me." When Jordan returned to treatment there were some uncommon thoughts about a need to avoid "killing" anything for fear of developing more guilt.

Traumatic experiences in combat were at the core of the PTSD vortex particularly for Jordan who saw dozens of deaths while assigned in the US armed forces. Jordan also had experienced the suicide death of an ex-spouse. I determined Jordan was appropriate only for individual therapy showing low levels of trust in others. Accordingly, Jordan isolated from others and latterly had an increase of intrusive thoughts. A retrospective look at suicidal emotions revealed some compelling evidence. Trauma had changed Jordan in radical ways from outgoing to avoidant of others. Jordan even noted, "I didn't know me anymore." In a similar fashion, Jordan remarked that while in deep parts of suicidal states it felt as if another had taken control– called "Hyde" or the "sinister" side. The paradox came in that Jordan said trauma also "awakened" a sense about, we found, the reality of death and before this awakening Jordan was "asleep" in life.

Jordan's suicide attempt was from the mouth of hell since a different person was in control who sensed only suffering without redemption or beauty. Jordan cited the reason because the horror of trauma was so stark that the only way to deal with it was to leave the body behind and, "symbolically die there" like some friends did. I sensed the crucial moment had arrived when Jordan's posture shifted and expression became pained. I asked, "What just changed?" Jordan expressed fear and began to cry. We remained in this moment for some time allowing it to process. Jordan found meaning in feeling; within feeling, Jordan said there was a real connection to the core self. From there we discussed a path to spiritual recovery of self by ascending from the horror of traumatic experience. Jordan agreed to the strategy to return from "exile."

Over a few months, Jordan improved in every way– mood, thinking, spirit, and physical appearance– as the depression came under control and "Hyde" was contained. For a while anyway. Ascending from the abyss of despair our bond deepened. Prior to that, Jordan's trust was not strong in part because I wasn't Jordan's first therapist, but I was the one who said Jordan's therapist had left suddenly. That caused the first break from treatment of about three months. The second break was a year long. Probably so Jordan could make those attempts at suicide. Returning with an air of honesty, trust deepened and that sacred moment when the pain was revealed became a catalyst for improvement. I just don't know where, how, or why it all went awry. Maybe it was from Jordan's Hyde character, something that remained concealed in shadow.

Jungian Shadow

Carl Jung (1875-1961) developed the concept of the human shadow complex explained as an unconscious, but living part of one's personality and possessing three levels (personal, collective, and archetypal). Jung said (paraphrased here), in The basic writings of C.G. Jung (1959), the shadow confronts every person reminding each one of his or her powerless nature and ineptitude. Shadow complexes have language and thought structures, but are submerged from general observation. Disowned traits, things people won't accept about themselves, are hidden in shadow. Jordan's shadow, Hyde, hid aspects, too.

Helplessness and ineffectuality spoke from Jordan's shadow to undermine conscious therapeutic progress. Authored from the shadow, Hyde reminded Jordan of perpetual helplessness tied to the horror of trauma and unremitting loss. I believe shadow contains the power to kill, as killing is not a trait most people are likely to own. Usurping control over Jordan, Hyde seems to have ultimately renounced life. Hyde at least had a name for shadow, but Hyde lacked any empathy for Jordan's situation or life. Without empathy or caring, Hyde becomes an efficient but heartless killer armed with tools of deceit, isolation, rationalization, numbing, and even addiction. Jordan's shadow consumed a life.

"Hyde"

What a maelstrom that must have existed within Jordan. Probably in most suicides, I suspect, based on the literature on ambiguity. A turbulent battle of opposites: one to live driven by survival opposed to death to end the struggle, thus stopping the torment. It was Jordan who made that distinction during assessment about those chaotic feelings.

Sadly, it did go all wrong. I wonder about how the sinister side of Jordan usurped the aspect of human free will. Perusing a mythology book, I came across Zoroastrianism (Hinnells, 1993) wherein God is conceived as wholly good and the devil evil. It explains that evil exists in humankind because of the choices we have based on free will to choose an evil or good path. I want to make it clear, I conceive of Jordan's suicide as neither evil, nor good, but to explore free will's role in choosing death over life.

Hyde (or whatever process complete with distortions) perturbed the system that was Jordan. Perhaps Jordan's shadow self convinced Jordan it was a good thing to destroy oneself as the self may believe it is essentially evil and the act of suicide is an ultimate sacrifice of redemption. This was reflected in Jordan's long-standing belief that Jordan failed to stop an event of horror. Another concept or alternative would be Jordan, in the grips of a suicidal crisis, may have perceived that life itself was evil so the only way out was through inevitable death. "Why wait?" asked Hyde.

If we can concede distortions exist, then we also must concede that Jordan's choices made during distortion were suspect. Options that may have been improvements over the selected death path were ignored, overlooked, discarded, or simply never came to conscious thought, suppressed by the shadow. Therefore, is it not the shadow that has usurped free will to implement the suicide as a solution scenario? I think so.

What went wrong? The news of Jordan's death at first was a shock to my system. As the reality that the death was a suicide sunk in, the weight of the truth was crushing. I learned this from Jordan's spouse. We had a few visits together to treat the grief and process the suicide together. However, at least for a while, this deepened my own sense of guilt and failure because I learned something of which I was unaware. Jordan had frequently researched ways to die, which created a transient worry for the spouse. Jordan would explain away this clear warning sign by saying he was just curious.

And there it was, the piece of the puzzle I had missed: Jordan actively planned to suicide. I wonder why Jordan didn't tell me? Another client had a lethal attempt and survived. Afterward, he told me he concealed it because he knew I would "talk [him] out of it." Although for Jordan I prefer to think these were Hyde's plans to die it was, after all, still a part of Jordan's personality that allowed Hyde to put the plan into action. In my own recoil from this new horror it was love's power which healed and still heals me. I have thought of this often. Did Jordan feel loved?

Resiliency

There is a wellspring of love within me. It is my bulwark against the onslaught of life in general with all its variations in effects on my life. Love backs me and fills me. However, that love also is present in my daily work as a therapist. This form of love keeps me centered to stay present even in the most horrible of situations. It served me well when I was speaking with Jordan's spouse, too. I do this job, no, calling, simply because I care about people. I think this is a resilient factor in that no matter what may befall me, I know deep down that love is illuminating my life from within.

I also believe the inverse can be true. Without the felt presence of love then what shields one from the horror? Would this not be a risk factor toward suicide if love were not felt? Or maybe worse, if one felt that one was unworthy of love's healing power? In these souls, the resilience of protection is not there. This seems borne out by literature on suicide prevention that frequently cites that a connection with others is a protective factor and open/communicating families are protective, too. Therefore, a social engineering solution to suicide prevention is to foster open communications done in a caring if not loving way. In this regard, I feel caring is a form of loving in the same manner that connection refers to a relationship.

Self-love, the caring and empathy for oneself, is important as well. Was this the missing protective factor in Jordan's case? Lacking empathy for self, in fact, based on self-hatred, guilt, shame, or whatever, Jordan acted as if the love or caring by others for Jordan had no importance or effect on the decision to die. Such a sad proposition in the last moments, not to know love.

Between Life and Death

I was listening to a song while waiting for a flight to attend a counseling conference in March 2009. It was a song of love a father has for his daughter that triggered an inspiration. Here's what I wrote on a large sticky note:

"While watching people in DFW (Dallas-Forth Worth Airport), it occurred to me that each face I saw was someone carrying a duality. One: someone loves them. But do we really see that? Know that? They love someone, too. Even the harsh, tired, worn faces I see are loved by someone in this "dangerous world," torn by fear, pressure, loss all in opposition to endless possibilities in that love.

Two: how do these folks, all nameless faces, carry the capacity for healing love, yet also possess the ability to destroy all that in suicide? Thus the duality.

While on the flight, I began to further this contemplation. I meditated a bit to study the effect of staying centered as well as calm my flying jitters. I began to notice my hands as I had them apart with the palms facing each other but not touching. They helped me understand the tension of opposites in energy terms (I could feel this). Like the duality I sensed in those "nameless faces" at DFW, I felt the duality of life and death in my hands.

Then I noticed the space between, the nothing between the left-right hands. Somehow that nothing was the crux of our existence, a focal point where all else pivots and all possibilities are born from nothing between life and death. In another way of thinking, it is a neutral zone between the opposite energies represented in each hand; it is neither good nor bad; it just is.

That neutral zone is the decision point or its crux, when one realizes that all the tension between life and death also has the nothing in the space between. It was an awesome experience to realize that the suicide dynamic also is in that great nothing. Each loved face in the crowd has this power to go beyond the mundane and realize the beauty of both in the great tension of opposites that can be tapped to examine the full potential in human existence.

While the tension is strong, it is likely felt as ambivalence to life and death. But with help that ambivalence can be used as evidence this tension does exist and also proves the duality as a true nature of humankind. Thus helping people understand suicide dynamics becomes a gateway to understand the awesome nature of self or the choice of annihilation to nothingness. It is the space between that can be tapped in the potential of the suicide dynamic.

Our human drive to survive is married to the knowledge of our impermanent nature. We are born to die. The life-death drives coexist with two fundamental capacities that in their purest forms are about survival, too. Loving, it seems to me, assures survivability of our species. It bonds us together in groups. The ability to kill is innate, Killing to protect our young, because we love them, or killing game to feed each other is a primitive drive, but is fundamental to who we are as humans. Side-by-side these forces generally coexist quite well.

Jordan was a loved face. Those same opposing forces were within Jordan and Hyde. The balance between life-death forces tilted to death as a choice. Jordan's death then, through its seemingly random and unforeseen impact, then created my personal crisis. So Jordan's death upset my usual dance of life/death and loving/killing forces through the random impact on my life and dozens of others. Balance between these forces vanished, creating ripples of crisis.

Addiction

I think something unpredicted collided in Jordan's world at the onset of suicidal thinking. The evidence was simple; Jordan's spouse knew of Jordan's preoccupation with death themes. Jordan's attention could be diverted for periods yet would eventually return to dwell with death again. Jordan was persistent in staying there which may well reflect the power of the shadow self. Ultimately, that preoccupation gathered the final and lethal plan for Jordan. Parallel to this, Jordan's spouse seemed to grow to accept that preoccupation. More likely it was Jordan's self-conditioning toward the means of suicide that also conditioned others this was the new "normal." In effect, a deception created from Jordan's desire to suicide.

According to Jung (1959), we cannot have a conscious personality without an unconscious shadow self. Jordan's frequent searching for a mode of death has the quality of deception powered by shadow. Hyde generated the illusion of normalcy to the outside world. But within Jordan it was more like a rehearsal to die. There was repeated exposure to the death theme which I think acts like an addictive drug.

I have thought about suicide as an addiction for Jordan because Jordan seemingly always resided in a death theme. The more that Jordan rehearsed this aspect, the greater the reinforcement of the drug as reward through anticipated release. During these rehearsals the thought and plan exist. However, what role does this addiction to the rehearsal-relief cycle build in order to cross the threshold to an action?

Perhaps, like drugs, the initial promise of release was the "hook," but subsequent promises held in the rehearsal-relief cycle born of the anticipation of death/release no longer produces enough relief so the ultimate release, death, will be the only solution. A person in that suicide dynamic, like an addict, begins to chase the illusion of release. In a manner of speech, addiction is never having enough and the anticipation must be rehearsed more often facilitating the transition toward the threshold when the action to die is embraced and death becomes the solution. Lethal, Jordan became the hardest to detect because the long period of time and energy involved not to be discovered created a wall of secrecy joined by the seduction of death's release from Jordan's waking nightmare.

Possessing both intent and capability, Jordan must have created the opportunity that generally would include isolation from others who may obstruct the suicide action phase. Death is chosen when the thought of death alone no longer is a sufficient release for the suicidal mind. I think this was Jordan's choice. Surrender, if you will, to the shadow's seduction. Lured by a promise from a part of self so deep that it isn't recognized as different at all. The shadow's promise of a release from Jordan's earthly hell must have been very powerful; likely a narrowed perception, this seduction prohibits the introduction of other alternatives.

Devices

My imagination is often a powerful ally. On occasion, it presents vivid details given some information. It is also, in part, my creative side full of possibilities. So, I picture Jordan doing research, day after day lulling those nearby into a false sense of safety or creating an illusion of normalcy. Then my imagination noticed something: what if Jordan was procrastinating? It sounded really odd when the phrase occurred to me so I gave it some more thought.

Procrastination may have a link to suicide. It would seem suicidal persons actually might be putting off the ultimate choice to end life until there seems to be no choice. In my experience as a therapist I figured that procrastinators put off their major decisions until the last moment to relinquish responsibility to time. They do this by setting up failure by not addressing the key issues they need to face. True, too, with suicide, right? The actual issues are not being addressed. Instead, the option to suicide avoids dealing with underlying issues in favor of the singular choice of never coping with anything ever again.

Another device used in suicide is deception. Shneidman (1996) refers to this as "dissembling." A year after Jordan died; I wrote one morning that clinicians may find nurturing a previously suicidal client important. Lethally suicidal persons lack empathy for themselves for if they had empathy for self the pain of existence could be accepted as part of the human condition. But therapists are part teacher, too, so I wrote how to help instill positive coping skills (Hankammer, Snyder & Hankammer, 2006). In my 2009 journal I wrote, "...clinicians must be wary that the shadow self could falsely accept this nurturing and provide the illusion of self-love in order not to be stopped," suddenly I was struck by Jordan's deception and cried as I was proofreading for this chapter. I had been deceived and it hurt because of the trust we had built over dozens of sessions spanning four years. Our trust contract was broken,

I speak of trust with others as the currency of relationships. Without trust, relationships suffer and are disconnected, shallow, closed-off, damaging, bankrupt, dishonest, defended, demeaning, at times, create hostility in an angry environment. With trust, there is a currency and, therefore, relationships are robust, open, creative, loving, cooperative, and honest. Trust makes therapy work.

Deception, which will violate trust has two targets: others and self. Deception by commission or lying and omission are its forms. Did a gap between Jordan and others separate to a maximum degree like a type of apogee from the usual orbit of relationships? Too far gone from others as to make them insignificant now to Jordan's life? Orbits of some comets are so far into space they are undetectable. Jordan, like a comet, became an insignificant speck in a vast universe, having a depth of loneness unimagined by those close to the sun.

Deception pervades the lethal phase. It's fueled by isolation, secrecy, and deep personal yet unresolved pain forming a toxic potion. Hyde cloaked in secrecy orchestrated this deception using a simple lie that nobody would understand Jordan's pain. Hyde's intent to kill Jordan wasn't accomplished until Jordan became an object instead of a person so Jordan can die as a thing as insignificant as a bug.

One of the complete truths of life is death. It's absolute. Wouldn't it seem true then that Jordan with designs to suicide was rushing headlong toward a reality while at the same time in a delusion which tricked the self into thinking nobody cares? Perhaps this is why suicide draws many people into its vortex. Since suicide and death are one in the same, the act of suicide embraces one of the three universal truths– death itself perhaps because the other universals (change and uncertainty) cannot be reconciled in any meaningful way. In other words, people who choose suicide are succumbing to the seduction of its release from the torment of life's constant change and vague nature.

Perception

Some of my times after Jordan's suicide were filled with comic relief of sorts. Yet even though the following story illustrates some of life's universals and the adaptive process in humor, it also gave me some insight on perception to crisis.

A funny thing happened to me on the way to teach a stress-reduction class. About an hour before the class was set to start I walked over to the classroom to check the equipment to assure proper function. Then I hit the first of many snags. My passwords would not work on the computer. I needed IT support but there was no phone in the classroom and I had forgotten my cell phone back in my office. I walked back and called for support. But I was told they couldn't help me without the serial number on the computer back in the classroom.

No problem! I thought as I trudged back over to the classroom. I have plenty of time.

I had my cell phone this time and called back to IT. No one answered. "Weird," I thought at the time. I tried again. Still nothing. I called later from my office. This time someone picked right up although I didn't recognize the voice. I didn't care. I was making progress. But once I made my request, the person on the phone declared, "Oh, you're in New Mexico?" Since he was in Georgia, he couldn't help at all.

Chagrined, I called the right local person who tells me how to log in to the computer. I logged into the computer and put the flash drive in the USB port. The projector whirred, but there was no picture. Tech support responded to my increasingly needy plea for help and arrived there in four minutes flat. They figured it was projector bulb that was out and there was a need for the AV support person.

While I waited, I noted I was getting thirsty with all the commotion and I saw this classroom had a water cooler. Lucky me! I also happened to have a pouch of drink mix. As I stood up I caught the lip of the cup on the water spout which pulled the cup out of my hand. The cherry– pomegranate drink fell to the floor splashing red liquid on my new pants!

I felt the rapid pulse of anger surge through me. Then the thought hit, "I'm getting stressed out right before a stress reduction class." And just that fast I began to laugh because I was minutes from a scheduled start time, I had no way to show my presentation, no one to show it to, and I had stained my pants. This is absurd! I thought as I chuckled.

The AV person replaced the bulb as people walked in for the presentation. We all had a laugh about my cooler experience as I found a way to blend this silly confusion into the stress reduction mode.

I determined you can't predict with any accuracy how a day will turn out and that class was proof of that maxim. You can predict that days like that will happen eventually in one's life. It is a matter of predictability to a degree. It's also about control and it's interaction with chaos or those nasty little random iterations spinning off the normal axis.

What does this means to suicide? Easy, it's comic proof that events can spin out of one's control, but that the perception of that event is key to the emotional response and behavioral choice. I shared my story with about fifteen people. Some laughed nearly out of control. Others responded by saying they would need some substance to make the day go away. I think those are reflections of the power of perception of an event in one's life. That perception can be crucial in determining the fate of a choice.

At least this story shows that life is unpredictable overall. What I now glean is that if the mind is prone to a set expectation, then a maladaptive response could be expected. But if the mind is prone to accept the unpredictable and often absurd nature of life, then an adaptive response like humor could show resilience. Once I chose humor, I had adapted to the chaotic situation and did not let the situation control my response.

Catharsis I

As I contemplated my conception of chaos in the death of Jordan, I think I now found the link to the ancient wisdoms, noble truths familiar in eastern philosophies. When these are intertwined without relief, the act of suicide becomes possible.

A sinister side exists in us all called shadow. Mapping of that aspect was done nicely by Carl Jung's work on the human shadow complex. Shadow resides more or less side-by-side within the complex human animal. Shadow battles incessantly, but usually unnoticed, resulting in behavior choices not always understood. Shadow is composed of aspects disowned from personality. This represents an internal disconnection of self to needs and identity. When shadow influences behavior, feeling, and actions, it seems chaotic as if emerging in an unexpected fashion, form, and intensity.

What if the shadow complex of the human ego actually embodies chaos and uncertainty? It might explain why human intelligence marginalizes the shadow part of ego. Shadow embraces the primitive and reactive part of the brain (mid-brain and stem areas) where emotion powers immediate response to threats. If so, then chaos has a home physically in the more primitive parts of the human brain as well as in emotion. Shadow, marginalized by human intelligence because shadow is so crude struggles to express only to be buried by busyness. When that sinister side finally got the best of Jordan, shadow was its real name and chaos was its game.

Chaos, acted upon, took a violent and abrupt end to Jordan's life. It blasted its way through to other people, communicating its message of uncertainty through the medium of death, reminding everyone that had a stake in Jordan's life how little control they had. It communicated the impermanence of life and the suffering Jordan felt. If Jordan accepted this suffering, freedom might have been found in its noble truth. Had Jordan embraced the wisdom that uncertainty and change is universal, would suffering been less than felt? However, Jordan's sinister (or Hyde self) was never recognized as the shadow self of Jordan. Shadow took control and was truly itself chaos contained in a human form. Forever altered, Jordan's helplessness was defined by a haunted and violent past.

What a cruel and beautifully unique form– a human being. Inside and out, the wisdoms mankind is destined to experience exist. Uncertainty (chaos) permeates the universe. Since we are all a part of the universe, we contain its noble wisdoms, its truths, and its seduction to things that would deny acceptance of either truth or wisdom. I suppose suicide in the manner of its violence is a poison of the first degree. Suicide is an aggression to the self intent on stopping the chaos felt within the person in intolerable pain. And still, knowing this now, I hurt so badly. I wept for Jordan, for me, for mankind's suffering. There is sweetness in this revelation of truth. The pain is sublime and unavoidable toward acceptance of absorbing Jordan's death. Through this suffering Jordan has given me truth and wisdom.

Initially, I recoiled from the horror withdrawing emotionally. That impacted my relationships in my family and at work as well. In a roundabout way, it was the destruction of my old ways clearing a path for a new beginning. What began as distraction into work ended in my deeper understanding of the suicidal mind

Catharsis II

Ultimately I realized my turmoil came from assumptions about how I thought the world should work. Those beliefs caused me great pain. I felt so responsible. I did blame me; no wonder it was hell. I felt full of poison and self-loathing for my failure to prevent a suicide I had guarded against for several years. A hell full of tears, nightmares, isolation, contamination, blistered by the searing heat of death, it destroyed so much of me that had to change.

Tears stung while sobbing made breathing harder, but no one could wipe away my tears because most of them stayed within me. Jordan's choice to suicide in some symbolic way killed me, too. I mirror in my pain the same anguish Jordan felt for the myriad of losses witnessed in hellish trauma endured over the years. Sometimes, despite all efforts to the contrary, I believe Jordan walked alone in life with only a sinister side there as if Jordan's shadow was the only company Jordan really knew. All of us, out on the periphery, were unable to break through. But the shadow was there walking over crushed dreams, broken by a vanquished past. A life trampled by death, destruction, and horror unresolved.

I bear testimony that Jordan's death slammed me, too. In me I have witnessed the symbolic death of the older, as-if world I once cherished. The Wayne I once knew was gone. Was I such a fool to live in the shadow of my assumptions? It was what I knew. Death, Jordan's that is, changed that forever or, rather, I choose now to allow the change.

Still the desire to numb out the pain is there like a siren call from my past begging me to return to the rocky shore. The effects of a crisis always seek solution. A fundamental change in a belief system is a crisis until accepted. Recognizing the death of the old me is a crisis of huge proportions. Ego was attached to keeping Jordan alive (my goal; not Jordan's). I did care. It's common for me to care about a patient, to use empathy and positive regard, plus be the best provider possible. I was at the top of my game, so to speak, when the game ended. But because I cared, the pain was (or is) immense.

Innocence or maybe ignorance is gone. Wisdom in the aftermath is the real product with the chance to convert pain, the death of innocence to battle my foe: suicide. Oddly, it seems, Jordan died in tragedy and yet it helps me find what I can believe about unchanging universal truths and human suffering. That is what it's all about, right? Suicide is concrete evidence of human misery, both in the act of completion and in how each death by suicide assaults so many to feel the pain of loss. Buried within the loss though, is rebirth, perhaps free from the fog of assumption and more life as it really is: stark, real, hard, needing love, truth, and the ability to handle unavoidable suffering of mankind. Maybe it's like being a Phoenix rising from the ashes, I feel hope and joy again that life as it actually is does work.

Jordan's Loss Now Helps Others

Recently, I had a discussion with a woman who was concerned her fiancé was going to attempt suicide. What got my attention was his behavior about dissuading her from helping. He would assure her he was safe and then send a coded message that said he was not. That message was, "If I did want to kill myself, you'd never see it coming anyway." It seemed he had the means and capability, but third hand it was difficult to determine lethal intent except through the impact it had on her.

She enlisted the help of a friend to secure his weapons and get him to counseling for his depression. I encouraged her to have his medications reviewed, to determine if he was taking them, stockpiling them, or was under dosed. I told her I thought he was at least moderately suicidal and needed assessment with her present to give her information about what she saw and knew to be true.

Afterward, I told her she was dealing with a temporarily-altered personality that was now in the throes of a crisis. I encouraged her to not take it personally because that crisis dynamic was trying to drive her off to create a better opportunity to die in isolation. The dynamic, I told her, was attempting to delude the self that everyone that matters will desert them and that makes it okay to die, alone. Treatment should assist her fiancé in knowing how the dynamic took over and how to use the energy contained in the dynamic to evolve the self instead of destroy the self. In turn, he converted his long-held secret suicidal energy toward a better life once he named and expelled the true source of pain he attempted to destroy. Today they are married, living peacefully.

Advice

As I worked on this chapter, I realized that understanding any suicide is to contemplate the nature of the human species. Fundamentally, I speak of the basic human nature in all of us, that when humans deny, attempt to control, or modify what I term universal truths, they are choosing to suffer. Truth will win out over a wish every time. Eventually, the truths of uncertainty change and death will happen whether we wish it to or not.

During my journey over the last few years, grappling with this loss, I have suffered, no doubt, in part because of my own ego. I grew angry at some point, too, using another block to acceptance until I recognized chaos about one year after Jordan died. Death also is a truth. Since I was using some blocks to acceptance, I made a choice to suffer since these blocks attempt to divert universal wisdom in the humble acceptance of life's uncertain and always changing nature. I learned that I would continue to suffer if I attempted to modify in any way the absolute truth of Jordan's death through "what if, if only, should have" kinds of thinking and this ignorance would prevent me from moving past the pain of Jordan's loss.

If you are to learn anything from my journey, it is this: if you have lost someone you love or a patient with whom you were invested, you indeed will suffer. This is natural. But you will continue to suffer if you choose to modify the character of the suicide. It was never yours to control, the same as life in general. We are along for the ride.

Close

Clint Eastwood played a gunslinger named William Munny in the 1992 film, "Unforgiven." What hit me was Eastwood's line after he and another killed a man they were hired to slay. Eastwood (William Munny) replied to his confederate's horror of the death something to the effect of "Killing is a horrible thing. You take all a man has or ever will have, too." The impact of that line has never left me. It describes death's truth, the impermanence of life, and that both men were uncertain of their own futures given what they just committed. The violence of that moment changed the younger man forever afterward having lost his romantic notions of killing. It was the death of his innocence.

I had evaded patient death by suicide for almost eight years. Honestly, I thought by that point one would never happen on my watch. I was wrong, really wrong, thus proving uncertainty once again. Yet after some time, I am still joined in the battle against a wily foe that kills more people every year than does homicide in the United States.

Nothing can make Jordan's suicide any different than what it was. Any insights I developed were part of my process to reach those cathartic moments. I first began to journal my erupting flow of consciousness about suicide eight months after Jordan died. My battle cry, "To find a great unifying or universal force" in all suicides compelled me to soldier onward. I don't know if I found any of that or not. What I did find was a way to forgive myself and to include a reminder that Jordan's suicide was never mine to control. I fought hard with Jordan to prevent it but together we could not. Jordan's spouse once remarked to me how much Jordan appreciated our time together and that I had made a real difference for a long time. So as another anniversary draws near, I've decided not to renew the annual contract of suffering for Jordan's suicide. Perhaps Jordan would like that.

References

Hinnells, J. R. (1993). Zoroasterianism. In R. Cavendish (Ed.). *Mythology: An Illustrated Encyclopedia*. Slovak Republic: Barnes and Noble Books. Pp. 40-47.

Hankammer, W., Snyder, B., & Hankammer, C. (2006). Empathy as the primary means in suicide assessment. *The Journal for the Professional Counselor, 26* (1), 5-19.

Jung, C. G. (1959). *The Basic Writings of C.G. Jung*. New York: Random House.

Shneidman, E. (1985). *Definition of Suicide*. Northvale, New Jersey: Jason Aronson.

Shneidman, E. (1996). *The Psychology of Suicide*. New York: Oxford University Press.

A New Journey

By Sharon Hughes
New Mexico, USA

In March 2009, I received a book from a friend for my thirtieth birthday. I enjoy reading, but just couldn't bring myself to start it. My mind was elsewhere.

It had been forty-eight days since my sister had ended her life.

The book (by Nancy Ortberg) was titled *Looking for God*. Of all the "things" I was looking for, I was fairly sure I wouldn't find them in that book. "Things" like how could my sister have taken her life? I knew her better than anyone and I never saw the signs. Or how could I stop crying all the time? Or what do I tell my two young boys when they ask about Aunt Casey– their favorite person in the entire world? Or how can I possibly be there enough to help her two children through this? Or how can I be polite when people want to give me their opinions on suicide and all I want to do is scream at them to SHUT UP! Yeah, I was pretty sure those answers weren't in that book. Or any book for that matter. So I put the book unopened on a shelf. Maybe I'd read it sometime down the road.

Fast forward to April 2010 (a little over a year later). On a Sunday morning, I got an email from Michelle Linn-Gust asking if I would be interested in writing a chapter for an upcoming book she was co-editing (this book). She and I had met about a month after my sister's death the year before. After reading her request, I was surprised, flattered, and pretty sure I'd say no. I told myself, "It's just too soon. Fifteen months is just too soon." What could I say to anyone walking this path that might give him or her hope? All these months later and I still barely had any hope for myself some days. Yeah, it was just too soon.

But I also was very aware that I was torn between saying "no" and feeling like I wanted to share what had happened. I needed to share my sister's story– through my eyes. After thinking on it all the next day I emailed her back, filled with uncertainty, and told her I'd do it.

Now, I wasn't so naive to think that writing this would be easy. I knew from the beginning that it would have its struggles. And has it ever! Writing this small chapter has been harder than anything I've ever put down on paper. Right away I learned that I needed to already be in a certain emotional "place" to write. Many times I would sit down to write and end up crying almost immediately. I would walk away from a blank page feeling like I was in way over my head. A few months into attempting to write (having only a few jumbled paragraphs) I remembered something a good friend told me after her mom passed a few months earlier. She said that she was "fine" as long as her thoughts just passed through her mind. It was when she really sat and thought of her mom (her smile, her laugh, her physical presence not being there any longer) that it became really difficult. She said that as long as she didn't think of her mom being gone as her reality, she was okay.

I related to that so much.

When I would sit down to write, my sister became "real" again. She was no longer just some long lost pain-filled memory that I had been trying to ignore. She was real. And she was gone. I would think of my sister's voice, or stare into her eyes in a photo or remember the inside jokes she and I shared or think about the far off plans we had made for our futures. It was in those moments that I'd miss her so much I almost couldn't function. So, needless to say, the writing was not going well.

On one particularly frustrating day I picked up that book– the *Looking for God* book I had gotten for my birthday the year before. It wasn't that I thought it held any words of inspiration that might help my struggling attempt at writing. It was more that I was starting to feel bad that I hadn't even started reading it. It was a gift, after all. Whatever the reason, I started reading, completely unaware that it held the words of wisdom that I needed to get my jumbled mess of thoughts into an organized chapter. So, through the tears, the uncertainty, and the frustration, I began.

Looking back, I had no idea that the morning of January 29, 2009, would be the beginning of a journey. However, in the months that have followed since my sister, Casey, took her life that is what I have come to realize. Her death forced me to embark on a journey. A journey that has taken me to places I never thought I'd be asked to go. Places like: more tears than I knew a person could cry, more anger than I knew I had inside me, more fear than I have ever felt, and more guilt and blame than I can handle some days. And yet, somehow I also have been taken to: forgiveness, acceptance, and a deep trust in God that I never had before.

Casey was my older sister (by two years) and my only sibling. She and I spent most of our early years growing up in Texas, bickering with each other. About everything! I can still hear our Mom saying, "GIRLS!?!?" She had to have wanted to scream sometimes, but she never let on. She just kept on loving us. She must have known we'd start to like each other one day.

That "day" didn't come right away. We seemed to be at odds with each other until we were both somewhere in our twenties. But the day did eventually come when we put all (okay, most) of our petty disagreements aside and started to enjoy each other as friends. Not just sisters who were stuck with each other, but real friends. Maybe it was maturity. Maybe it was growth on both of our parts. Maybe we learned how to overlook each other's shortcomings and appreciate each other for who we were. Or, maybe somewhere deep inside I knew my time with her was limited. More than likely, it was a combination of all four.

It also wasn't until my twenties that I ever saw my sister struggle with the family illness– depression. Mom struggled with it before and after our births. An aunt has struggled with it. And, their dad (my granddad) also struggled with it. He struggled so much that in 1963 he took his own life. Because of this, we had grown up talking openly about how bad depression can get. We also grew up hearing about what suicide does to a family. Apparently, "hearing about it" wasn't enough for my sister to see how deeply it destroys a family.

Early in life, I just thought she was too serious. I used to jokingly call her a "worry wart." She called herself that, too. She was the first to admit that she needed to have more fun. Less worry, more happiness. If only it were that easy. My life (and my sister's life as far as I knew) had been okay. Sure, we had our hurts– our wounds from life. Growing up in a single-parent household hadn't always been easy. But we were strong. Wounds heal. What I didn't know was that depression isn't a childhood wound. It is an illness.

Even though we talked openly about depression in our family, for some reason there seemed to be a shame base to it– especially for my sister. I think this only added to her denial. She would be the last person (literally) to admit she suffered from it.

In January 2004 (soon after Casey's second child was born) I saw "it." Depression. She had a brand new baby boy as well as an eight-year-old daughter. She and her husband were also in the process of buying a new home (that would need renovations) and she was still working a very demanding part-time job.

Needless to say, she was overdoing it having just given birth. So after struggling a few months she met with her pastor and a then doctor to talk about the depression. She was given a prescription medication. I know she felt ashamed to even think she had depression. But I also know she felt even more ashamed that she was taking a prescription medication for it. She took it for two weeks and then quickly stopped because "it hadn't worked." My sister was a very smart person; she knew two weeks wouldn't have been enough time for it to "work." Because of the shame, I think two weeks was all she could bear of it.

Yet even through all of this she still insisted on throwing me a baby shower. She loved parties! She used any excuse she could to throw a party! Christmas parties were her favorite, but any party was fine with her. They were always tons of fun and our baby shower was no exception. It was wonderful! We had a co-ed baby shower with a John Deere theme. She chose this knowing how much my husband loved his John Deere tractor. And because we knew we were having a little boy. She always was thinking about what would make other people feel special and we certainly did feel special that day. She wanted it to be perfect so she hand made almost everything (invitations, decorations, etc.) herself. I still have the John Deere tractor decorations she and my aunt made as well as the hand-made invitations. They were special to me then, but they are more special to me now. They are one more reminder of who she really was.

After the shower (in April), she didn't slow down one bit. She was working too much, sleeping too little. Running on empty. On top of everything else, she had slipped a disk in her back. She needed to slow down and recharge. In my eyes, it looked like she was just overdoing it.

But through her eyes, I think it looked very different. More like an unshakable hopelessness. A feeling of absolute dread. A horrifying fear of the future. I didn't see any of that at the time. I was eight months pregnant with my first child and very preoccupied with making preparations for our new baby. I thought she would catch up on sleep and be just fine.

My son was born the following month (May 3, 2004– on his due date). The next year was a whirlwind of activity. To say I was "out of touch" during the first year of motherhood would be an understatement. I was overwhelmed with life. I was still working part time and exhausted with the neediness of my new "bundle of joy." I won't say that I suffered from true postpartum depression (because it came on so long after he was born), but, about six months after his birth, I came closer to being depressed than I had ever been, or have been since. It was the most helpless, hopeless feeling. I remember being so tired, overwhelmed, and frustrated that I couldn't see many bright spots in my life. I remember seeing a couple walking through a parking lot to return a stack of DVDs they had rented. I sat in my car and cried. I was certain I would never be able to watch a movie again. And I really believed that I would never sleep a full eight hours again.

A few months later I could see how incredibly silly that way of thinking was. But at the time no one could have convinced me otherwise. I thought that phase of my life was never going to change. To me, the future looked scary. And it felt even scarier.

I think my sister must have had similar thoughts, only worse. She must have felt that hopeless, helpless, scary feeling many, many times before taking her own life. I felt "it" that once and that was more than enough; it lasted a few weeks and was gone. That's not to say that I never have experienced a depressed day here and there. I definitely have. But none of them have been like that dark feeling of depression I had after my first son was born. Thankfully, those awful feelings have never returned.

Sadly, I don't think my sister's dark feelings of depression ever completely left. I think they just got quiet sometimes. But I don't think they ever got quiet enough to silence the terrible anxiety she had that "it" could and would return at any moment.

Regrettably, I can't say for sure when her depression in 2004 ended. I just know that at my son's first birthday (in May 2005) she was there being her helpful, funny, friendly, careful, giving, hardworking, big hearted, compassionate, thoughtful, and sometimes controlling self.

The following year (2006) my second son was born and Casey was right there to help out. I cannot remember any specific times that she was outwardly depressed. However, I do remember her mentioning a few times that she was having very uncomfortable abdominal cramps. But she had always struggled with painful cycles, so I just assumed it was a normal part of that. She was very busy, but always seemed happiest that way. In addition to almost single-handedly caring for our aging grandmother's needs (for the past year) she also enrolled in online classes through a local college. She had taken classes on and off again since high school and was working toward a teaching degree.

In 2007 my sister's busy life continued. Her abdominal pain had not gotten better so in the summer of 2007 she decided to find a doctor. She despised doctors and hated the hospital setting– except for the years in high school when she volunteered at a local hospital. She was always volunteering for this or that. She loved being of service.

In September of that year she finally saw a doctor. They diagnosed her with endometriosis. She was given some medication and told it would "fix" the problem. It didn't. In October they ran more tests and discovered she also had a cyst on her left ovary. They told her she would need another ultrasound in a few months. If the cyst wasn't gone (or considerably smaller) she would need surgery.

In 2008 she went in for the second ultrasound. It showed she would need surgery. She told us that she had read about the surgery and it didn't sound like a huge procedure, but that it was surgery all the same. I know she was relieved to finally know what was causing the pain, but not thrilled that she would need surgery.

That same year (2008) I heard her say (many times) that she wasn't sleeping well. She said she was only getting a few hours of sleep each night. On top of that, she said she was having nightmares. Thinking back, I'm shocked to realize how unsympathetic I was about that. If there is one thing I understand (from having children), it is how important sleep is. One of the deepest hurts I still have is realizing how many times my selfish nature stopped me from being there for her. Being sisters, we had an obligation to be there and support each other. I am so sad knowing I wasn't there for her during times she needed me. And, I am equally sad that she's not here for me. I still need her so much. We all do.

On June 18, 2008, she had the surgery to remove the cyst on her ovary. Almost immediately, she knew it hadn't completely fixed the problem. In August, she returned to the hospital for a full hysterectomy. In my heart, I feel that if the doctors and nurses had done a better job of following up after the surgery they would have seen the signs of depression. However, I am fully aware that depression was something she had battled with before. But she had won. I firmly believe that the hormonal imbalance created by the hysterectomy made fighting back impossible. From the surgery on, she was not herself.

Looking over emails and instant messages between the two of us (thank God I am a pack rat even with computer correspondence) I can clearly see that something changed in middle of 2008. Too soon after her surgeries she seemed to have an attitude that she was unstoppable. She didn't take time to heal. She immediately took on even more than before. They bought a new vehicle and drove to Colorado and back in one day. She started an Avon business as well as a bread business on top of already having a part-time job. It was as if she thought she had endless energy. I thought differently. I remember commenting to my husband, "I hope she doesn't crash too hard." I worried about the burnout I knew she would eventually face. I knew she couldn't have a major surgery and take on that much without it affecting her in one way or another. But, I never, never thought it would affect her in the way it did. I never thought she would take her own life because of it.

Mom and I have discussed many times over these last eighteen months that if someone had asked us to make a list of 100 people we thought were at risk for suicide she would not have been on the list. Depressed or not, she would not have been on that list. I think this is partly why her death has been so extremely painful, especially for Mom. She felt that because she had struggled so long with depression herself (and watched what it did to her dad), she should have been able to prevent it. She should have seen it coming. If only it were that easy. But it wasn't. Sadly, no one (family or friend) saw the signs or clues that she was that depressed. We all thought she would reach out and accept the help that was available (whether it was personal offers of help or prescription medicine help) if things got too bad. We thought she would get past this depression just as she had in 2004. No one saw how awful it had become. I don't think my sister even saw how awful it had become.

My sister and I rarely spoke of depression. It was a topic we didn't like discussing. Depression had caused a lot of hurt in our family. I think we were both a little scared of it. To be honest, I still am. But in October the topic came up and she openly expressed her fear that she had manic depression. I could sense the embarrassment in her voice when she said it. I told her that if that was the case, help was available. I tried to remind her that she wasn't the only one who had it. Not just in our family, but people all over the world. Over the years, I had never thought of my sister as having manic depression (referred to these days as bipolar) but looking back I can see so many times that she was unusually "up" or "unusually" down. Maybe this is why her "behavior" after her hysterectomy wasn't so alarming to me. I'd seen it before.

As October rolled on she started showing signs of frustration with her businesses, as well as life. Still she continued full speed ahead trying to get both her businesses up and going. She was so excited thinking that once they took off they would finally be debt free.

But in November she seemed to lose hope. I didn't realize it then but it was more than just a lost hope in her bread business or her Avon company. It was a lost hope in herself. I think when her bread and Avon businesses didn't take off immediately, after she had poured her heart and soul into them, she felt like she had failed. She had spent quite a bit of money to get the businesses going, and told me how awful she felt about increasing their debt. I think what she didn't tell me was how much she now thought of herself as a failure.

By the following month (December 2008) she was more depressed than I had ever seen her. The U.S. economy had begun its nose dive and she had all but given up on the success of her businesses. She was crying much of the time and so drained of energy that she couldn't do much of anything. We talked almost daily (by phone or email) and each time she would say the new day was "darker" than the one before. She still wasn't sleeping well and had taken on another part-time job to help with Christmas expenses. I found myself not knowing how to help or what to say. Any suggestions I gave, the answer seemed to be, "No, it won't work," or "I've already tried that." I thought being there for her, listening and trying to encourage her, would be enough. It wasn't.

Christmas was normally such a happy time for her. She loved the shopping, the decorating, and the gift giving. But she was so depressed that she couldn't even enjoy it. Prior to her death, I would have told you that even through the depression Christmastime was a happy time for her. I would have told you that I remember laughter, a family game of Scrabble, a birthday cake for my Grandma's ninetieth birthday, and smiles on Christmas Day. I would have told you about the fun we all had being together at Mom's house. And we did have fun. But now when I look back on it, I see that something huge was brewing. She was withdrawn, sad, and distant. She was off in her head. You could see it. Almost like a deep daydream.

A few days after Christmas, I asked if she would come to my house and spend the day with us. We live about an hour outside the city and I thought it might help to get out of the hustle and bustle. So, on the 31st she came out (with my niece and nephew who were going to spend the night) to sled in the snow and hopefully enjoy the country. What a wonderful day we had! I gave her a pedicure and we made lunch together. And we laughed! We had not laughed together in months. We enjoyed sledding with the kids and just being silly. During that day I told her about some of the issues I was having in my life and we talked about some of the issues she was having in hers. But more than anything we just enjoyed the day and each other.

However, when it came time for her to leave (I can't remember where she had to be) she visibly changed. The sadness I had not seen all day returned. Standing on my front porch, she told me she didn't want to go. I asked her if she would come and stay with us for a week or so. She said she couldn't. She had too much going on (her children's school, her work, life in general). We talked a while longer, hugged a few more times and then she finally turned and left. I will forever hold a special place in my heart of her standing there not wanting to leave. That just wasn't my sister. She was never a touchy-feely person. To her, goodbyes were supposed to be quick and there was no time for long, drawn out, tear-filled farewells. Little did I know, less than thirty days later she would say goodbye for the last time.

The following month (January 2009) was similar to December but with one huge change. She wasn't crying or showing emotion at all.

Her son's fifth birthday was on the sixth of January. My sister said she didn't feel up to planning a party so I brought my boys and some crafts over. We made "shaggy dogs" out of red yarn and paper towel tubes. The boys played and she and I talked. At one point, she told me what a good mom (and aunt) I was because I did stuff (like crafts) with the kids. But it wasn't really a compliment. It was more of a way she could beat herself up because she hadn't had much energy for stuff like that lately. I tried to remind her that I didn't always have energy to do stuff with my kids. Just like everyone, I had good days and bad days. I tried to reassure her that all moms go through times where they struggle. But looking back, I know she didn't hear me. She was already so convinced she was a bad mom, not just a mom who was struggling.

Later that day, on her son's birthday, our mom came over. She too tried to talk with my sister, but it was getting harder and harder to have a conversation with her. The only way I can describe it is: she seemed to be locked up tight inside herself, unable to get out. I have one picture from that day that shows this "locked up place" perfectly. She is sitting at their kitchen table wearing a red coat. For the last few months she had worn it almost constantly because she always was cold. Sadly, I now know that being cold is a sign of a hormonal imbalance. In this photo she is so far away. You can see it in her eyes. She was emotionally somewhere else.

A few days later (on January 11) my youngest son had his third birthday party. It wasn't until after the party that I realized she hadn't helped me dish the cake, keep track of who gave what gift, or any of the things she normally helped with during parties. Both of these birthdays should have been more of a wake-up call for me. I saw that things were worse than they had been, but I just didn't know what to do. I wish so badly that I had been able to see that she was unable to reach out for help.

Her thirty-second birthday was on Monday, January 26. The previous year we had gone to play Bingo, saw a movie, and had lunch together. But now she didn't even want to leave the house. Knowing she didn't want to go anywhere for her birthday, I told her I would come over and give her a pedicure. And Mom came over and made lunch. The kids played and both Mom and I tried to remind her how special she was. Birthday or no birthday she was important to us. We talked. We listened. Nothing worked.

The following evening (Tuesday, January 27) I went to her house and insisted that she go somewhere with me so that we could talk. Having two children in the house made talking, with no distractions, very difficult. After about thirty minutes trying to convince her to leave she finally agreed to go with me. She had to wake up extremely early (about 3:00 am) for her job so I assured her I would have her home by 8:00 pm. We drove to a local coffee shop and for the next two hours I tried to get her talk about what was really troubling her. I knew that their finances were weighing heavily on her. And, I knew she felt discouraged that her businesses weren't taking off. But I also felt strongly that there had to be more to it.

Like I said, getting her to talk was very difficult. Because she was so distant and emotionally unavailable, most of the words we spoke that night were my own. She would listen and occasionally say something but mostly she just sat; locked up tight inside herself.

Looking back to that night, the thing I saw the most was guilt; especially with regard to her kids. She seemed to feel so sad thinking she was not being a good mom.

When I drove her home that night she didn't get out right away. She sat in my car long after we had hugged and said our goodbyes. We talked a few minutes more, but she was so distant that it almost felt like she wasn't there. More than anything, she would just stare off into nowhere. I didn't want her to leave but I knew she had to get up very early the next day. I told her I would talk to her tomorrow and that she should get some sleep.

I have such regrets over my lack of compassion that night. She was being hard enough on herself. She didn't need anything but complete love and support from me. Sadly, I didn't give her that. There were times throughout that evening that I was very honest with her. Looking back, I should have only given her acceptance and love. I regret I spoke even a word of criticism or offered well-meaning advice. I wish I'd let her sit in my car as long as she wanted. I wish something about that night would have helped. I now fear it only made it worse.

The following day, Wednesday, January 28th, my boys and I spent most of the day on an outing with friends. I remember wanting to ask my sister to come, but decided against it. I was almost certain she would say "no." With the way their finances were, I thought the cost to get in would only add to her stress. And she would have never allowed me to pay for it so I decided to not even bring it up. I always will wonder if things might have been different had I asked her to join us.

When I arrived home that night, about 7:00 pm, I called her. Her husband answered and told me that she was already asleep. Because of her job, going to bed early wasn't all that unusual. But looking back, it didn't sit right with me. I asked him to have her call me if she woke up. Otherwise, I'd call her in the morning.

I never got to make that call.

The following morning, Thursday, January 29, my phone rang. It was 7:12 am and I was sleeping in. My two boys, who were normally very early risers, hadn't woken up yet. I was sleeping soundly with no clue that all of our lives would soon change forever.

My niece (and Casey's twelve-year-old daughter) called me after she and her father found my sister in the family's main bathroom unconscious and not breathing. I answered the phone still half asleep and heard her say to me, "Aunt Sharon, I need you to come to me. You have to come to me now." She never had called me upset before and I could tell she was frightened. Her next words to me made me gasp, "My mom hung herself."

My first feelings ranged from complete disbelief to an odd feeling of calm. I remember thinking that she must be overreacting or that she was confused. After all, she was only twelve, I thought. I think it was that thought (that she was confused) that allowed me to stay calm.

I cannot remember whom I called next, Mom or my husband. I just remember feeling that I didn't want to show on the outside what I felt on the inside: panic, fear, and a complete loss of control. Even now, eighteen months later, that feeling is still with me. I don't want people to know what is going on with me on the inside. I've gotten very good at portraying an image of "everything is fine." However, quite often that couldn't be further from the truth. I don't remember what I told either of them. I just remember trying to stay calm.

Next, I frantically called my mother-in-law (who lives next door) to see if she could watch my children. There was no answer, so I quickly dialed my sister-in-law who lives across the street. I didn't want to tell her what was going on. Looking back, I think the shame already had begun to set in for me.

The drive that usually took forty-five minutes instead took me twenty minutes. During the drive, my niece called to let me know the paramedics had been able to get her breathing again. I had no reason to think that wasn't wonderful news and was very relieved to hear that. I would soon learn differently.

When I made it to town and turned down my sister's street, I saw two police cars parked in front of her home. I can't even begin to describe what that felt like. I had never known anyone in my adult life who had the police called to their home; much less my sister.

When I walked inside the officers were finishing paperwork. They asked who I was and told me not to enter the bathroom. I was told it was "still under investigation."

Almost immediately after arriving, I called one of my closest friends and told her what was going on. She immediately left work and drove to my sister's house. As soon as she arrived, she offered to watch my nephew (who was too young to go the hospital) so that my husband, niece, and I could go on to the hospital. But I didn't want to leave right away. For the first few hours, I cleaned and tried to make things more presentable. Depression had not been allowing my sister much time to clean. And I didn't want anyone to judge her for a messy house. What a ridiculous thing for me to care about but I did.

My friend and I cleaned and talked and tried to not think about what was happening at the hospital. But as the hours passed and we hadn't left, I started to realize how much I didn't want to go to the hospital. I was so angry, confused, and scared. And still a part of me didn't see the need to rush to the hospital. After all, last I heard, the paramedics had been able to get her breathing again so she was going to be okay. Right?

At about 2:00 pm that afternoon, we finally made our way to the hospital and found my sister's room. It was the worst thing I had ever seen. She was hooked up to full life support machines and covered with a white blanket. Only her face, feet and hands were visible. I walked in, picked up her hand, kissed her forehead, ran my fingers through her hair and, in my mind, without being aware of it, started saying my goodbyes.

It wasn't until then that I was told there was no brain activity and that they didn't expect her to ever regain consciousness again. We spent the next day and a half in the ICU. Sadly, my sister was not "there" with us. She was still unconscious with no brain activity.

Whether it was my body's way of protecting me, or total shock (or both) I still secretly held out hope that she would regain consciousness. I never thought she was going to die. Never. Not one time.

That first night (Thursday evening), Mom decided to stay with her at the hospital. I can't imagine what that must have felt like to stay there in a hospital room with your first-born child barely clinging to life. I pray I never have to. And I pray my mom never again has to experience the hurt suicide causes. She has seen so much in her life.

My husband (Ben) and I left the hospital late that night to go home to our boys. All they knew was that I had left early that morning in a rush. They had no idea what was going on. And I didn't quite know what to tell them. Deep down I really thought she would have made some improvement by morning and they (as well as her son) might be able to go see her.

Ben and I have been together since I was sixteen. We have had our share of problems and seen our share of troubles over the years, but through everything he has continued to be my rock. Dependable. Loving. Thoughtful. Strong. I can fall apart with him and know he will love me through it. That night was no exception. As we were driving home, I couldn't stop saying, "I can't believe she did this. I can't believe she did this." After repeating that a few times, my husband took my hand and said to me, "Sweetie, SHE didn't do this. Whatever took over her brain did this."

I immediately knew what he was referring to. And I knew he was right.

Now I was not (nor am today) a very religious person. In my adult life God, Jesus, and I have gone round and round. But I knew the moment my husband spoke those words that he was right. Whatever "took over" her brain was to blame. Not my sister. Not God. Not Jesus. Call it the "devil" or "evil" or whatever you want, but that was the cause. I call it both. To me, they are one in the same.

I believe, slowly and cautiously, filled with trickery that "evil" started making my sister believe she was worthless; a failure at everything from a bread business to a mother. Slowly, she started to believe terrible lies about herself. Before she knew it she was so lost in a dark forest of lies that she wasn't even able to talk about the things that were troubling her. Slowly, she started to believe that she didn't even deserve to breathe the air anymore. She became convinced that we would all be better off without her. Then, at some point, that evil put in her mind a "way" out. And, in a terrible moment of desperation she took that way out.

My sister was not a poor me-type of person. During everything (the slipped disk in her back, the endometriosis, the depression, etc.) she never complained. She just wasn't someone who would have chosen suicide to "end her pain." When I hear people say, "What a selfish thing to do" I have to remind myself of the truth. Casey was one of the most unselfish people I have ever known. I firmly believe that in her mind she thought it was best for everyone. I don't believe she ever realized what it would do to her family.

She and I had talked many times over the years about our father leaving his family. Leaving us. Neither of us could understand how a parent could ever do that to his children. So I can say with absolute certainty that this was not her choice. It was a moment of pure desperation. It wasn't thought out. It wasn't planned. It wasn't what she wanted. She would never, never, never have left her children.

Friday morning, January 30, while getting ready to go to the hospital, Mom called to see where we were and to give an update. She said that Casey had made no improvements. She said the doctors said it would be only through a miracle that she would regain consciousness and brain activity. Mom also said that the doctor had asked to have a family meeting with us. I couldn't believe what I was hearing. No improvement? Only through a miracle? A family meeting? I told Mom that we were on the way and that we'd be there soon.

At about 1:00 pm we met with my sister's ICU doctor. What a kind man. He first explained the situation from a medical standpoint. He then explained it from the standpoint of a son who had recently lost his father. He told us that only a few months prior he had been faced with the same decision we were facing: whether or not to disconnect life support. He told us that aside from a miracle from God, modern medicine had done all it could do for her.

Earlier in the day, my husband had hooked up a CD player in my sister's room. We thought it might help stimulate her brain if we played some of her favorite music. After the family meeting I knew nothing but a miracle would stimulate her brain.

Once we heard our options, we cried, we discussed it as a family, we asked questions. But we really only had one choice. So we made the hardest decision any of us had ever had to make; we decided to disconnect life support that evening.

At approximately 7:20 pm (with Randy Travis singing "Gospel" in the background), we turned off the breathing machine. And just like that...she was gone.

In my book, *Looking for God*, Nancy Ortberg writes (p. 181):

"On the other side of beginnings are endings. Endings teach us how to begin, what we should center our lives upon, and what is really important. Life has to be grounded in things that can never die, can't be stolen, and can't get taken away."

For me, that simply left God. Deciding if (and how) I wanted to continue a relationship with God has been one of the greatest struggles for me throughout this journey.

After Casey died, I left her ICU room and went into the hospital bathroom to cry. After coming out of the stall I looked at myself in the mirror. Who I saw looking back surprised me. I saw, for the first time, me. Just me. I realized in that moment I had really always been us. My older sister and me. Now, it was just me– alone. I went back into the stall and cried some more.

After losing her and returning to my "normal" life, I went through all the emotions. Shock, anger, sadness, waking up in the middle of the night thinking it was a dream, crying almost nonstop, confusion, not wanting to talk or even think about it anymore and wanting answers yet having none.

But mostly I was angry. I would get so upset that she hadn't left a note. Or talked to someone, anyone. And as for God, why hadn't he intervened and stopped her? I knew he could have.

The first five or six months were filled with complete shock and disbelief. Then I slowly started having days of acceptance. They didn't last long, but I felt I was moving toward a place of healing. Right after she died I felt alone in that bathroom. But that didn't last. Within a few days I started to feel her with me. I know that everyone has their own unique opinion on this and I can't explain mine, but through everything we were still sisters and I still felt her in my life. I still do today.

Ten years ago, a friend of mine lost his daughter (and only child) in a terrible car accident. A few months after she had passed I said something to him so terribly insensitive. I asked him if he had considered adoption. As if he could replace her?

It was only after one of my husband's family members suggested I find someone to replace my sister with (only two days after she had died) that I remembered making that awful comment to him all those years before.

My friend and I hadn't spoken in years. But as soon as I remembered having said that to him I sat down and wrote him a letter. I apologized and explained that I had just lost my sister and I fully understood how hurtful my comment must have been. After receiving my letter, he called. He said he didn't even remember my comment and he forgave me. He said he had learned early on that people say things just trying to help or to fill the awkward silence. Through him I was shown the power of forgiveness. So I was able to easily forgive the person who had suggested I replace my sister. As well as many more well-meaning comments from people who just don't understand. They were only trying to help, just as I was so many years ago.

I have now learned that most of the stupid comments people make are only because they have never experienced such a deep loss. My friend puts it this way: he says in order to understand what this walk is like you have to be a "member of the club." Meaning, you have to have lost someone so close to you that they were a part of you. Otherwise, you can't comprehend what the loss feels like. Sadly, if you're reading this, you're probably a member of the club. I am so sorry for your loss.

Early on, a few well-meaning people asked, "Are you allowing yourself time to grieve?" What did that mean? Was I supposed to schedule in a certain number of minutes per day devoted to grieving? Thankfully, no. My friend told me to not allow anyone to put a timeline on my grieving. He said that if I didn't give my feelings enough attention they would just take it. Even if I tried to ignore them, they would always find me. And they did. Granted, it wasn't always during the most convenient times, but the emotion always came. His words gave me relief that there was no right or wrong way to grieve.

Then, on November 6th (about nine months after my sister passed away), I received a call from a friend. She told me that a mutual friend of ours had taken her life the evening before. Her death ripped open all the wounds that my sister's death had created. I never thought I would EVER have to deal with another suicide. Yet there I was facing it all over again.

The Sunday after my friend took her life, her pastor gave a sermon on "God's grace." In it, he said, "We cannot out-sin God's grace." I desperately needed that. Since hearing it, I have never again wondered about where my sister is. Casey is in Heaven and I will see her again. I still miss her like crazy but I no longer worry about her. Now, when I cry, I know I am not crying for her; I am crying for me.

Aside from my husband, my mom has been the most supportive person in my life. She has influenced my thinking in ways I would have never come to on my own. Without her gentle, wise, loving reminders of the truth, I would still be lost in anger. Watching her handle her daughter's death, she has become one of the greatest teachers in my life.

Only days after my sister's death, Mom reminded me of something her mom (my grandma) had said after her husband (my mom's dad) had taken his life more than forty years ago. My grandma said that her husband had suffered from a "mind attack." Just as the heart attack victim suffers from a heart attack. Without question, my sister had a mind attack. And it killed her. Forgiveness comes easily when I am able to stay in that frame of mind.

One day while Mom and I were talking, she said something that made me (for the first time really) think deeply about the matter of true forgiveness. She said she wondered if we really are doomed to live what we can't forgive. My sister had never forgiven our dad for leaving us. Yet that is exactly what she ended up doing to her family. And Casey had never forgiven our mom for having depression. Yet that is exactly what my sister faced. Casey had never seen Mom's depression as an illness. She always saw it as a weakness. My sister thought that Mom could overcome it if she had only been a little stronger; tried a little harder. I am not (nor was my mom) suggesting that my sister's inability to forgive is the only reason for her suicide. I know it happened because of a variety of reasons. But I do think forgiveness (or the lack thereof) played a major role.

Mom also shared with me her view on God's intervention. She said she felt God had intervened. She said that if my sister's husband had found her even five minutes earlier she might not have passed away after the life support was disconnected. She said there was a chance my sister could have been a vegetable the rest of her life, still in the hospital. No brain activity and unconscious. Thinking of my sister, still in the hospital, unable to live and unable to die is a nightmare I can't imagine. Thanks to Mom's words, I am now thankful for God's intervention, too.

My husband and my mom's strength have been so comforting. Through both of them, I am reminded of God's love. And that reminder makes me want to continue to pursue a relationship with Him. Without their guidance I would have given up on God and Jesus a long time ago. Sometimes when I find myself wondering where their strength comes from, I have to remind myself that their strength comes from the Lord. Just as He told us it would. And that gives me strength because I know it is available to me as well.

My niece (who is now fourteen) is amazing. What a gift she is in my life. We were close before, but she is so very dear to me now. She has handled losing her mom in a way I never could have. Almost immediately, she started going to professional therapy. I think that outlet has been so valuable to her finding a place of peace and healing. We also have frequent heart-to-heart talks about anything and everything. She has helped me heal in ways no one else could have. My hope is that I have helped her heal as well. I realize that her walk through life will not be an easy one without her mom. But, she is finding her way. Talking, crying, healing, and continuing to lean on God. I am so very proud of her.

And, my nephew (who is six) is also doing well. He is a bundle of energy and the spitting image of his mom. I doubt he will have many memories of her but I intend to help with that as much as I can. I have started both her children scrapbooks for when they are older. My hope is that those books will be reminders (should they start to question) how very much their mom loved them.

Without my husband, Mom, niece, family, and a handful of the most amazing friends, I wouldn't have been able to move ahead with my life. I still have days where I struggle with forgiveness and anger. And some days sadness still envelops me like a fog. But thankfully most days I am able to come to a place of peace with my sister's death.

My only wish for this chapter is that some of what people have shared with me helps you on your journey, too. Healing does come.

Reference

Ortberg, N. (2008). *Looking for God.* Carol Stream, IL: Tyndale House.

RESOURCES

Web Sites

American Association of Suicidology
www.suicidology.org

American Foundation for Suicide Prevention
www.afsp.org

International Association for Suicide Prevention
www.iasp.info

Suicide Prevention Action Network
www.spanusa.org

Suicide Information and Education Center
www.suicideinfo.ca

Suicide Prevention Resource Center
www.sprc.org

Internet Bereaved by Suicide Support Groups
The main web site is www.pos-ffos.com

To join POS (Parents of Suicides) or FFOS (Friends and Families of Suicides), email Karyl Chastain Beal (arlynsmom@bellsouth.net) and ask for an application, or to go to *http://health.groups.yahoo.com/group/parentsofsuicides/* to sign up for POS or to *http://health.groups.yahoo.com/group/ffofsuicides/* to sign up for FFOS.

If you are worried about yourself or someone you care about in the United States, please call the National Suicide Prevention Lifeline at 1-800-273-TALK (*www.suicidepreventionlifelife.org*). You also can call this number if you are grieving and need support.

If you are in another country and seeking resources, the International Association for Suicide Prevention (www.iasp.info) web site offers information for various countries.

ABOUT THE EDITORS

Michelle Linn-Gust, Ph.D.

Michelle Linn-Gust, Ph.D., is an internationally known author and speaker about suicide prevention and postvention issues as well as the importance of dog companionship, particularly after loss. She is the author of several books including *Ginger's Gift: Hope and Healing Through Dog Companionship*. Her first book, based on the suicide of her younger sister Denise, *Do They Have Bad Days in Heaven? Surviving the Suicide Loss of a Sibling*, inspired siblings around the world in their survival after a loved one's suicide. She is the President-Elect for the American Association of Suicidology. Michelle lives in Albuquerque, New Mexico. Read more about Michelle at *www.michellelinngust.com*.

Julie Cerel, Ph.D.

Julie Cerel, Ph.D., is a clinical psychologist on the faculty in the College of Social Work at the University of Kentucky. She grew up in Atlanta, Georgia, attended Kenyon College for her undergraduate degree and The Ohio State University for graduate school. She completed a clinical internship and fellowship at West Virginia University in child clinical psychology and a post-doctoral fellowship in suicide prevention at University of Rochester. She has been active in suicide prevention for over a decade with most of her work focusing on suicide bereavement and postvention. She is the author or co-author of more than twenty academic publications and her research has been funded by the Substance Abuse Mental Health Services Administration (SAMHSA), the Nation's Alliance on Mental Illness (NAMI), American Foundation for Suicide Prevention (AFSP), and Suicide Prevention Action Network (SPAN USA).

ABOUT THE AUTHORS

LaRita Archibald, founded HEARTBEAT Survivors After Suicide, Inc., support groups for suicide bereaved in 1980, two years after the suicide of her 24-year-old-son. A member of the American Association of Suicidology since 1979, she was among the founders of the Survivor Division in 1984, co-chaired the Division 1993-1994, chaired the first national survivor conference in 1989, served on the AAS School Education Committee, the *Surviving* newsletter editorial staff, and is certified as an AAS Crisis Worker. LaRita was among concerned Coloradoans forming SPARE, the first state suicide prevention organization and in 1993, LaRita co-founded the Suicide Prevention Partnership/Pikes Peak Region. Upon request of Schriever AFB Wing Commander, LaRita co-authored a Crisis Support Team program manual, developed teams at Peterson and Schriever AFB and traveled to USAFE, Ramstien, Germany, three consecutive years to train teams. LaRita has three sons, nine grandchildren, one great grandson, and lives in Colorado Springs with, Arch, her husband of sixty years, and, Snickers, their Yorkie.

Mary Chandler Bolin, Ph.D., is a licensed psychologist and director of the University of Kentucky Counseling Center. She is a national senior master trainer for QPR [Question, Persuade, Refer] gatekeeper programs, is the co-primary investigator for the university's SAMHSA grant for campus suicide prevention, and has served on the Kentucky Suicide Prevention Group [KSPG]. Her professional affiliations include APA, KPA, AUCCCD, and IACS, for which she serves as chair of the accreditation board. When not working as an administrator, therapist, or consultant, she enjoys touring with the Lexington Singers and dancing the Argentine tango.

Dottie Granger lives in Baton Rouge, Louisiana, where she helps suicide survivors through the local crisis center. She enjoys visiting and making memories with her two daughters and sons-in-law. She also enjoys traveling, especially to the beach yearly with her canasta card-playing friends.

Wayne Hankammer is a licensed professional counselor employed by the federal government as a Critical Incident Stress Management Specialist and instructor. Wayne has sixteen years experience in suicide prevention. Wayne was assigned to

Security Forces at Ramstein AB Germany and there trained with his friend LaRita Archibald in Crisis Support Teams. That experience led to his career in counseling. He has written on both suicide and post-traumatic stress disorder. He lives in New Mexico with his spouse of eight years. They love to travel to places in the sun.

Adrian Hill practiced law for thirty years on Toronto's Bay Street and enjoyed a second career teaching and writing texts, manuals, and articles on addictions, mental illness, and wellness as well as developing assistance programs for lawyers and judges across North America, Europe, and Asia. Adrian was a board member for nine years and served as president of the Canadian Association for Suicide Prevention. He also was a core writer and the national editor of Canada's Suicide Prevention Strategy and has lectured about suicide prevention and bereavement on four continents. He is the father of an airport firefighter and a veterinary surgeon, and has been the dance critic for a national newspaper, a paramedic, and the breeder and trainer of Greenland Huskies.

Sharon Hughes is a thirty-something native Texan now living in the Southwest. She is a full time stay-at-home mom and wife. She has two young boys (ages six and five) and a husband of almost ten years. Sharon spends most of her time juggling the delicate balance between time for herself and family time. When she isn't running after her ever-active boys, she is putting her red hair up in a baseball cap and trying to find the lighter side of life. In her spare time (whatever that is), she loves, camping, water-skiing, horses, scrapbooking, college football, dancing, and traveling.

Wesley H. "Buddy" Knox is a lifelong resident of Baton Rouge, Louisiana. He spent ten years as a criminal deputy with the East Baton Rouge Sheriff's office before working as a logistics manager for a large paper manufacturer and as the Director of Trade Development for the Port of Greater Baton Rouge. His proudest accomplishment is that he has been married to his wife Betty for fifty-four years and from this marriage there have been four children, fourteen grandchildren, and thirteen great-grandchildren all of which he says are the light of his life.

Doreen S. Marshall is a licensed psychologist and professional counselor living in Atlanta, Georgia. She is currently Chair and Associate Professor in the Counseling Department at Argosy University, Atlanta. She also is a member of the board of directors for the American Association of Suicidology and a member of the Survivor Council of The American Foundation for Suicide Prevention. Her professional interests include suicide prevention and postvention, trauma, and professional issues in counselor education. She enjoys reading, cooking, and most of all, spending time with her toddler, Augustina Jane.

Nicole Masco Morton lives in South Central Wisconsin with her best friend (who happens to be her husband), their energetic son, and their new baby daughter. She is currently on hiatus from pursuing a second career in elementary education to be a stay-at-home mom and CEO of the Morton household. When she's not spending time with her family, Nicole will most likely be found strolling the aisles at the local Target.

Diana Sands, Ph.D., lives in Australia and is the Director of the Bereaved by Suicide Service, Sydney. For more than two decades she has worked as a clinician, educator, and researcher in the area of suicide postvention, prevention, and intervention. Diana loves curling up with a good book on the veranda of her home overlooking the beach, under the dappled shade of the magnificent Australian eucalyptus trees

Janet Schnell, MSW, is the middle child of Don and Mary Lou Schmitt. She grew up in a family of five children who were born one year apart. Janet always had a special connection with her parents and siblings. She never expected her baby brother, Kent, would die by suicide when he was thirty. After his death, Janet knew she had two roads she could travel–follow Kent's footsteps or make a difference. Starting college at the age of forty to pursue a Master's degree in Social Work, which she finished in 2010, she continues to reach out and make that difference. After her brother's death, Janet and her family started Survivors of Suicide of Dubois County. She is the president of the support group. Janet is a suicide prevention (QPR), intervention (CALM), and postvention (Connect) trainer. Her husband Jerry has been by her side for twenty-six years. They have one son, Kevin, age twenty.

Lois Two Bears is an enrolled member of the Standing Rock Sioux Tribe. She and her husband, Tony, met in 1981 and live in Cannon Ball, North Dakota. Lois is a lifelong resident of the Standing Rock Sioux Reservation with the exception of time served in the military where she received training as a Patient Administration Specialist. She and her husband live with their grandson, Koltyn Two Bears, and their family pet dog, Happy. Lois has worked for the Standing Rock Sioux Tribe since 1990 in various programs. She is currently employed as the Community Health Educator, a job she began in March 2003. In her spare time, she enjoys reading, sewing, and watching girls and boys basketball games, also known as Rez Hoops! But most of all, Lois loves her grandchildren very much and enjoys spending time with them.

Mark A. Wilson lives in Baton Rouge, Louisiana with his wife Lisa, who is a nurse practitioner, and near their children, Jackson, who attends the University of New Orleans and is in the Naval Architecture program, and, Lara, who attends Louisiana State University Veterinarian School and is in her fourth year. Mark is the vice president of sales for a national software firm selling software to public safety departments. Mark and Lisa enjoy vegetable and rose gardening, and cooking up fish, gumbo, shrimp, oysters, and crabs. Every chance they get, they spend time on their Hatteras yacht on the Gulf of Mexico.

Mark C. Wilson works as a producer on a news and current affairs radio show in Auckland, New Zealand. To unwind, Mark enjoys spending time at his central city home working in his small garden which he does to avoid doing DIY work around the house. Mark continues to work with those bereaved by suicide and often shares his experience of loss at conferences and in the media. Ultimately what Mark is really looking for is a beach on which to read a good book and relax. Mark lives with his partner Annabelle and they are expecting their first child in March 2011.